The Power

of Agency

ALSO BY ANTHONY RAO

The Way of Boys

The
Power
of
Agency

The 7 Principles to Conquer Obstacles, Make Effective Decisions, and Create a Life on Your Own Terms

Dr. Paul Napper, Psy.D. and Dr. Anthony Rao, Ph.D.

St. Martin's Press
New York

The names appearing in the book's anecdotes and in the consulting and clinical stories have been changed. To further protect the privacy of individuals, identifying information has been altered. In a few cases where it was not possible to protect the privacy of individuals, stories are based on composites of people we have known and worked with over the years.

www.stmartins.com

Design by Karen Minster

The Library of Congress Cataloging-in-Publication Data
is available upon request.

ISBN 978-1-250-12757-0 (hardcover)
ISBN 978-1-250-22563-4
(international, sold outside the U.S., subject to rights availability)
ISBN 978-1-250-21349-5 (ebook)

Our books may be purchased in bulk for promotional, educational, or business use. Please contact your local bookseller or the Macmillan Corporate and Premium Sales Department at 1-800-221-7945, extension 5442, or by email at MacmillanSpecialMarkets@macmillan.com.

First Edition: March 2019

10 9 8 7 6 5 4 3 2 1

For our loving parents,

Donald Napper and Betty Griffin Napper

and Salvatore Rao and Rita Rao:

You were the first to give us agency.

Contents

Preface

We'll start with two simple premises: 1) Most people these days feel overwhelmed by life, and 2) this feeling prevents them from making decisions, *acting* on them, and doing the things necessary to live the lives they want to lead. In short, they feel stuck.

If these premises apply to your life, we are confident we can help you. The combination of principles put forward in this book have proven tremendously effective for people just like you. However—and it is a *big* however—it's quite possible that the burden of reading an entire book and adopting a series of principles, not to mention *thinking* about the time and energy required to do these things, will only add to your sense of overwhelm.

So we'd like to suggest the following:

1. You are under no obligation to read this book.
2. Should you decide to read on, you are under no obligation to finish.
3. Should you finish, you are under no obligation to adopt all seven principles we recommend.

These three points are all another way of acknowledging something you have but may feel you've lost: *agency*. Our mission is to help you find it.

INTRODUCTION

The Age of Anxiety and Overwhelm

Leslie and Josh entered the office and sat down on two chairs placed roughly parallel across from the therapist. They thought they were there to fix their son, who'd recently begun acting out at school.

The therapist began by asking about their daily routine. Leslie launched into a description of that morning. After an hour spent getting ready for her part-time job (which was part-time in name only), she woke up her three boys. Tired and irritable, they resisted, and it took too long to get them all started on their days. Soon, texts from coworkers began flashing on her screen, reviewing the details of an essential meeting that would begin only an hour and a half later—an important customer was threatening to jump ship. She counted on having a half hour that morning to prepare—she'd been too exhausted to do it the night before.

Somehow, as this thought was occurring, her mind had performed the complex calculation of what had to happen and in what order to get everyone fed and out the door so that she could arrive at her meeting a full five minutes early. Lunches had to be made. Book bags, instruments, and homework had to be located and packed up. Breakfast—the most important meal of the day as most guilty parents remind themselves—had deteriorated from fresh fruit and pancakes on Monday to peanut butter smeared on once-fresh bagels later in the week.

Amid all of this, the boys, sensing a vacuum, grabbed a few more minutes of screen time instead of putting on their shoes. Still, as was usually the case, she'd managed to get everyone where they needed to go on time, including herself to work, but never without the sense that the day was on the edge of being a minor disaster before it had even begun.

Recalling these details, Leslie's arms tightened across her chest. Her voice, clipped and fast-paced, now rose, weariness turning to anger as she transitioned to her husband's performance, or lack thereof, on the average morning. She refused to look at him as she described his ability to float above the morning scrum.

Josh, for his part, assumed the alienated grimace of the perennially misunderstood and underappreciated as the room now looked to him. He sighed wearily, defeated, as he began to defend himself. He was overwhelmed, he said, running his business. His workdays started early and ended late, and still he never felt as if he was doing everything he needed to. He was having to travel more than ever to stay connected to his customers—never mind doing the important work of trying to sign on new ones. When he got home, he was spent. It was hard to be present with the kids, and most of his and Leslie's time was taken up by trying to get on top of everything, keeping the house running and getting it set up for yet another day. And each day, every day, it began again.

Leslie and Josh eventually returned to their son's struggles at preschool. Left hanging in the air, though, was a much bigger problem.

What We're Hearing

One of us (Anthony) is an experienced child and family psychologist (and the therapist who worked with Leslie and Josh), and the other (Paul) is a management psychology expert who helps business leaders improve their performance. We work with different people who arrive at our doors seeking to tackle challenges and work toward goals in very different realms of life, from successful executives to stressed-out parents like Leslie and Josh. And yet we've been struck in recent years by a significant and troubling commonality in the way people from all walks of life describe the things that compelled them to seek a coach or therapist:

- They feel overwhelmed by life.
- They struggle to make choices and decisions.
- They often feel stuck, adrift, or thwarted.

When we drill deeper, they often describe a burgeoning insecurity or anxiety, the source of which they can't quite identify. Those working full-time watch their calendars fill up months in advance, and those with children have a second and similarly demanding calendar. All talk about losing the power to cope with the daily flood of demands—emails and the constant interruptions from electronic devices.

Many report feeling unhappy with where their careers have taken them (note the passivity in this description) but feel too overwhelmed to do the hard work of figuring out how to get to a better place. And it isn't just adults. Children and teens have also become captive to a destiny they haven't chosen. By middle school, they already feel they're under the gun to achieve, to build résumés. A seventeen-year-old high school senior neatly summarized what so many of us are feeling:

Nearly every minute of my day,
everything I do isn't what I care about.

When you listen closely to what people are saying, you hear deeper problems that, when viewed from a psychological health perspective, are alarming.

Increased isolation and social disconnection permeate their stories—people tell us that they find fewer opportunities to connect with the people they care about. They can't find the time to visit friends, be with spouses, or check on parents or extended family. Spontaneous, enjoyable social moments are rare.

And we hear mounting complaints about a loss of freedom to explore new things or do the things that make people feel energized and fulfilled.

We hear unsettling phrases about a lack of real *humanness* in people's lives:

> Everyone is distracted. My spouse is lost in his own world.
> My friends seem like they are just going through the motions.

Older people are observing noticeable changes in their communities. Gary, a pastor in Minnesota, described how his congregation seems constantly harried and on edge. People no longer linger after church and rarely connect outside of Sunday mornings as they used to. Further, his congregants seek out his help much more than in years past. While he loves the counseling part of his work, he wonders why people are having so much more trouble coping. "This wasn't how it was just ten or so years back," Gary observed. "People seemed to be more self-reliant then, but now they seem more lost. They aren't sure what to do." We asked Phyllis Schimel, a licensed social worker, what she's observed among the New Yorkers who come to her psychotherapy practice. Phyllis has been seeing patients for six decades, and she, too, notes an alarming trend. "I've seen the pressures climb over the last few decades, there's no doubt," Phyllis told us. "It's a part of life now. Things are faster. They really started accelerating in the '80s. It's not going to go away. We're in a race to adapt—trying to catch up constantly—and the effects are significant on our body and mind."

We spoke with a fifth-grade teacher in Arizona. Sue has sixteen years' experience and noted that she's observed differences in her eleven-year-olds. "Other teachers are talking about this at meetings and in the break room," she said. "Students seem more agitated—more fidgety. Some of them look exhausted and tired. They need more help staying on task. In the afternoons, many have a hard time staying alert. And this is noticeably worse year after year." Parent-teacher conferences have become more emotionally charged, too. Parents—much like their kids—come into these meetings worn out and nervous. They have a boundless need for reassurance that their child is "on target." They demand and then obsess about metrics showing where their child stands academically. This, in turn, ramps up Sue's anxiety. She says she finds it harder to stay focused on what she does best, which is educating youngsters and preparing them emotionally and socially for middle school. Instead, she feels pressured from all sides to prepare them for college. To her, the treadmill-like quality of it is mystifying:

> No one stops to question if what we're doing makes sense.
> We just keep doing it.

Here's what we observe from our respective practices: The pace of life has accelerated to a level beyond that to which most of us can fully adapt. The result is a series of negative feedback loops that, left untended, can quickly spiral out of control. To wit:

- We exist with a constant buzz of worry and anxiety that we're not doing everything we're supposed to be doing.

- This creates a negative feedback loop in which we can't get things done because we're anxious, and our inability to get things done makes the list grow and grow, leaving us ever more anxious.

- All this anxiety also makes us seek distractions (Facebook or Netflix, anyone?), making it harder to be present for others, hurting our relationships. As we become isolated, we tend to become depressed, and this, too, makes it harder to get stuff done . . . leading to more anxiety.

- When it comes time to make a decision, reaching *any* decision becomes difficult, whether it's "Should I stay in this job?" or "Where should we go on summer vacation?" or even "What should we do for dinner tonight?" We can't quite seem to figure out how to weigh our options. And so the deal doesn't get done, vacations aren't taken, and dinner is last minute and stressful.

For the past two to three decades, professionals have focused on stress. We've been recommending stress management, a healthier lifestyle, medications, and in some cases, psychotherapy to help our clients and patients get back on their feet.

But it turns out this approach is only symptom management.

There is a bigger problem.

The Critical Role of Human Agency

What we're witnessing in our practices, and indeed across every spectrum of the human experience, is an increasing number of people who have lost their ability to adapt to stress—with the result that they lose the ability to direct their lives. Psychologists refer to this as a *loss of agency*. Agency is what allows you to pause, evaluate, and act when you face a challenge—be it at work, home, or anywhere else in the world.

Agency is about being *active* rather than *passive*, of reacting effectively to immediate situations and planning effectively for your future. When you become too overwhelmed and lose your agency, you can no longer evaluate your circumstances, reflect on the challenges and opportunities you're confronted with, make creative decisions, and then act in ways that open up possibilities for a meaningful life on your own terms.

In simpler words, agency is what humans have always used to *feel in command of their lives*. With it, people are able to live in ways that reflect their interests, values, and inner motivations. Building agency is central to what therapists and consultants like us do in helping people improve their lives, and it has been debated and written about by mental health scholars for years.

And yet only recently has it begun to penetrate the popular consciousness as essential for coping with the obstacles that life throws our way and building a healthy fulfilling life. Its erosion is linked directly to the crisis levels of anxiety we see in current times, for physiological reasons we'll get to below, and because when we don't have agency, problems fester, and plans don't get made, leaving us with a constant sense of worry about the things that aren't getting done and the impending consequences of inaction.

According to data from the World Health Organization, the United States has been ranked as the most anxious nation on earth, with at least one in five—a full forty million Americans—currently diagnosed with an anxiety disorder. Many more people are hovering just beneath that clinically diagnosable line, absorbing and carrying around unhealthy amounts of tension, worry, and fear, which produce more distraction, restlessness, and fatigue.

And then there's the destructive physical process set off by uncontrolled anxiety. Researchers know that at the cognitive and biological level, intense and chronic emotions such as fear and worry interrupt people's healthy, normal thinking skills. In these moments, a chemical reaction occurs in the brain that disconnects people from fully employing their critical-thinking skills and navigating thoughtfully toward better options and solutions. We've all experienced this. The more upset we are, the less we can stay calm and act deliberately. When being upset, stressed out, and worried becomes chronic, people often become exhausted and just want to give up and stop trying. Biologists use the term *allostatic overload* to describe this type of problem. In short, exposure to ongoing high angst wears down the body's normal ability to adapt and adjust, and it can sever the connection to the mental skills people rely upon to regulate their mood and make good decisions. Adrenaline is part of this, chemically speaking, but it's the buildup of cortisol—the primary stress hormone left in adrenaline's wake—that builds up, and we need to keep a closer eye on. It causes long-term physical damage to the body. It can also leave us experiencing anxiety and depression, which only further dismantles effective thinking.

Not surprisingly, our children aren't spared. Shockingly, researchers have observed that starting in the 1980s, typical school-age children began reporting higher levels of anxiety than child psychiatric patients of the 1950s. And this continues its upward climb. More concerning, rates of suicidality and self-harm have doubled over the last decade in young people, according to the Vanderbilt University Medical Center.

Pediatrician Dr. Gregory Plemmons recently told Susan Scutti of CNN, "An increasing number of our hospital beds are not being used for kids with pneumonia or diabetes; they were being used for kids awaiting placement because they were suicidal." More high school students, including college-bound teenagers, are taking their own lives. Sadly, it's no longer a rare event.

Statistics show that more than half of college students who visited their campus counseling centers between 2015 and 2016 did so because they were feeling too much anxiety. This is a generation that is experiencing intolerable stress. Anxiety has taken over depression as the top complaint by college students seeking counseling.

In everyday conversation, we hear greater numbers of people talk about feeling *overwhelmed*—this is the word they most often use. When asked to elaborate, they describe periods of confusion and mental exhaustion where they lose the ability to focus and feel they can't keep up with what is being demanded of them. They report a range of symptoms that may last a few minutes to a few days and can include flashes of panic, a desire to flee, trouble staying calm and focused, and becoming overly aggressive or, the opposite, shutting down and becoming passive. They may experience rapid breathing, sweating, waves of nausea, or muscle tightness. As a result of this, they essentially lose access to their full human faculties. Psychologically, we understand them as having exceeded their personal capacity to cope with and adapt to stress. Experiencing the state of overwhelm can feel like experiencing a clinical anxiety disorder, but while its symptoms are significant and debilitating, they don't last long enough to qualify as a clinical disorder.

We often tell clients that experiencing overwhelm is like seeing an automobile dashboard warning light going on; something is happening that they need to pay attention to. But most people, when feeling overwhelmed, don't stop to focus on figuring out the problem and mitigating the causes.

Instead, most motor on. And that is when the problems start.

What's Different Today?

What's changed to bring on this age of anxiety and overwhelm? Here are some of the cultural drivers and changes we see in personal habits:

- **Always-on technology.** Cell phones, tablets, and larger screens dominate our homes and work lives. Too much screen time, almost independent of the actual content consumed, is associated with anxiety-like symptoms, including agitation, impatience, and restlessness. Importantly for our purposes, it robs us of quiet, reflective time when we might find time to focus on our lives.

- **Competitiveness stoked by metrics.** We have become a culture obsessed with measuring everything—from test scores to goals scored in youth soccer games to monthly sales targets and number of steps taken each day. All of this measurement leaves us reflexively struggling to compete with others on whatever metric the outside world deems important. The minute you start thinking in these terms is the minute you lose your ability to think about and seek that which *you* really care about.

- **Loss of human connectedness.** The availability of cheap and high-quality entertaining diversions and the rise of social media as a substitute for person-to-person contact have paralleled an increase in isolation. Increasing isolation leads to elevated stress hormones and is correlated with anxiety and depression, both of which diminish agency.

- **Less physical movement.** More time sitting at home means less time spent in active pursuits. Lower exposure to outdoor and natural settings fuels stress and increases hyperactivity. We all know that we feel sluggish and isolated when we sit around the house by ourselves and energized and connected when we're out doing things with friends and family, and the latter feelings are essential to agency.

- **Always working.** Our interview subjects tell us that work, for many of them, has increasingly encroached on their private time. They report more time at the computer on nights and weekends and less time outdoors. They take remote meetings at nights, on weekends, and during vacations. Kids have more homework and "vacation packets" to occupy them at times when they used to be out running around with their friends. Most significantly, people report there are fewer moments in their lives to experience themselves as separate from the complex systems and fast-moving tasks required of them to simply get through the day.

In short, individuals' and families' lives have become increasingly isolated, overscheduled, and fraught with economic anxiety and worry about how they're not measuring up or what they're missing out on. And as with the proverbial frog in a slowly heating pot of water, people often don't realize how much worry they are carrying around until it gets to the boiling point. Exposure to chronic high tension, often in a silent, steady way, leads to more frequent episodes of feeling overwhelmed and a resultant loss of agency.

The good news is that it doesn't have to be this way. There is a series of simple steps you can take to restore your agency and regain control of your life. We'll start by unpacking the concept of agency just a bit more, and then we'll show you how to restore it (we say *restore* because you already have it).

Common Questions About Agency

There is often a moment in our sessions with clients and patients when we pause and say something along the lines of "I know you feel overwhelmed, and I want to tell you two things: 1) There are good reasons why you feel the way you do, and 2) I have found that there are specific practices that have proven highly effective in helping people restore control of their lives, through what we call their *agency*." They usually respond with the following questions:

- **"What are the core features of agency?"** Agency is, fundamentally, the ability to slow things down, focus, and size up your current situation and make good decisions. This comes from developing a capacity to *pause, reflect, and deeply consider* where you find yourself. In its highest form, agency allows you to step outside of yourself and assess the quality of your own thinking and feelings, a concept that psychologists call *metacognition*. This is all another way of saying that agency allows you to see your life accurately and envision it as it *could be*—and plot the steps to get there. Note some things that agency is not about: "productivity" or "high performance" (although it does bolster both).

- **"How do you know when you are lacking agency?"** The most common symptom is the feeling of being stuck in an unsatisfying place, overwhelmed by everyday life, and unable to clear your mind and organize your thoughts to figure out how to get unstuck. It often involves feeling controlled or held back by outside forces—your work situation, or people in your family or your community, for example. Lack of agency often involves experiencing considerable doubt about your proper place in the world. People often describe a sense of going through the motions without a true direction or confidence in their future. In more extreme cases, people say they feel like they're drifting through life and not truly connected to anyone, even friends and family.

- **"What is eroding my agency?"** We are in a period of profound and accelerating change to our day-to-day lives, and this produces a commensurate need for us all to adapt—and to do so without the benefit of a guidebook or road map. When the capacity to adapt is overtaxed for an extended period, the resultant increase in anxiety, if elevated and chronic, leads to a decline in agency.

- **"Does everyone have the capacity to develop a higher level of agency?"** Absolutely. Agency is a human capacity that can be learned. Indeed, human history itself can, in many ways, be seen as a quest for agency. While some people appear better at adapting to difficult situations and show more agency than others, this is because they have learned to do so. Each of us may have greater agency in some domains of our lives than others. The important thing for your purposes is that there are specific and proven practices that can help you develop your agency no matter what your baseline.

How We Developed the Agency-Building Principles

One of the great parts of our jobs is that we often get to hear people describe their approach to solving difficult problems at work or home, and in doing so we learn about their intuitive, trial-and-error methods for building agency. For example, Paul once coached a senior-level executive, Steve, who was feeling uncharacteristically defeated at work. Steve reported being worried and preoccupied to the point that his ability to make decisions was being severely compromised. This was both new and highly unsettling for him and, even more unsettling, he didn't know exactly what was causing it. Hitting the Pause button periodically over the course of several months to carve out room to reflect more deeply on his situation allowed him to arrive at a creative solution. While hesitant at first to even consider questioning his life's ambition to be CEO of a large public company, he ultimately embraced the idea of taking himself off the CEO track as he began to see himself and his options in new ways. Coming to the realization that his long held ambition was in conflict with the reality of what it entailed, he decided to embark on a new path in venture capital incubating startups and mentoring aspiring entrepreneurs. The act of deliberating and initiating a bold, well considered life change that was in sync with his core passion and values left him confident in his ability to thrive no matter what the future brings. This is the essence of agency.

Steve is just one example of a client from whom we've learned about agency in practice. Our work gives us privileged access to the inner worlds of many people who are successfully pursuing their passion in life. These are people from many walks of life, including teachers, athletes, business leaders, law enforcement officers, healers, and scientists, among others. What unites them is a remarkable degree of self-possession, confidence, and personal agency. We've witnessed many of them adapting and thriving despite the high-stress stakes of modern living.

To add to the baseline of information provided by our clients, we conducted in-depth interviews with a diverse group of more than a hundred people across the country to more deeply understand what high-agency people are doing differently to adapt and prosper. Including people from different racial, class, and geographical backgrounds gave us the widest breadth of material possible to further define and hone the principles to build agency. The questions, while standardized, were flexible enough for us to dig at deeper stories and experiences about how people coped with uncertainty and overwhelm. It was surprising how many different types of people we interviewed demonstrated some of these skills. The principles that emerged seem to be universal, but in most cases, people weren't aware they were following them until we pointed them out and gave them a name. We worked to fully distill the different techniques and practices we learned about during our interviews into a final set of clear, specific principles. We continued to field-test them in our ongoing clinical and consulting work with very positive effect.

What emerged from our observation and study were specific behaviors that promoted adaptation and coping, and certain ways of thinking and mind-set that promoted self-awareness and good judgment. Most importantly, we learned that these capabilities could be developed. Putting these principles into use doesn't require a special talent that only a lucky few are born with. We firmly believe that people only need to be shown the steps and given some encouragement to stick with them to make progress.

In addition to what we learned from our clients and interviews, we recognized the good-sized cottage industry of alternative health practices and self-help products that have arisen to address the age of overwhelm. Some people unplug at scheduled times. Others do yoga, meditate, or practice other forms of mindfulness. Others focus on a discipline like long-distance running or hiking, or knitting or slow cooking as a way to bring meditative mindfulness back into their lives. These are effective ways to quiet the mind, retrain the self to focus closely on one task, or to be less sedentary. We recommend some of these practices in our book, but it's important to note that none of them by themselves address the larger problem.

And so we've sought to bring together a set of principles that anticipate and disarm the flood of "stuff" headed your way every day that gets in the way of living the life you want to lead. These principles, and the practices and techniques from which they are derived, aren't designed to be deployed only at times of pain or crisis to dull specific symptoms like stress, though they often have this effect. They are designed to be integrated *habitually* into the fabric of your everyday life—to become part of what you do whether feeling good or bad, happy or sad, empowered or stuck. They provide a healthy, research-backed framework of acquirable life skills to help you to creatively adapt and flourish in twenty-first-century society.

While we've been recommending many of the practices and techniques outlined in this book for years, it was not until stepping back and reflecting on what works best and why that we recognized the degree to which they cluster around seven distinct principles. These seven principles can be practiced in a myriad of ways; hence, you will find many techniques and tools. We've integrated the most cutting-edge research in the field of positive psychology, including research on confidence, resilience, grit (long-term perseverance and passion), cognitive behavioral therapy (CBT), intuitiveness, and the benefits of physical movement. Ultimately, it was the integration of our work experience and interview findings with theory, research, and known best clinical practices that enabled us to distill the most essential elements to building agency into an actionable series of seven principles.

Focus on Building Agency Rather Than Reducing Anxiety

When we set out to write this book, we were struck by one thing above all. We observed a link between people's general confidence and their ability to meet significant challenges. It seemed that those who were confident more of the time—that is, they were feeling more in charge of their lives and connected to their sense of agency—reported less anxiety and overwhelm, *even when they were placed under highly challenging, pressured situations.*

For us, this was a eureka moment. It wasn't just that less anxious people felt more confident but that *confidence itself fended off anxiety and moments of overwhelm.* There is a biological parallel here. The sympathetic nervous system (which ignites fear and aggression when the brain perceives threat) and the parasympathetic nervous system (which returns the mind and body to calm and homeostasis) work in this seesaw way.

The breakthrough idea we had is this: Instead of trying to lower people's worry or anxiousness (as many practitioners now do with pills and therapies), we attack it from the other end. We encourage a confidence that can actually *help keep stress away.* And we do it by figuring out what empowers people, what gives people greater capacity to cope and adapt, and nurturing that. Our theory was that the resulting confidence would neutralize—or at least keep at bay—the negative emotions that so often drag people down.

We started integrating this approach into our work, explaining the concept in simple terms to adults, teens, and even kids as young as seven. First, reframing "problems" was key. We started telling people, *You don't necessarily have anxiety because you're an "anxious person" or that it's a given that there's a "disorder" beyond your control boiling up from some mysterious biological place.* We told them to frame what they were feeling more as *an erosion in their confidence.* Uneasiness isn't the problem, we said. In fact, angst is the natural response that warns you that something is wrong, so we don't always want to rush to sedate it. The real culprit involves actually being overwhelmed by real things happening in the world all around you. The solution, we explained, would be found in incorporating the daily behaviors and ways of thinking that we have found build confidence in other people so they can better handle whatever life brings them.

Everyone has agency within them waiting to be unlocked.

That includes you.

WHAT YOU'LL LEARN

The Seven Principles

The Seven Principles for Building Agency

The erosion of agency is a serious, widespread problem. Fortunately, we all have powerful adaptive abilities at our disposal. We have developed seven targeted principles for you to follow to increase your level of agency and keep it at a healthy level. You will find a range of simple, effective practices embedded in each principle:

- **Control Stimuli.** Cutting back the number of distractions in your immediate environment increases your ability to choose where your attention goes, improves your level of concentration, bolsters creative thinking, and makes you less susceptible to impulsive acts and poorly thought-through decisions.

- **Associate Selectively.** Surrounding yourself with healthy, empathetic, open-minded, candid, and supportive people will boost your mood, elevate your motivation, and improve your overall health and well-being.

- **Move.** Focusing on movement, and on the nutrition and rest necessary to keep you active and in balance, increases mental and physical strength and stamina—essential building blocks to all body and mind functions.

- **Position Yourself as a Learner.** Actively questioning, listening, and learning as part of your daily routine gives you a deeper understanding of the world around you, enabling you to continuously expand your knowledge and capabilities.

- **Manage Your Emotions and Beliefs.** Cultivating greater self-awareness helps you to identify and bring order to strong feelings and beliefs that could misguide you, allowing you to navigate life with greater confidence.

- **Check Your Intuition.** Learning to access your intuition, and ensuring that you use it wisely rather than impulsively, provides valuable guidance as you make your way through challenges.

- **Deliberate, Then Act.** Using a defined deliberation process allows you to identify and weigh options in a contemplative, inclusive, rational way before making important decisions and positions you to take positive, clear, decisive actions.

How the Principles Work

We call the first three principles—*Control Stimuli, Associate Selectively,* and *Move*—the Behavioral Principles. These self-management principles are the easiest to learn and develop. They consist of practices that help free up the mind from negative influences and get you moving in the right direction.

We call the next four principles—*Position Yourself as a Learner, Manage Your Emotions and Beliefs, Check Your Intuition,* and *Deliberate, Then Act*—the Cognitive Principles. These are more challenging to learn and develop, as they require a shift in your awareness and a change in how you manage your thinking and emotions.

As you master the practices associated with the seven principles you will become more open to learning and better able to keep strong feelings and distorted beliefs from derailing your judgment. You will also be better able to tap your inner wisdom at moments when there's no obvious answer sitting in front of you. And finally, you will start to put new ideas to work in your life.

GETTING STARTED

Taking Inventory of Yourself

Where Are You Right Now?

We developed the Agency Practices Inventory below for you to assess your current level of functioning within each of the seven agency principles. The goal of the inventory is to give you a sense of which principles are your strongest, which you need to bolster, and which you need to begin addressing immediately.

If you'd like to go even deeper we suggest enlisting a friend, spouse, or coworker to fill out the inventory as they see you, to give you additional perspective. By comparing your results to theirs, you can further strengthen your level of self-awareness.

Upon completing the inventory, choose one principle that interests you to begin working on. As you gain mastery of that principle, you can move on to others. You'll begin to feel how they complement each other, and soon you'll start using them more proactively in an integrated fashion. Our clients tend to describe this as challenging, invigorating, motivating, getting back on course . . . *a kick*, as one younger client told us.

Test Yourself: Agency Practices Inventory

Below are a number of statements that may or may not apply to you. For each item, please indicate how well the statement describes you. When finished, add up your responses to obtain your total score.

AGENCY PRINCIPLE ONE
CONTROL STIMULI

	1 Not at all true	2 Hardly true	3 Moderately true	4 Exactly true
1. My focus is interrupted throughout the day.	1	2	3	4
2. I do not have time to relax in peaceful locations each day.	1	2	3	4
3. I am bombarded by things demanding my attention.	1	2	3	4
4. I cannot seem to keep my thoughts in the present moment.	1	2	3	4
5. There are too many distractions around me.	1	2	3	4
6. I lose track of good ideas.	1	2	3	4
7. I feel disorganized most of the time.	1	2	3	4

TOTAL SCORE ITEMS 1–7 _____

IF YOU SCORED:

10 or lower: *Control Stimuli* is a strength for you. Work to maintain this advantage by keeping your skills in this principle current. Focus on the tool kit and strategies as you read the chapter.

11-17: You will benefit from further developing this area. Brush up on the basics of *Control Stimuli*. Give this principle more attention to bolster and increase your level of personal agency.

18 or higher: This is a significant gap area for you. There is an opportunity to build agency through developing this principle more fully. You will want to make it a high priority to read more about how to *Control Stimuli* in your life.

Go to page 36 to read how to *Control Stimuli* in your life.

AGENCY PRINCIPLE TWO
ASSOCIATE SELECTIVELY

	1 Not at all true	2 Hardly true	3 Moderately true	4 Exactly true
8. I'm not able to spend enough time with my friends.	1	2	3	4
9. Most of my social interactions are online.	1	2	3	4
10. The people around me do not challenge my thinking.	1	2	3	4
11. I spend so much time helping others I do not have time left for myself.	1	2	3	4
12. I feel drained after spending time with those whom I care about.	1	2	3	4
13. I don't have as many close friends as I would like.	1	2	3	4
14. I feel disconnected from the wider community.	1	2	3	4
15. The people I spend time with stress me out.	1	2	3	4
16. The people I love are not there for me when I need them.	1	2	3	4

TOTAL SCORE ITEMS 8–16 _____

IF YOU SCORED:

14 or lower: *Associate Selectively* is a strength for you. Work to maintain this advantage by keeping your skills in this principle current. Focus on the tool kit and strategies as you read the chapter.

15-24: You will benefit from further developing this area. Brush up on the basics of *Associate Selectively*. Give this principle more attention to bolster and increase your level of personal agency.

25 or higher: This is a significant gap area for you. There is an opportunity to build agency through developing this principle more fully. You will want to make it a high priority to read more about how to *Associate Selectively* in your life.

Go to page 59 to read how to *Associate Selectively* in your life.

AGENCY PRINCIPLE THREE
MOVE

	1 Not at all true	2 Hardly true	3 Moderately true	4 Exactly true
17. When I am busy, I may not notice my body's signals (e.g., hunger, exhaustion, stress).	1	2	3	4
18. I am often stuck sitting all day.	1	2	3	4
19. I often feel sluggish.	1	2	3	4
20. I don't keep track of how active I am.	1	2	3	4
21. Exercise is not part of my regular routine.	1	2	3	4
22. I don't sleep well.	1	2	3	4
23. I cannot find the motivation to exercise regularly.	1	2	3	4
24. I feel exhausted at the end of the day.	1	2	3	4

TOTAL SCORE ITEMS 17–24 _____

IF YOU SCORED:

11 or lower: *Move* is a strength for you. Work to maintain this advantage by keeping your skills in this principle current. Focus on the tool kit and strategies as you read the chapter.

12-19: You will benefit from further developing this area. Brush up on the basics of *Move*. Give this principle more attention to bolster and increase your level of personal agency.

20 or higher: This is a significant gap area for you. There is an opportunity to build agency through developing this principle more fully. You will want to make it a high priority to read more about how to *Move* in your life.

Go to page 97 to read how to *Move* in your life.

AGENCY PRINCIPLE FOUR
POSITION YOURSELF AS A LEARNER

	1 Not at all true	2 Hardly true	3 Moderately true	4 Exactly true
25. Doing new things makes me feel uncomfortable.	1	2	3	4
26. Making mistakes discourages me so much that I give up on learning new things.	1	2	3	4
27. I react defensively when people disagree with me.	1	2	3	4
28. I don't like to ask questions.	1	2	3	4
29. I don't like working with other people.	1	2	3	4
30. I don't care to learn about viewpoints different from my own.	1	2	3	4
31. I avoid situations that are challenging.	1	2	3	4
32. I don't enjoy taking classes to learn new things.	1	2	3	4
33. Most of my learning was in the past.	1	2	3	4

TOTAL SCORE ITEMS 25–33 _____

IF YOU SCORED:

13 or lower: *Position Yourself as a Learner* is a strength for you. Work to maintain this advantage by keeping your skills in this principle current. Focus on the tool kit and strategies as you read the chapter.

14-22: You will benefit from further developing this area. Brush up on the basics of *Position Yourself as a Learner*. Give this principle more attention to bolster and increase your level of personal agency.

23 or higher: This is a significant gap area for you. There is an opportunity to build agency through developing this principle more fully. You will want to make it a high priority to read more about how to *Position Yourself as a Learner* in your life.

Go to page 127 to read how to *Position Yourself as a Learner* in your life.

MANAGE YOUR EMOTIONS AND BELIEFS

	1 Not at all true	2 Hardly true	3 Moderately true	4 Exactly true
34. I am confident my beliefs are right.	1	2	3	4
35. I feel angry when I hear something I don't agree with.	1	2	3	4
36. When something has upset me, I cannot stop thinking about it.	1	2	3	4
37. It is difficult for me to challenge my negative thoughts.	1	2	3	4
38. The same old feelings come up a lot and get me down.	1	2	3	4
39. My worries often take over.	1	2	3	4
40. I believe most things in life are outside my control.	1	2	3	4
41. New information does not change my beliefs.	1	2	3	4
42. My emotions come up fast and pull me off track.	1	2	3	4
43. I don't know why I can be so emotional.	1	2	3	4

TOTAL SCORE ITEMS 34–43 _____

IF YOU SCORED:

14 or lower: *Manage Your Emotions and Beliefs* is a strength for you. Work to maintain this advantage by keeping your skills in this principle current. Focus on the tool kit and strategies as you read the chapter.

15-24: You will benefit from further developing this area. Brush up on the basics of *Manage Your Emotions and Beliefs*. Give this principle more attention to bolster and increase your level of personal agency.

25 or higher: This is a significant gap area for you. There is an opportunity to build agency through developing this principle more fully. You will want to make it a high priority to read more about how to *Manage Your Emotions and Beliefs* in your life.

Go to page 176 to read how to *Manage Your Emotions and Beliefs* in your life.

AGENCY PRINCIPLE SIX
CHECK YOUR INTUITION

	1 Not at all true	2 Hardly true	3 Moderately true	4 Exactly true
44. I generally go with my first instinct.	1	2	3	4
45. My gut instincts are always right.	1	2	3	4
46. I don't go to sleep for the night if I'm wrestling with a problem I haven't solved.	1	2	3	4
47. I don't have time to check in with how I'm feeling.	1	2	3	4
48. I am not aware of how my body is feeling in the moment.	1	2	3	4
49. When solving an important problem, I can't move on until I have figured out what to do.	1	2	3	4
50. My gut feelings tell me everything I need to know.	1	2	3	4
51. I don't need to question what my gut instinct is telling me.	1	2	3	4
52. I don't have time for activities that involve creativity.	1	2	3	4

TOTAL SCORE ITEMS 44–52 _____

IF YOU SCORED:

13 or lower: *Check Your Intuition* is a strength for you. Work to maintain this advantage by keeping your skills in this principle current. Focus on the tool kit and strategies as you read the chapter.

14-22: You will benefit from further developing this area. Brush up on the basics of *Check Your Intuition*. Give this principle more attention to bolster and increase your level of personal agency.

23 or higher: This is a significant gap area for you. There is an opportunity to build agency through developing this principle more fully. You will want to make it a high priority to read more about how to *Check Your Intuition* in your life.

Go to page 222 to read how to *Check Your Intuition* in your life.

DELIBERATE, THEN ACT

	1 Not at all true	2 Hardly true	3 Moderately true	4 Exactly true
53. I am quick to judge new situations.	1	2	3	4
54. I often get stuck deciding between a few options.	1	2	3	4
55. It is difficult to decide what is most versus least important.	1	2	3	4
56. I second-guess my decisions after I have acted.	1	2	3	4
57. I prefer to let others make decisions for me.	1	2	3	4
58. There's rarely time to stop and think, so it's best to act quickly.	1	2	3	4
59. I rarely need to question my assumptions.	1	2	3	4
60. My procrastination interferes with reaching my goals.	1	2	3	4
61. I don't reach the point of acting on my decisions.	1	2	3	4
62. I rarely stay on track to complete my plans.	1	2	3	4

TOTAL SCORE ITEMS 53–62 _____

IF YOU SCORED:

14 or lower: *Deliberate, Then Act* is a strength for you. Work to maintain this advantage by keeping your skills in this principle current. Focus on the tool kit and strategies as you read the chapter.

15-24: You will benefit from further developing this area. Brush up on the basics of *Deliberate, Then Act*. Give this principle more attention to bolster and increase your level of personal agency.

25 or higher: This is a significant gap area for you. There is an opportunity to build agency through developing this principle more fully. You will want to make it a high priority to read more about how to *Deliberate, Then Act* in your life.

Go to page 247 to read how to *Deliberate, Then Act* in your life.

Your Results: There Are Many Ways Forward

The seven principles can be used in an à la carte manner, but we've found that becoming skilled at the seventh principle, *Deliberate, Then Act,* tends to be most important and has the biggest payoff in terms of building agency. It's this final principle that allows people to make high-quality decisions grounded in intelligent, rational thought in accordance with their best interests and closest-held values. We've put it last because we've also found that mastering at least some of the first six principles provides a useful foundation for developing this seventh and most critical outcome-oriented principle.

And remember this: The people whose lives you read about here, who have figured out how to reclaim their agency and harness it to keep overwhelm at bay, were not born talented in the use of these principles. Most have worked through trial and error for years to get where they are. In this book, we're offering you a more direct path to the same result.

TIPS FOR GETTING THE MOST OUT OF THIS BOOK

How We Designed the Seven Principles

We didn't design the principles you'll explore in this book as a stress-management tool or a means to mindfulness. We also haven't designed them to be like a medication or clinical technique to lower unwanted "symptoms," although, grounded in serious science, they offer those potential benefits—because building one's agency through these seven principles delivers important homeostasis, or equilibrium. People we work with report feeling more balanced, calm, and less stressed as they gain greater confidence and conscious control of their decision-making in their daily lives. Medical and psychological symptoms like headaches, elevated blood pressure, worry, agitation, and fretfulness—all of which are exacerbated or caused by stress—decline. We believe this is because agency, and the practices that help develop and maintain it, protect you from overexposure to overwhelm. Your body goes through a great many negative reactions when under such pressure.

We designed the principles to address all parts of yourself and all the areas of your life so that you have one effective system or protocol to follow—the most powerful strategies and tools at your disposal for most every challenge and need you encounter.

Here are tips that will improve your reading of this book and make developing human agency easy and most effective:

1. Find a good spot to read, listen, and think.
Choose a quiet, private spot to read, a place where you can avoid being interrupted and can listen to your own thoughts. Remove devices—it's

not enough to turn them off because they'll still distract you. Listen to music (without words) or white noise on earbuds if it helps you shut out distractions. You need a clear head and the space in your mind to begin building your agency.

2. Make notes.

Circle, underline, highlight, make notes as you read. If you're listening to this book, have a notepad handy devoted to all your ideas and reactions. This is important because so much of our best thinking can happen in the moment and be forgotten once we have moved on to something else.

3. Read with your shields down.

Borrowing from *Star Trek* lingo, it's important to have your shields down—that is, to keep open to the possibility that the principles in this book can help you as they have helped others. It's perfectly natural for negative or defensive thoughts to enter your consciousness (for instance, "I'm too lazy to keep this up" or "I couldn't possibly make time for that"). Don't judge yourself for feeling that way; just allow the thoughts to occur and let them go.

4. Pace yourself and build momentum by starting with less challenging principles.

We recommended starting with one principle that feels easily attainable; reading the chapters in order isn't entirely essential. We have found that this order tends to be optimal for our clients, but that doesn't mean it's the only way to proceed.

5. If you get stuck, learn to relearn.

If you're struggling with your focus—feeling you're not getting into it or find yourself drifting—you may want to start with chapter 4, "Learn Always and in All Ways." For some of us, it has been a long while since we've been active learners. Learning can be thrilling, but it does tax the brain, and sometimes the brain pushes back against what's new or different. But, like riding a bike or having once played an instrument or spoken another language, it comes back as you push through. Chapter 4 will orient your brain back to the days of being an active learner.

6. Keep data—record and plot your progress and setbacks.
Devote a small, simple agency notebook to keeping track of how things are going as you read and try out the principles. Daily diaries of progress—just a few lines—are terrific and valuable. With this data, you will be able to see trends, areas for improvement, and obstacles to address.

7. Share the experience.
Share your insights and experiences of the principles with people you trust. As you talk about human agency with family, friends, colleagues, coworkers, and close neighbors, you are committing more to the principles you're working hard at. You may also help someone else who wasn't aware that they, too, can have greater agency in life. People will share their experiences and stories with you. You may learn something new about yourself in the process. You won't feel you're the only person on the planet with the desire to improve yourself and gain more control and happiness in your life. Talking about the principles and showing people the real efforts and changes you are making will reinforce your gains and encourage you. You will integrate them into your life, and soon, they will become more organic—a part of you.

A CLEAR HEAD

THE PRINCIPLE
Control Stimuli

Managing your exposure to external stimuli will increase
the quality of your thinking, the quality of your judgment,
and the quality of your life overall.

Most of us have had that moment when we're sitting at lunch with a
friend and find our fingers reaching for our smartphone or glancing over
their shoulder at the baseball game on the TV screen over the bar. And
most of us have come to hate these moments, which undermine our
human connections and leave us feeling uneasy as a result, but we feel
powerless to fight them. There's just too much stuff competing for our
attention, everywhere.

New York Times columnist David Brooks touched a nerve with a col-
umn on the constant distractions of everyday life. The line that really
struck home with us:

> I am losing the attention war.

Information overload is the collateral damage of an ongoing war for
our attention. We have a whole range of devices and apps designed to be
addictive. They, combined with ever-expanding data sources, can help
us do our jobs better and enrich our leisure time. But increasingly, all

they do is overwhelm us, robbing us of the agency necessary to do what we want to do or need to do.

Fortunately, it's possible to build mental firewalls so that you can focus on what's important, whether that means putting your phone in a drawer in the other room or gently removing yourself from a distracting situation until your immediate goal is achieved. Learning to control environmental stimuli is a great source of agency because it involves us taking an active role in determining what environment is best for us.

Agency Begins with What You Let into Your Mind

Think about what children are like when they're overwhelmed by information. Throw too much at them and they will become hyperactive, explode into sudden silliness or crying, have tantrums, or shut down and emotionally check out. Some kids literally cover their ears and eyes or try to escape from places that overwhelm them.

Adults are generally better at sublimating their sensory overload—at least for a while. We don't throw tantrums (most of the time), but we do show specific signs when we are losing the battle with stimuli. Sensory overload in adults looks like this: tension headaches, sleepless nights, sore and tired eyes, problems concentrating, irritability, anger, loss of temper. Many adults live with some collection of these symptoms every day, powering through with a combination of determination and resignation.

Do you know that little spinning wheel you sometimes see on computers and phones when they're having trouble processing? Many call it the *beach ball of death.* It means the computer, overwhelmed by too much information, has stalled.

While the human brain seems to have unlimited capacity for information, it, too, has a tipping point. Information overload, which occurs when our brains are taking in too much sensory information at any one moment, is a real state, and one experienced with increasing frequency.

One common example of how we overload our brains with information is *multitasking.* While Ed prepares breakfast for his son each day, he often finds himself "checking in" to view work emails and (guiltily) social media, going between the toaster, his phone, and stealing glances at a second screen—the television—to get weather, news, and traffic updates before the two of them run out the door. On some mornings, it's expanded to three screens, with Ed's laptop open on the counter to scan a work spreadsheet or something else that he has to deal with at work later that day.

Is Ed's situation unusual? Not as much as you might think. All of us are handing over our attention to devices, sometimes two and three at a time. Ed could put the agency principle of *Control Stimuli* to good use at the start of his day by being more aware of where he puts his attention, respecting the processing limits of his mind, and taking steps to exert more control over his behavior in the few precious minutes he has with his son during breakfast. The true cost of his habits each morning goes beyond what's happening with the neurons inside Ed's brain. There is the irretrievable cost to the experience of simply being present and enjoying the company of his ten-year-old son at the beginning of each day.

There are people who have learned to block unnecessary stimuli well before their own internal processor breaks down, who protect their memories from getting bogged down and distracted by random messages. They're able to circumvent added stress and focus on what truly matters to them.

Monica is a woman in her late twenties holding down two jobs while trying to get her career off the ground. She told us that her work involves using social media to network several hours a day, and she relishes opportunities to take a break from electronics.

There are still some places that are free from digital noise. Monica told us that she has started visiting a church daily to grab some peace and quiet between shifts. "Quiet and calm are commodities," Monica said. "I can go in there for a few minutes during my lunch break and recharge. The quiet allows me to think, to be alone with my own thoughts."

Use Your Agency: Take yourself to quiet and screen-free spaces.

Incoming Data Takes a Lot of Energy to Process

External stimulation takes many forms and isn't inherently bad. In its best forms—great books, films, music, for example—it can inspire, teach, and motivate us. It can be the fuel that moves us closer to our desired goals. It can help us survive and adapt to change. It can come in forms that provide us better data to do our jobs more effectively, or find a good restaurant, or it can provide us with important downtime. When controlled and chosen selectively, it doesn't tire us out—and, in fact, it can help us elevate and maintain a more positive mood.

But external stimulation has to be controlled, particularly at times when 1) you have to get something done or 2) you're overwhelmed. And fortunately, even in this age when entire business plans are built around creating addictive stimuli, you can actually learn to control them.

You may have noticed some colleagues who are good at controlling stimuli. We know one such person, Deborah, a highly energetic Fortune 500 marketing executive with a particularly good reputation for her strategic thinking and her personal warmth. Both, in fact, result from a decision early in her career to actively shape the ways she receives and processes information.

Deborah told us that it took years of hard work and trial and error to figure out how to intentionally make best use of the volumes of data and stimuli coming her way. Her abilities in this regard have increased her productivity and, more importantly, made her work more meaningful and impactful and made her a particularly helpful colleague because she rarely seems overwhelmed or stressed.

Like most of us, Deborah has a large number of interactions with colleagues, clients, and stakeholders each day. They come in many forms. Emails. Texts. Voice mails. Skype. Slack.

Deborah has figured out something many of us have not—because there's no way to respond effectively to every single request or query, or to process all the information we receive, or determine how much of it is actually useful, we have to take steps to reduce it.

Use Your Agency: Think about how you can get incoming information packaged and trimmed before it gets to you.

So how does she do it? She communicates to her team the importance of presenting information in digested form.

"I am not interested in receiving a raw data dump from others," she told us. "This helps to keep my head uncluttered. I don't allow information in unless it's absolutely needed, and I let people know this."

Her approach is surprisingly straightforward. "I enlist the support of others to help me," she says. "I tell people up front what I need and what I don't need." This has made her a better leader. "I ask people to go out and learn a subject and to bring me the learnings they have distilled down. I want to know what they think—then I can ask them probing questions to help me learn as well. My approach keeps me from micromanaging, which would pile anxiety back onto my colleagues. And it gives them a chance to learn even more."

Putting this strategy into practice is simple, to a degree, but Deborah says it requires her to be vigilant and disciplined in insisting that her team follow her communication style, because with so much information coming in, it's easy for her colleagues to backslide. Deborah says that she provides reminders regularly, such as at the start of meetings.

Best of all, her method has begun to filter down to the way her team communicates with each other. "This method has caught on, though, and others are using it," she adds. Now the whole team works to better *package and trim information* instead of just passing along unfiltered data.

The Problem: We Are Blind to the Volume of Stimulation We're Surrounded By

One estimate showed that 34 gigabytes of data and one hundred thousand words of information reach the average person's eyes and ears each waking day. By the time your head hits the pillow tonight, you will have been pitched five thousand ads. As outlandish as this may sound, exposure to data continues to climb every few months as technology advances.

Surprisingly, many people have become inured to the digital turbu-lence around them, unless you sit them down in a quiet moment, as we have, and ask in detail about their daily habits.

Lynn is a single mom with two young boys who felt that the start of the new school year was going pretty well. We asked her for details. Upon giving it further thought, her face changed. "The mornings are actually tough going," she said. There wasn't enough time to get herself and her family dressed and fed in time for work and school.

Lynn saw her hectic mornings as a *time management problem,* but as we heard more, it was evident that the problem had more to do with *in-formation management.* Jason, her oldest at seven and a half, "just stares off into space most mornings and won't eat breakfast—or sometimes he'll just engage in nonstop chatter." Oliver, her youngest, is six and is more focused and feels almost overly compliant and solicitous. Comparing them, Lynn wondered if Jason has an attention deficit problem.

But after some questioning, we learned an important bit of data: There is a small TV perched upon Lynn's kitchen counter. Further, in the morn-ings, it is always on, tuned to one of those fast-paced morning shows, with their mix of cheery banter and disturbing news items. Further, she sometimes gives the kids her iPad as a reward for good table manners. Finally, Lynn, often stressed at the prospect of being late to work, not to mention the constant patter from the TV, will add to the stimuli by venting her stress or staring at the clock and sighing.

The children are surrounded by stressful stimuli. One copes by zon-ing out, the other by becoming overly compliant. As Lynn adds to that stress herself, the whole environment becomes self-reinforcing. We sug-gested that she begin by turning off the TV and putting away the devices and allowing herself enough time to avoid stressing about being late.

Know Your Potential Enemy: The Four Primary Sources of Stimuli

Stimuli can be anything that is registered by your senses. For the pur-poses of bolstering agency, there are four primary sources you'll need to recognize and pay attention to that cover most of the bases.

- **Baseline stimulation.** This is the everyday stimuli that comes from where you live and work, from interacting with your family and engaging in social relationships—the so-called tasks of daily living. You may not think of your daily interactions and activities as sources of stimulation, but to the brain they are. Much of it—such as interactions with people you love or respect—often invigorates and motivates you, but as in the case of Lynn's effect on her children, baseline stimulation can turn toxic at times. For this reason, assess the amount of positive and negative stimulation you experience in your recurring day-to-day routines.

- **Background stimuli.** This includes all things like ambient noise, music, lighting, vibrations, and crowding. Sometimes background stimuli can be pleasant, like rain hitting a skylight. Positive sources can stimulate thinking and creativity; for example, some surgeons play classical music in the background of the operating theater. But negative background stimuli, especially when excessive, causes stress and fatigue; behind the scenes, the brain has been working nonstop to block out or adjust to the sensory assaults. Compared to baseline stimulation, background stimuli are less obvious and sometimes nearly invisible, but their cumulative effects are considerable and negative. You might think of them as a kind of sensory pollution. Homes and offices are bombarded by new technologies that bring with them a cacophony of simulated voices, beeps, pings, and alarms, while outdoor sources of noise range from your neighbors' leaf blower to the *beep-beep* of a backing up trash truck.

    High levels of noise, heat, and lighting can all negatively impact mental performance. And noise has been shown to release the stress hormone cortisol. Research indicates that excessive cortisol impairs the prefrontal cortex (the part of your brain that helps you regulate executive functions—your ability to plan, reason, and control impulses). These functions are essential to many of the practices that promote agency, as we will show you in later chapters.

> **Use Your Agency:** Cut down background noise
> where you can in your environment.

- **Complex systems.** These are largely technology driven. Examples include such things as navigating the world of health-care plans, banking and insurance options, and even dealing with your cable TV remote control. Again, you may not think of such things as stimuli, but your brain does. Anyone who needs a phone number changed or wants to dispute a cable bill or address a health-care benefit has quickly learned that the process can be anything but straightforward. What might have taken five minutes and a single call to a live person twenty years ago now involves multiple calls, automated menus, and spreadsheet comparisons, all of which require time and mental focus.

  You've probably noticed by now that frustration with complex systems can make you frustrated to the point of anger! Beneath the frustration, anger, and alienation one feels is a brain experiencing too much information and having a hard time processing and digesting it.

  Carlos is a bank manager in South Carolina who knows all too well how complex systems are affecting his job and his customers. His bank has been growing, and it's been developing more products and financial services that it promotes online. This has made it harder and more confusing to navigate the bank's website. His customers are pushing back, wanting simple products and an easy-to-use interface without continually being marketed to. He said, "I get it. They want to do their banking and move on with their lives."

- **Digital stimuli.** Digital stimulation is primarily carried into our brains visually via screens, such as smartphones, tablets, laptops, desktop computers, TVs, and, very soon, virtual reality devices.

  In children and teens, where screen exposure is likely to affect developing brains and sensory systems, researchers have reported alarming concerns. These include delayed language development and problems with executive functions, insomnia, poor posture, vision problems like myopia, obesity, cardiovascular disease, social aggression, depression, and anxiety.

Anthony's Notes from the Office:
The Accidental Cell Phone Vacation

A sixteen-year-old patient told me he dropped and broke his smartphone while getting off an airplane. He was en route to visit family in the Middle East.

His parents decided not to replace the phone until he got back to the States after the summer. Six weeks later, he was sitting in my office with his parents to talk about the start of his junior year. To the surprise of all, he hadn't asked to have the phone replaced.

He admitted he really didn't miss having it. That led to a discussion about the pressures of social media—Facebook, Instagram, Snapchat, and the constant volley of texts he normally received. He said it stressed him out because it was hard keeping up with everyone and everything. He also recognized that this upcoming academic year would be a challenge and he'd need to stay focused on school if he was going to have a shot at a decent college. He looked relieved not to have the burden of the technology. In time, he'd get another phone, but he was experiencing a different life without it. He joked that it must have been fate or divine intervention that made him drop the phone because he doubted he would have made the decision to forgo the phone on his own.

Many screens—and the stimuli they bring to us—are ones we own, but more are showing up in places where it's more difficult to control our exposure. Out in the world, no matter where your eyes land, there is likely to be a screen nearby competing for your limited attention.

Erin is a mom of three who recently told us about the assaultive digital screens she encountered at a gas station. "I jumped," she said. "A woman's voice started barking loudly at me. I thought someone had snuck up behind me and was angry." Turns out, the screen was advertising junk food and pitching credit cards. Erin felt momentarily off-kilter and couldn't escape because she was tethered to the gas pump purchasing gasoline for several minutes.

Erin registered a growing sense of irritation building up inside her. She told us the loud and visually frenetic ads had also captured the attention of her kids, who were peering through the backseat window. She rolled her eyes, adding, "As soon as I got back in the car—you guessed it—they started begging me for a soda and snack from the convenience mart." Erin is considering going to another gas station farther away that—for now, anyway—doesn't have screens.

> **Use Your Agency:** Pay attention to the various venues and businesses you frequent. Do they surround you with noise, harsh or excessive lighting, heat or cold?

Brock, a quiet analyst who travels frequently for work, told us about the screens he encounters in taxicabs. These screens are positioned only inches from riders' faces. He's figured out how to mute the volume as soon as he gets inside the cab, but it angers him. Cab rides used to be downtime for him, he explained, and he feels resentful having almost every free moment of his day invaded by what he calls "mindless chatter and consumerism."

Screens are now appearing in quiet places once devoid of such technology, like museums and libraries. Even outdoors is being intruded upon, with the sides of some city buildings being wrapped in eye-arresting digital screens.

Take Control of (and Design) Your Living Space

Two facts are indisputable. First, we live most of our lives indoors. Secondly, these spaces impact our levels of concentration, the quality of our thinking, our emotions, and our biological well-being. With this in mind, be more aware of the spaces in which you live and work, and when feasible, have a hand in designing those spaces to improve your cognitive functioning and health to enhance agency.

Will changing your living space impact you in any measurable way? There's ample scientific evidence that it will. Nancy Wells is a professor of human ecology at Cornell and holds a joint Ph.D. in psychology and architecture. Along with colleagues, she has studied a wide range of environments and their influences on behavior and coping skills, such as how the design of schools encourages kids to move or not move and how open kitchen plans influence how we eat. One of her research studies showed that living closer to natural settings served as a stress buffer for children.

You don't have to spend thousands of dollars to gain a meaningful impact from changing your living space. Start small. Clutter has a negative impact on your thinking and productivity, so consider uncluttering your spaces first to lower distractibility and improve organization. Screens and devices should not be in bedrooms or places you want to encourage relaxation and meditative calm states. Their presence alone, even when turned off, sends a signal to your brain to desire high stimulation. Ideally, screens should also not be present in rooms where you take meals. Lastly, it is helpful to designate a space specifically for deeper thought and self-reflection, like a reading room. The general operating principle here is that creating quieter, calmer spaces in your living environment will enhance your ability to put your attention where you want it, which improves your level of agency.

Make Changes to Your Living Space to Best Appeal to Your Senses

- *Your eyes:* Lighting matters. Is it too harsh, too bright, too dim? Create sitting areas close to windows or beneath skylights to expose yourself to natural light and to outdoor settings. It will help set your biological clock and circadian rhythms and fend off feelings of depression, especially in the shorter, darker days of winter.

- *Your ears:* Music can motivate or soothe, energize or distract, so think about what you listen to. When trying to focus, background music should be instrumental, although there is room for your own individual preferences here. Natural sounds have been found in some research studies to lower blood pressure, perhaps in part because they block out extraneous noise. If you live in a busy urban setting, you can download nature sounds free from many sites. And quietness in your living space is always healthy.

- *Your nose and mouth:* Candles and room diffusers scented with pleasing herbal fragrances help people feel attached to nature and invoke a calm state, but keep in mind many people react to strong artificial odors, as they can be distracting or overwhelming. Food smells can be distracting, too, but residual food smells can also stimulate our appetite in a healthy way—and many of us hold deeply fond memories of what was cooked in the kitchens of our youth (cookies, anyone?). A bowl of healthy fruit on a counter or a basket of assorted teas suggests to the mind more healthy eating habits and the value in pausing to take breaks and refresh oneself during the day.

- *Your skin:* Textiles and fabrics that come in contact with your body can signal a range of body and mind associations, such as feelings of

(continued)

warmth, coolness, and security. If you live in a large, open space, simply hanging a fabric can divide spaces and can give you a sense of greater privacy and security and eliminate visual distractions from other rooms. Pillows or textile hangings also can lower extraneous noise.

Meet the Extreme Vetters

For some people, controlling stimuli is a conscious, daily task because their jobs or lives depend upon it. Surgeons and pilots, for example, take measured steps to control stimuli in surgical suites and cockpits, respectively, to lower distraction, increase focus, and minimize potentially fatal errors. People with photosensitive epilepsy think about where their eyes go and avoid triggers, such as averting their gaze from flickering lights and avoiding certain theater or theme park experiences.

Milking a Snake Requires an Empty Mind

Jim Harrison does one of the most dangerous jobs in the world, and it requires a special kind of focus. Surrounded by almost two thousand poisonous snakes at the Kentucky Reptile Zoo, Harrison extracts venom for medical use. According to reports in *Business Insider* and *The New York Times*, he faces these life-threatening reptiles daily.

Harrison says he practices maintaining an "empty mind" during his work, controlling the stimuli of his own thoughts. Any thought can break his focus. He's been bitten ten times in forty-one years, has had one of his fingers amputated, and his heart has stopped four times. With remarkable calmness, he says in a video for the zoo's YouTube channel: "I died, and I came back and it hurt."

Other people go through life experiences that force them to become more acutely aware of stimuli in their surroundings. This happened when Zach returned from his second tour of duty in Afghanistan and was diagnosed with post-traumatic stress disorder, or PTSD. His symptoms are not as bad as those of some of his troop mates, he told us, and since serving in the military, he's become acutely attuned to the stimuli around him. He practices healthy hyperawareness, consciously considering where he is and the stimuli his brain is likely to absorb. Managing stimuli in this way, he's able to keep symptoms of combat-related stress at bay.

Another veteran we spoke with learned to practice healthy hyperawareness, too. Rico is a retired barber who worked in a busy city salon. Fumes from buses crept in when the door to the salon was propped open during warmer months, and the smell was similar to the diesel fumes from helicopters back in Vietnam, and that could ignite PTSD symptoms. Rico said he realized that it was best for him to work at the back of the salon and take cigarette breaks a block or so away in a small park where there were no buses and trucks.

We have something to learn from the extreme vetters. When you're doing something critically important, you need to be fully aware of the level of baseline and background stimulation around you. It can ruin your concentration and sabotage your performance. And if you're in an emotionally vulnerable place, seriously consider the amount and type of stimulation you're exposing yourself to. This will help you to keep your mind calm and your feelings under better control.

A Deeper Look: What's Happening on the Inside?

Distraction is only part of the resulting problem caused by information overload. Most of what comes at you—and much of what gets inside—may not be helpful or needed and in many cases could be harmful. Unwanted stimulation is constantly crossing critical neurological thresholds, getting past biological brain filters that help separate noise and unwanted messages from the meaningful information people are trying to seek and pass along to live their lives effectively.

In essence, too much noise is getting through and creating confusion, loss of self-direction, and stress. Sound engineers call this *a bad signal-to-noise ratio*. Businesspeople talk about the *law of diminishing returns*. Studies show that as distraction increases, performance is watered down, more errors are made, biological energy gets drained, and our emotions become overstimulated.

The cumulative result of all these events is that we lose the power to make good decisions for ourselves and for those we love. We're no longer in the lead. We're simply continually reacting to all the information coming at us.

Your remarkable sensory system is the pathway into your brain, particularly through your eyes, but there are other routes—ears, nose, mouth, nearly every centimeter of skin, as well as the muscles and joints beneath the surface. All these pathways are eagerly and constantly pulling stimuli in. That's the job they're designed to do. Your brain must deal with all that stimulation and accept, sort, prioritize, filter, process, and then react to all those stimuli constantly in real time.

The challenge is straightforward: You need to control stimuli prior to the point of entry.

Each of us needs to be more like Deborah, the executive who learned to create filters around what information came to her and what she worked to keep out. We need to consider our daily exposure to information in similar ways if we're to build and maintain personal agency.

Truth or Fiction? Slow the Pace and Volume of Information to Know the Difference

Daniel Gilbert is a psychologist at Harvard University who knows how not to be gullible. Through his research efforts, he's discovered why we end up believing falsehoods. Turns out, when someone tells you something—anything—your brain must first accept it as "real" or "true" to begin to evaluate its accuracy.

One possibility is that you quickly hold on to a piece of information as "truth" while you check your memory for what you may already know and then do a quick logical comparison. Does it add up? Does it jibe with known facts or what you have already experienced? If not, you doubt the information before placing it into the "untrue" information storage box of your mind.

Sounds fine, right? The problem, according to Gilbert, is that we tend to assume all information is true until otherwise noted. And because information is coming at us so fast from so many directions, we quite often don't have time to do a proper evaluation. Our brains get taxed. Lies, for example, if heard over and over, are frequently accepted as truths.

To guard against this, slow things down. Don't let people interrupt you or talk over you. Don't passively expose yourself to information from fast commercial media, such as advertising and opinion-based news programs that pander to your emotions and beliefs. Seek out quality information sources, such as newspapers and public radio and television. They may seem slower, denser, and not as easy or fun, but your mind will be processing better information at a slower pace. The bottom line is to limit your exposure to fast talkers and suspect information.

Boredom Is Good

As entertainment has become more portable, it has become possible to avoid any moments of *boredom*. Most of us resist boredom—we count on Hulu or Netflix to get us through doing the dishes or watch sports highlights as we eat our breakfast. But an emptier mind is freer to move in the direction of intentional, deeper, and more creative thought. Developing the capacity to be alone with yourself facilitates reflection, which is a building block of agency.

In today's highly stimulating world, ironically, many of us become agitated when we *don't* have anything distracting us. We don't like having our phones out of reach. In a series of eleven studies, reported in 2014 in the journal *Science*, subjects left alone in a quiet room with their own thoughts didn't report it as an enjoyable experience. When given the opportunity, subjects actually *preferred to administer electric shocks to themselves* instead of "being left alone with their thoughts" for periods of only six to fifteen minutes. This is madness!

Every few months, new digital devices come to the market. Our exposure to digital stimulation is increasing. It fills more of the space we used to have available between thoughts, between social encounters, between activities. These opportunities to experience downtime, moments of quiet, peace—really any type of restorative mental break—may be diminishing.

Make boredom a habit. Consider the advantages of allowing yourself to have occasional states of monotony. You're not distracted, you're not overstimulated, you have increased access to your fuller attention, and you have better powers of concentration and focus. The blankness of time and task provides more cognitive space for what comes next. The stage is set to marshal your thinking skills and satisfy the (temporary) void with something potentially very meaningful and deep. When you relabel "boredom" as a part of a calm mindfulness experience, it can become incredibly satisfying. A suggestion to get started is to set aside brief periods of time for this and then make them longer as you can tolerate more.

My Cell Phone, My Self

Might our clever digital companions be taking ownership of a piece of our mental capacity—some of our attentional bandwidth? We constantly touch and interact with them, we cradle them in our hands, we have them accompany us wherever we go, we rely on them, we get nervous when separated from them, and we panic when we believe they're lost. Many of us sleep beside our phones and wake up to them. For many of us, they're the first thing we reach for and touch each morning.

In a 2012 TED Talk, psychologist Sherry Turkle, founder and director of the MIT Initiative on Technology and Self, warned, "Those little devices in our pockets are so psychologically powerful that they don't only change what we do, they change who we are." Dr. Turkle is a pioneer in exploring how people relate to technology and its effects on those around them. We urge the reader to take nineteen minutes and watch this TED Talk to more fully appreciate why *Control Stimuli* is our first principle and why it's essential in developing and maintaining human agency in the twenty-first century.

Of her many observations, Turkle warns that screens are interfering with children learning how to be alone and quiet, an essential skill for them to develop self-reflection and deeper thinking. At this point, many of us fear, or even loathe being bored or simply alone with ourselves. These natural and healthy moments of downtime have been redefined as something to be avoided, "a problem to be solved" in Dr. Turkle's language. As soon as quiet, stimulation-free moments appear, we reach for technology to eliminate them.

Thaasophobia is an obscure term that might show up on the popular TV game show *Jeopardy!*, but it's becoming a more common feature in the families we work with. It's the fear of boredom and idleness.

Anthony's Notes from the Office: The Need to Be Constantly Plugged In

The "twins," as their parents efficiently refer to them, are identical, energetic seven-year-olds with matching summer buzz cuts. When they are asked to step out of my office for a few minutes so their parents can talk more privately, a row ensues. They protest and flat-out refuse unless they get a device. "I'll be bored!" one of them screams, while the other starts crying.

To be fair, they're entering an unfamiliar place, a barren cold spot—my wireless sitting room with *only books, small toys, and magazines.* Fear emerges on their faces. Eyes like saucers, mouths agape, clenched hands near their mouths, and yes, some of it is exaggerated, but their dad reflexively hands over his phone while their mother digs in her bag for the "travel iPad." As if supplied with pacifiers, the boys calm once they have screens, and they leave. Ten short minutes

(continued)

later, I step out to get them. They're at opposite sides of the room, their faces close to glowing screens, and they don't look up. I could have been a stranger entering the room, and they didn't notice. It takes some energy to unglue them from their screens, and this time, they're protesting for another reason: Now, they want to stay put.

While Turkle is "still excited by technology," she believes "we're letting it take us places that we don't want to go."

Media Requires a Warning Label

Cigarettes, alcohol, and commonly prescribed pharmaceuticals like Adderall and Prozac all come with warning labels. Has the time come for warnings to accompany the use of media, particularly social media? Is there unhealthy or unsafe exposure or dangerous doses, so to speak? On the surface, this may sound preposterous, but as you read these brief research findings below, ask yourself if you might rethink your exposure to media and start controlling it for yourself.

- A study in *The Journal of the Association for Consumer Research* found that the closer you are to your (turned off) smartphone, the more it acts like mental kryptonite. Simply keeping it anywhere near you distracts you and can lessen your capacity to think.

- The more time people spent on Facebook, the worse they felt and the less satisfied they were with their lives, according to University of Michigan researchers in a 2013 article for *PLOS ONE*.

- People watching news coverage of the 2013 Boston Marathon bombing reported higher acute stress two to four weeks after the tragedy than people who had direct exposure to the events at or near the bombings, wrote researchers in *Proceedings of the National Academy of Sciences of the United States of America* (*PNAS*) journal.

Because of studies like these and our clients' own awareness that enslavement to their phones is not good for them, we've found that many of our clients are starting to rethink exposure to their electronic devices. They're managing how much time they're "on," much like they monitor how much time they spend in the sun without sunblock, or how they space out x-rays at the dentist's office, or how much fish they eat that may have higher levels of mercury.

There's one more serious risk to consider. Social media, gaming, pornography, even seemingly innocent YouTube exploration, many now believe, can become addictive. While researchers are working hard to determine how addictive digitally delivered media is—or even if these forms of media are addictive—those of us who work with people to improve their daily performance and manage struggles are seeing this problem of addiction grow. Why is digitally delivered media hard to quit?

In terms of social media, the attention and validation you get from others is among the most powerful, potentially addictive social rewards you can experience. It may sound like a stretch to think of those innocent jolts of pleasure from Facebook likes, Instagram comments, contact requests on LinkedIn, or seeing your Reddit posts move up in popularity as mini shots of a euphoria-inducing drug, but studies are suggesting that we should be taking a serious look at how our brains respond when we're on social media. A groundbreaking study using functional MRI scans, conducted at the UCLA Brain Mapping Center and published in 2016, found that when teens viewed photos on Instagram that had more likes, it stimulated a region of the brain that also responds to highly rewarding things like chocolate and winning money.

Stopping these socially charged rewards coming at us is very hard, and for some, it's nearly impossible. They often come at you intermittently, and when that happens, you are getting dosed with rewards much like a gambler does sitting in front of a slot machine for hours, pulling levels or tapping screens. You are in a rigged, algorithmic system that's designed to keep you engaged for as long as possible.

Beware. Unpredictable (and frankly unearned or not terribly meaningful) bursts of good feelings and excitable digital moments are the most difficult to step away from—or, as behavioral scientists say in studies on rewards systems in lab rats, *the most resistant to extinction.*

Tips to Balance Your Use of Social Media

Here are some of the tips that we give to our clients to protect themselves from too much social media distraction:

- Don't have your social media feeds open all day. If you conclude that they're important to you, set a specific time or times during the day when you will use them and a time limit (and no more than two hours a day total). There are tools provided by Facebook and Instagram, as well as in the settings of many phones, to set your own time limits and monitor your daily use. When you are on, use them intentionally or with a specific goal—*I will catch up on my friends or the media people I follow*—and limit your use to accomplishing that goal.

- Weed out and eliminate social media apps you don't use or really need.

- Say "no" more frequently and decline more invites or participation on sites, and opt out of irrelevant webinars, group lists, email lists, and unnecessary updates.

- Balance your social life. For every two hours you spend on Facebook, have two hours of real face-to-face time with real friends.

- Kill the screens when socializing. Cell phones draw our brains away from quality human contact and interactions.

- If you've recently moved—as students do when they first move to college or as adults do when relocating for a new job—remember that this is an especially important time to significantly reduce your use of social media. Staying virtually tethered to the people you already know won't get you face-to-face with your new community. Get off screens and start developing a real network of new friends.

The American Psychological Association (APA) goes further. The APA recommends regular *digital detoxes*. The APA's 2017 *Stress in America* survey found a startling 86 percent of adults report being constantly or often connected to their electronic devices. To detox, the APA recommends finding regular times to *completely* unplug and stay away from *all* devices. Doing so, the organization says, will lower stress, maintain better mental health, and help break the chronic compulsive behavior many of us have to constantly check in with our electronic devices—reaching for digital stimulation to fill every free moment of downtime.

Pay Attention to Your Attention

Where we choose to put our attention is a momentous decision. Our attention is a precious commodity that defines our ability to be effective agents for ourselves.

Ask yourself right now how many interruptions you've experienced in the past twenty minutes, either from a text, screen, another electronic device, or an interruption from inside your mind, such as a nagging feeling of impatience to jump onto something else.

You may not have total control of where your eyes go or roam, but you ultimately have conscious control over where they stay. Spend an hour, or a day, or a week really paying attention to where your attention is going. Where does it get hijacked? Those screens that draw your eyes in don't play fair. Places that are noisy will also steal your attention. Determine the settings and people most likely to scatter or disrupt your attention.

Meanwhile, consider what you lose by not being more in charge of your attention. What have you been missing? What *aren't* you thinking about? Imagine the places your mind could go if you created the space for it to happen.

YOUR AGENCY TOOL KIT

REMOVE YOURSELF: Seek a quiet space by yourself when you need to reflect and concentrate.

FOCUS: Place your conscious attention onto what is of most importance *now*.

FILTER: Seek only the information you need for the current task. Ask for help from coworkers, family, and friends to prefilter raw information whenever possible.

AVOID THE JUNK: Minimize your exposure to distracting and misleading "junk" information.

MONO-TASK: Ditch multitasking except when it's absolutely necessary.

LOSE THE PHONE: Turn the ringer off and leave the phone in another room except when using it. If you are somewhere where you can't do this, put it away, turn it facedown, and generally keep it out of sight as much as possible.

TAKE NOTES BY HAND: Go analog with pen and paper.

LIMIT SOCIAL MEDIA: Just as you should never eat potato chips from a large bag without doling out a small portion, you are best off setting prescribed limits to social media use before starting.

EMBRACE BOREDOM: Know that time devoid of stimuli is a precursor to more intentional, deeper, and more creative thought.

GET OUTSIDE: Take a walk at least once per day for twenty to thirty minutes in all seasons, preferably in nature and without your phone.

BE HERE NOW: Close your eyes, relax, or meditate at least once per day for twenty to thirty minutes to be more present in the moment.

BE ON GUARD: Identify disinformation early to defuse it.

THE COMPANY YOU KEEP

THE PRINCIPLE
Associate Selectively

Spending time with empathetic, optimistic, open-minded people and weeding out those who have the opposite qualities will boost your mood, elevate your motivation, and improve your health.

Human beings are social animals—we all need some degree of interaction with other humans for basic survival as well as psychological health. And it turns out that our relationships are crucial to our sense of agency—or lack thereof. When we associate *selectively*—that is, with careful consideration, and when we surround ourselves with friends and family and communities who encourage us to reach our full potential, affirm our values and difficult decisions, reality-check us when we've behaved badly or are stuck in negative thinking, identify and nurture our talents, and cooperate in solving problems—we develop a broader confidence that extends to other parts of our lives. In turn, when we allow a pattern of negative or undermining behavior by close associates to go unchallenged, our agency is diminished, with sometimes dire consequences.

Associate Selectively is one of three Behavioral Principles presented in this book, along with *Control Stimuli* and *Move*. You'll notice that what these principles have in common is that they involve engaging in conscious behavior to cope actively with the world as it comes at you, as opposed to passively taking what the world gives you. Together, these principles free you up to move through life with a greater sense of confidence and self-efficacy.

Associate Selectively is essential because we express agency within the context of our relationships with others. Think about how a weekend spent with old friends or a vacation with a loving partner and family can send you into the next week with a powerful confidence that you'll be able to tackle whatever challenges it may bring. On the other hand, think of those moments when you feel withdrawn from friends and family or when they seem to be undermining you and how that can leave you feeling tired and sapped of energy.

The positive people in our lives can help get us past our worst versions of ourselves—and help move us to a more fully formed state. We cannot know or fully experience ourselves without real connection with others. Many people we think of as having high levels of agency will say something similar to this:

> You want to associate with people who are the kind of person you'd like to be—people who inspire you to learn and do things you might not believe are possible. Being around such people will move you in this direction. And *the most important people* by far in terms of this are your closest friends, family members, or your life partner.

It can't possibly be emphasized enough how important these people are. They represent your core inner circle. And they are critical to your level of agency.

Conversely, having a life partner, close friend, or business partner who unsettles, stifles, or, worse yet, abuses you can bring your agency to a screeching halt. Even a hostile neighbor who continually demands unrealistic things of you or spreads destructive gossip can impede your ability to think and act.

Making Choices to Keep Your Closest Relationships Healthy

Most of us were encouraged by our parents to choose our friends carefully, but of course, associating selectively does not mean jettisoning important relationships as soon as they become challenging. It does, however, require addressing negative, unhealthy patterns in relationships *early*. If a close relationship cannot be repaired or renegotiated to arrive at a healthier place, we sometimes have to make the hard decision to move on.

We saw this up close in one of our clients, Gail. She loved her fiancé, Tyler, but they seemed to be going in opposite directions. Gail's career had taken off in the six years since they graduated from college. Tyler, on the other hand, had been unemployed for nearly a year and was escaping into video gaming instead of looking for work. He was also smoking pot with a frequency that could no longer be described as recreational. To make matters worse, he'd begun to resent her success and had begun making cutting remarks that undermined her confidence.

Tyler was stuck in a bad place and soon began to make a serious impact on Gail. She found herself beset by doubt and worried about the future at a time when she should have been buoyed by her success at work. She was less motivated to take her morning run, which she'd always looked forward to and which had considerable physical and psychological benefits. Her motivation at work suffered, too—somehow Tyler's failure to grow alongside her made her feel more ambivalent about her own work. It was hard to enjoy success while watching someone she loved flailing on a self-destructive path.

Tired of feeling stuck and so unclear about her options, Gail decided to take a long weekend by herself to reflect on her troubling situation. She unplugged from email and social media.

Reflecting on her situation over the weekend, she came to the realization that she was paralyzed from taking any significant action because she was pretty sure Tyler wasn't going to turn things around anytime soon, and yet she feared never finding anyone she loved as much as she loved him and the possibility of being alone forever.

What Gail did next was in some ways a model of agency. While it was a bit scary at first, she attempted to focus on her main fear to assess its validity. Calmer reflection reminded her that she both made friends easily and enjoyed the process of meeting new people. Removed from the day-to-day drag of her relationship, she realized how much her confidence had been worn down by months of conflict and tension with Tyler. She saw for the first time that she was emotionally drained and stuck in what had clearly become a dysfunctional relationship. Gail came away from her weekend with the unshakable realization that living together had become unhealthy for both of them, and she decided to take the bold step of moving out. This decisive action, taken after much deliberation on Gail's part, restored her sense of confidence and agency. Her work life also improved once precious mental energy was freed up. And best of all, it also saved her relationship with Tyler, as they were ultimately able to communicate openly and honestly with each other and work through their problems.

One of the core principles of agency is that reflection combined with decisive action opens up potentially better paths and opportunities. Gail exercised agency by not muddling along indefinitely in an unhealthy intimate relationship racked with doubt. She also showed agency by making the decision to move out only after some careful deliberation, rather than impulsively walking out on Tyler. Imagine how Gail's relationship with Tyler might have looked six months or a year down the line if she hadn't taken the time to think more clearly and make the difficult decision she made. The more time spent in the relationship, the more she would have begun to see it as normal—likely getting pulled into distorted thinking and leading her to unintentionally further enable it.

Interestingly, the opportunity arose to reflect on this with Gail more recently. When asked what would have happened if leaving Tyler hadn't worked out, Gail reflected on her strong sense of agency. "Well," she said, "that was very likely. I also told myself that if things didn't work out, I'd be closer to meeting someone new and possibly better for me."

Healthy Boundaries Underlie Healthy Relationships

Suzanne is a gifted and hardworking student who saw her grades plummet during her sophomore year at college. A little like the characters in the TV show *Girls*, who spend a lot of their energy reacting to the needs of one another, Suzanne is a caring listener who became mired in her roommate's constant neediness. Her moody and often pessimistic roommate monopolized her time with stories of her latest dramas, turning Suzanne into a kind of 24-7 therapist. As a result, Suzanne found herself feeling more irritable and distracted and less trusting of others.

Think about it. Do you have someone in your life who invariably makes you feel worse? Do you do something about it or just let the situation continue?

Suzanne felt a sense of inner conflict. On the one hand, she really liked some things about her roommate and wanted to be a good friend to her. She had to admit, too, that in some ways she liked having someone who needed her that much and valued her advice. On the other hand, her roommate was in constant need of attention as one problem turned into another. In time, Suzanne became resentful and realized she couldn't go on this way.

The *True Friendship* Test

For those who are uncomfortable saying no and setting boundaries, there's often a need to think more deeply about whom they call a "friend." Genuine friends are rare and worth finding and holding on to. Often, we have to remind our clients that their time and friendship is valuable and that they shouldn't give themselves away to others too easily. And yes, there are a few clients whom we coach on being a better friend to others. We give them these points to consider in their quest to recognize what a true, close friend really is:

- A true friend doesn't hesitate to lend an ear. They are ready and willing to have a conversation with you. They're good listeners. They

(continued)

can hear you out patiently when you have a problem, without interrupting or forcing their views on you.

- If you're in a jam, they offer their time. They're willing to drive you to
the airport, help you move some heavy boxes, or take you to a doctor's appointment. And they do so without complaining or making
you feel guilty.

- A true friend will support you as much as you support them. Think of
a balance scale. If you're investing more into a relationship than you
are getting back, then the scale tips. You want to have equity in
what you put in and get out of relationships, especially with your
closest friends.

Acting on a friend's advice, Suzanne started spending more of her
time outside the dorm among more positive-minded friends and discovered that she enjoyed the quiet and lack of drama of the library and a
particular outdoor seating area during her breaks each day. This simple
way of creating boundaries made a big difference. Her resentment abated,
and her focus on her classes improved. And, interestingly, although her
roommate was angry at first because Suzanne wasn't always available,
she soon adjusted. She had to face some of her problems on her own or
with the help of other friends and became less needy.

Securing time with more supportive and emotionally healthy
people—the basis of *Associate Selectively*—is all the more relevant when
you consider how we human beings are socially and biologically wired.
People are constantly gravitating toward one another. We're always
watching and monitoring one another. This continual observing is called
social referencing. In addition, when nearby people are displaying strong
emotions, like sadness or worry, our brains will mimic these same emotions automatically. Feelings are contagious. That's because we have
mirror neurons. We'll explore both of these in more detail shortly.

Be Aware of How You Feel and Act When in the Presence of Others

To associate selectively, you need to be aware of your own feelings, stress level, and related behavior. The next time you find yourself suddenly ill at ease—which could mean you find yourself flustered, or feel your heart start to race, or you suddenly are heading out the door or to the kitchen to do some mindless comfort eating—reflect and ask yourself, *Who is in the room, or who did I just talk with, or what did I just experience? What's going on around me?* Fear, worry, and other negative emotions register quickly and often pass from one person to another with few or no words. This is how you can identify if you've "caught" someone else's "emotional virus."

If you spend an evening, for instance, with people who drink heavily, does that erode your ability to keep to your goals of limiting your own drinking? If you're having a productive workday, how much do you get derailed by an interruption by a snarky colleague? If you're volunteering for a committee at your community center or religious institution, do you think about staying home just to avoid another committee member who is a force field of complaints? An awareness of when your energy or mood or behavior is being affected by others, both positively and negatively, is the first step in getting better at associating selectively.

Even our physical health and our susceptibility to medical diseases are related to the company we keep. What we eat, how much we sleep, how sedentary we are, and how much exercise we get is strongly influenced by the people we choose to associate with. Always stay aware of yourself when you are around others, and if you are not comfortable, change locations or speak up!

Use Your Agency: Keep in mind that stress and anxiety is contagious. Pay attention to when your mood suddenly changes for the worse. Did you "catch" something from someone whom you might want to avoid in the future?

Tamara, an athletic woman in her late twenties, offered to drive her friends for a long weekend of skiing. She told us how odd it seemed, and how uncomfortable she felt, that as soon as they were on the road, her friends took out their phones and started texting. The car got completely silent. "It just felt so weird that they saw it as dead time," she said. "I told them, 'Hey, we should be catching up. We don't get a lot of time together in one place anymore.'"

The good news is that, with practice, you will become better at detecting—and then avoiding or managing your reaction to—the people around you who are frequently swimming in their own private thoughts or negative states of mind. You can say something, as Tamara did, or navigate away from people so that their distress does not pull you in and trigger your own. Conversely, you will be able to better detect those people who lift your spirits and support your goals and move to secure closer relationships with them.

We were impressed that Tamara spoke up. Most of us might not say anything and just keep driving in silence, but that would likely lead to feeling resentful or alone. The moment Tamara describes was brief, maybe not highly significant, but it nicely illustrates how often these micro-moments of associating with people happen every day. Be aware and proactive to enhance your associations with the people around you.

> **Use Your Agency:** You are not obliged to give yourself over to others—not your time, not your energy, not your happiness. Give yourself permission to question or say no to situations that pull you down.

Get Comfortable Saying No More Often

This is an especially important skill to practice around authority figures, family, and highly persuasive individuals. Like a muscle that you want to keep flexible and strong, saying no and setting limits about where and how you spend your time requires ongoing attention and practice.

Saying no can be as simple as saying, "I wish I could do that, but it's not possible for me." Create a simple phrase and rehearse it many times before you meet up with people who are highly demanding.

Don't feel you must apologize. You don't have to say you're sorry if you don't want to go out for drinks with colleagues, or if you don't want to buy Girl Scout cookies from a colleague who is selling on behalf of his daughter, or if you don't want to take on a volunteer project. Just say, "No, thanks, but I hope you have a good time / I hope you sell a lot / I hope it goes well." Saying *sorry* implies that you think you've made a mistake or that you are regretful.

We understand that this can be difficult. For many people, saying *sorry* has become an automatic phrase, but consider using that word sparingly. Don't feel like you need to use it when saying no to requests for your time.

Mitigate Negative Interactions When It's Impossible to Escape Them

It's not always possible to walk away from difficult people. Workplaces are particularly challenging. You come into direct, prolonged contact with groups of people under stress. In that environment, it is all too easy to pick up negative emotions, and it can seriously rob you of agency.

Sean's work life is a great example. A thirty-two-year-old former marine, he is physically fit with a no-nonsense demeanor. The way he carries himself, speaks, and makes eye contact projects confidence, not anxiety. Yet since leaving the structured environment of the corps, Sean finds himself under considerable stress. He is working two jobs, and the pressure is coming not from the hours but from the people who surround him. "I get these negative vibes," Sean recently told Anthony. "And it's getting to me. I don't know why."

One of his jobs is managing a busy waterfront restaurant. As he tells it, the restaurant environment is a magnet for drama. There are ongoing feuds among the waitstaff. People try to triangulate him to choose sides— petty political games among coworkers that lead to deliberately messing up orders, slowing down service, and not taking up the slack when the crowds show. It drives him crazy.

"By the time I get home, I'm worked up," he said. "I can't fall asleep and, trust me, I can usually sleep anytime and anywhere." He likes many things about his job, and he wants to stay; it's a great way to meet people and to challenge himself while also making good money. What bothers Sean most is being around people who don't do what they're supposed to do.

As Sean's story illustrates, it's best to keep to a minimum the time you spend with draining friends or coworkers. Watch out for people who talk more than listen—they are essentially treating you like an emotional dumpster. They leave you with a headful of their anxieties and negativity.

Anthony's Notes from the Office: The Power of Shrugging It Off

When he walked into my office for one of our sessions, Sean's furrowed brow and clenched jaw spoke volumes about the stress he was under.

"Maybe it's time to quit the restaurant job," he announced. The pettiness of his coworkers was driving him nuts.

I told him to stay put in the job if he liked it and use the *Associate Selectively* principle I'd recently taught him. Sean liked the strategic psychological operations (PSYOP) technique—selectively ignoring certain people and navigating around the drama to keep his mind clear. He approached the challenge like a military operation, and with practice, he got good at it.

Sean's strategy sounds simple, although for him it proved extremely effective: He realized that a simple shrug or smirk would suffice at times, allowing him to walk away and ignore provocative coworker spats. He also discovered humor's potency and gave himself permission to reconnect with his, as he put it, "goofball self" whenever he felt an uncomfortable or awkward moment approaching.

As Sean got to a place where he could maintain his strong work ethic yet not let the behavior of others drag him down, his level of anger diminished and his agency increased.

In later sessions with Sean, we delved deeper into what was setting him off. I explained that people can pick up negative moods around anyone anytime, but they are most susceptible around people who push their buttons, and that often goes back to their upbringing. In Sean's case, it traced back to his two demanding parents, who doled out love only when he met their needs. They also fought with each other and put Sean in the middle. Sean tried to do the right thing and worked harder and harder to take care of everyone else's needs. Working at the restaurant, he found himself getting pulled into triangles and trying to manage immature personalities, which was a throwback to his childhood and teenage years. Knowing the reason why he was more susceptible to others was helpful, but it was the actual use of selective association that allowed Sean to opt out from engaging in most of these negative interactions.

Managing interactions with family members who drain us presents special challenges. We want to spend time with family members, even if it's stressful; walking away is not always an option. But tactics like Sean's can still be incredibly useful: shrugging or making a lighthearted joke when family members or friends become negative or competitive. We know one couple who imagine their loud, self-absorbed in-laws as characters in a Woody Allen movie and encourage each other to keep talking even when these other family members interrupt them or try to dominate every conversation. This couple has found some humor to tap into and has made it a game they can share rather than allowing their emotions to rush in and upset them at every holiday dinner.

Use Your Agency: Don't engage in negative interactions if you don't want to. Develop strategies that allow you to block out unhealthy interactions that deplete you of your energy.

Mirror Neurons and Other Forces at Work

Sean was able to recognize the drain that his coworkers had become on him. Partly, this drain comes from the way we are hardwired.

The human brain has evolved over many thousands of years to pick up any and all potential threats and negative feelings expressed by those nearby. Neurobiologist Dr. Charles Stevens, a nationally recognized expert at the Salk Institute's Molecular Neurobiology Laboratory in California, told us, "There's a neural basis for how we share emotions. Cells in our brain will fire in the same way as the nervous system that we're watching. Our nervous systems respond similarly—are linked— they mirror each other—to whomever we are observing and close to." As if tethered by invisible cords, we are wired to replicate the moods of others—including worry, anxiety, and sadness—just by being in the same room. The positive moods of others are just as easily replicated.

Other research shows that moods can spread among networks of people like a social contagion. Sociologist Nicholas Christakis of Harvard Medical School and political scientist James Fowler of UC–San Diego looked at data from a twenty-year study that included information on the social networks of 4,739 people. Called the Framingham Heart Study, the research followed people from 1983 to 2003. The results were startling: On average, they found that for every happy friend in your social network, your own chance of being happy rises by 9 percent. For every one *unhappy* friend, your chance of being happy *decreases* by 7 percent. Happiness—as well as unhappiness—was essentially spread and shared.

Paul's Notes from the Field:
Address Your Stressors Head-On

I'd arrived at the conference room early to find Abby, a young, high-potential business leader, waiting for the meeting to begin. After a few minutes of catching up with me, she commented, "Paul, you seem wound up—are you worried about our meeting today? Is there something I should be concerned about?"

I smiled and released a breath. "No," I reassured her. I explained that I'd been in back-to-back meetings all day without a break. Abby had picked up tension in my body language through social referencing. It was adding to her stress as she and I were waiting for her boss, and her boss's boss, to join us. We both had a good laugh over it, and she noticeably relaxed before the others arrived. The meeting went well.

Abby was smart not to simply sit with the tension I'd carried into the conference room. It would have been easy for her to mistakenly attribute it to herself—or speculate that there was impending bad news related to her work performance about to be delivered. Associating selectively isn't only about avoiding people who create stress in you, which isn't always possible. It's about addressing the stressor head-on when you first notice it.

So always ask for clarification. Don't assume that what you're sensing is directly related to you or that it must continue. Tension can often be defused by facing it squarely.

Just how much are we influencing each other? Researchers are suggesting that our neurons fire in ways more similar to our friends than to strangers. A study published in 2018 in *Nature Communications* tracked the functional MRIs of people watching a wide range of movie and television clips from *America's Funniest Home Videos* to debates on CNN's *Crossfire*. Those who reported being socially closer showed more similar cortical activity. The study raises the strong possibility that the more we associate with others, the more neurologically synchronized we become. Or, perhaps, we simply gravitate to people who think more like we do. Either way, to bolster agency, be mindful of how much you share or absorb other people's ways of thinking. It is very comfortable to spend time with similar people, but consider if this might be limiting or influencing you in any unusual ways.

Health behaviors and habits are an important example. Like emotions, they can be picked up and shared between people. When you're in the company of others who eat poorly and are sedentary, you can unknowingly adopt these unhealthy habits and your health will be affected. Over time, you can even develop a serious metabolic disease such as type 2 diabetes, as researchers have noted. Fortunately, the opposite is true. Spending more time with people who have healthier life behaviors will help you adopt behaviors that keep you healthy.

Also in Action: Social Referencing, a Biological and Social Mechanism

Social referencing involves looking at other people and taking your cues from them. It starts early; infants and toddlers engage in social referencing instinctively. They look toward their parents and caregivers in confusing moments because they don't know if things are safe or if they should be worried. It's how they survive.

As we grow into adults, we also engage in social referencing, and although we do so less intensively than we did as infants, it remains a basic human skill that carries through adulthood, and it ties in with the goal of associating selectively in some interesting ways.

Raquel is a young woman, about twenty-five, who grappled with a fear of flying all her life. Her husband didn't share her fear of flying, and it was a source of tension. He wanted to travel, and Raquel's dread was a limitation.

Questioning her about what made her most worried, Raquel said that any kind of turbulence would make her afraid that something bad was going to happen. She would shut down and nearly have a panic attack. In talking with her, we learned that she flew very infrequently, so she never got used to the feeling of being in the air. That was part of the problem—she was not habituated to the experience.

Our suggestion was that she use social referencing to her advantage. Hone your focus, we said, on the people on the plane who have way more experience in this: the flight attendants. Look at them and only them. Look at their body language. Look at their faces. Speak to them. If anyone knows when something real is scary, it's them, because they have vastly more experience in this. If they don't seem scared, you shouldn't be scared.

Raquel was able to use this technique along with deep breathing. It calmed her down enough to fly more often, and fear stopped having as great a grip on her. Although the anxiety to fly still comes and goes, she is able to joke about it, another helpful tool to conquer the anxiety.

People depend on social referencing in a variety of situations—from tempering their fear of flying, like Raquel did, to projecting calm to others in time of crises. That was the case for Olen Kalkus, who was headmaster of a private school in Princeton, New Jersey, when the shootings at Sandy Hook Elementary School, in Newtown, Connecticut, happened in 2012. On that awful day, twenty young children were killed at the school, along with six adult teachers and staff members. Across the country, people were understandably on edge after the massacre, especially at schools. Kalkus told us that in those first few days and weeks, he noticed people watching him more closely. He believed they were trying to pick up on his moment-to-moment reactions to determine if he was feeling anxious. Unknowingly, they were scanning him, socially referencing someone in charge for signs that they were safe.

Kalkus said he made a point of looking everyone in the eye when talking and always speaking in a measured, calm, and reassuring voice during that stressful time. He knew that as headmaster, using social referencing this way would make his school's students, staff, and parents feel securer. He saw his job as providing this steadying influence. When possible, he stood close to others—and often used that as a way to reduce the anxiety that had built up. A handshake or even a hand on someone's shoulder, he says, made a difference.

Use Your Agency: Be aware of when you are picking up emotional cues—both positive and negative—from other people. Pay attention, too, to when people are looking to *you* as a point of reference for insight about how to react.

Maintaining Agency in Groups

As we have seen, social referencing is particularly powerful when there are elevated emotions. We've all been in large crowds, such as concerts, where everyone is excited and singing and moving in unison. We look around and pick up the vibe, so to speak; the happiness in those situations is contagious. But we've also been in or seen large groups of people who feel angry and tense, and it doesn't take much for a crowd like that to become aggressive and out of control.

When people push one another to think alike, there's a corresponding pressure to act, and sometimes that means acting in ways that are contrary to our individual needs or values. Sometimes *groupthink* and *tribalism* can lead to dangerously impulsive behavior. A political leader fanning people's fears to enter into an unnecessary war is one extreme example. Teens egging each other on to drink too much is another troubling example; so, too, are business situations when office executives participate in bad behavior, like telling sexist jokes or boasting of unethical shortcuts. Use the principle of associating selectively to help you avoid getting pulled into these situations. It helps you to lead yourself more and follow the herd less.

If others in a group around you look worried, or if the tone seems suddenly different in some way, you'll automatically pick up on these signals. It happens in groups big and small. At home, parents pass worry and stress to their children, and vice versa. It happens in classrooms with teachers and students, in workplaces among coworkers, in informal social settings and in more formal settings—basically anywhere people congregate. It happens in crowds, as when the fear of missing out on certain products or opportunities pushes people into primitive aggressive actions—for example, excited holiday shoppers on Black Friday hoping for a bargain can quickly turn into a mob that stampedes and harms others.

Why do we have this evolutionary skill to pick up emotions in groups? We're designed that way because we need to know if something bad is going on and if we're under threat. We're built to pick up potentially threatening cues that something might be wrong at any moment. Most of the time, we're not in any danger. Still, we are tethered to the emotional feelings of those around us just in case.

Your Personality Is a Factor

People pleasers and hard workers are especially susceptible to the needs, anxieties, and negativity of others. It can work in their favor to try to please others in the group because they feel rewarded for this effort, but they are also taken advantage of quite often if they repeatedly and unwittingly give more than they receive.

That's why it's important to associate selectively. Think carefully about where your brain is at all times. Is it around people who react rationally and calmly and approach the world with openness and good cheer? Great! But if it is around people who overreact, are mostly pessimistic, and are looking to pull you into their problems, you need to move out and find healthier people.

Here's an exercise to help you become aware of how often you pick up cues while in groups.

Next time you find yourself in a group and something unexpected or uncomfortable happens, look around as if you're a psychologist or an anthropologist studying human social behavior. Stay detached. Maybe someone makes a racist or homophobic comment. Maybe an elevator temporarily stalls between floors. Maybe someone at a gathering is drunk and obnoxious. Observe what happens. People turn toward each other to see reactions. If the moment grows tense, people scan each other for who may be in charge or who might know what to say or do. Don't do what most people reflexively do in these seemingly stressful moments and reference others. Instead, step outside of the moment briefly and be a keen observer and you will be thinking more independently.

Mirror neurons are at work, social referencing is at work—and all of it is automatic, unless you stay aware of what's going on. You want to avoid catching other people's worries, like a virus, and spreading them around. Instead, size people up and ask yourself, *Who around me seems to be overreacting and getting agitated?* Avoid listening to or moving toward those people. Then ask, *Who seems most reasonable and measured at the moment?* Approach those people, either in the moment or afterward, to ask what they think is going on. This is an active way to practice and engage your skill of social referencing.

Associate Selectively in *All* the Worlds You Inhabit

We typically socialize most with our families and closest friends, but there are broader ways to think about associating selectively. An important part of associating selectively goes beyond just choosing supportive friends; it involves a mind-set where you see yourself as an important participant in the various rings of community that make up your life. Some of us never make it out of the inner ring, and that is a shame, for there is nothing like the agency that comes from participating and contributing to a community outside your immediate circle. So take a moment to think about the various worlds you occupy beyond your friends and families. There's your local community. Your church. Athletic centers and communities based on mutual interest, such as your softball league. The corner pub where you run into familiar faces. Obviously, your state, region, and country. And your planet. Assess your level of involvement and connectedness. If we are talking about your town or state, do you keep up with local news? Do you stay informed about pressing issues? Do you vote? Would you ever consider volunteering your time to be part of solving a problem? Do you recognize the ways in which these matters influence your quality of life, your level of agency?

The Power of Expanding Circles

As art school was nearing its end, Jonah, a photographer, was planning to leave Michigan and head back to New York City, where he grew up. Job prospects were good in advertising and graphic design, and there were a lot of freelancing opportunities. Jonah's parents were excited to have him return home, and his on-again-off-again college boyfriend was moving to Brooklyn.

Then something unexpected happened. Over semester break, Jonah visited an exhibition at a gallery showing an artist whose photographs of downtown Detroit—simultaneously beautiful and horrifying, showing the decay of a neglected, once world-class city alongside emerging signs of vibrancy—mesmerized and inspired him.

When he got back to school, he visited parts of Detroit shown in the photographs that he'd previously avoided. He discovered that many artists were setting up studios in the city's abandoned buildings. These new communities rising up from the ashes spoke to him deeply as an artist. It bolstered his identity as a creative person with positive messages and offered unique opportunities to professionally connect. He felt an instant connection and desire to be part of this movement.

Jonah decided to spend at least a year after graduation living in one of these new artist communities. He would expand his circles of association in the process, becoming a part of the building of a new community and furthering his career at the same time.

Selective association at this level means choosing to actively participate in the larger communities surrounding us in order to influence them in positive ways so that they, in turn, are healthy and supportive communities for us to develop and express our personal agency.

Pramila Jayapal made history in 2017 as the first Indian American woman elected to the U.S. House of Representatives. To us, she is important as a case study in building a social network from the ground up, associating selectively to establish and move her life forward in a meaningful way. Pramila first arrived in the United States, by herself, at the tender age of sixteen. Imagine showing up at a college dorm, knowing not a soul, significantly younger than everyone else, having grown up in a radically different culture on the other side of the world.

Pramila took measure of her new world and got busy creating a community around herself. "I was deeply attuned to those early surroundings. How do I learn everything I need to learn from the people who looked and acted so different from me at that time?" She recognized the need to develop a social support network. She knew she needed guidance to help her make better decisions in a world whose rules and norms she didn't fully understand. She forged healthy, new relationships one by one.

After college, she earned an MBA from Northwestern and then got a job in finance but quickly started questioning the direction of her life. "I kept feeling like I wasn't quite doing what I was meant to do—knew I wasn't quite happy," she told us. Next, she took a position in sales and marketing with a medical company. "Back then, I was the only person of color selling defibrillators in West Ohio and Indiana. I would go out on emergency vehicle calls—I went to people's homes and got to know their kids and spouses. I'm selling equipment to these people, and I needed to know who they were." Her intuition kept nudging her. "I trust myself—I trust my inner feelings—and let them guide me," she said. She soon made a significant change in the direction of her life once again, this time moving toward public service and social justice.

She founded the advocacy group Hate Free Zone to address the rise of hate crimes toward immigrants in the aftermath of 9/11. She registered new American citizens to vote. She served on mayoral advisory committees in Seattle and won a state senate seat in Washington in 2014.

Running through her life story is a strong and consistent focus on the value and the importance of communities in people's lives. She now works from her position as a congresswoman to strengthen communities and to help the newest arrivals to the United States to successfully build lives here as many previous generations of immigrants have done before them. This is challenging work that often requires her to manage strong emotions, such as fear and doubt, both in herself and in others, to get things done. "I choose to stay positive," she explained. "I'm an eternal optimist in terms of my beliefs about the world and other people. I always see the good in people."

The Social Fabric of Your Life

Realize that you can be both supportive of and supported by any of the communities that you encounter in your life. The key is your active involvement, your active choice to associate. You can probably see how this would be true in your local town, where volunteering to coach a team or joining a crew improving a playground benefits you and your community. But what about places that are less obvious—say, the towns through which you commute briefly on a daily basis? It starts with the mind-set that you are a guest of the community you are traveling through and that you should show respect. In our hometown Boston, ground zero for aggressive driving, you occasionally will see a sign some community member has placed along the roadway imploring drivers: *Please Drive Like You Live Here.*

Jeff is a prototypical Angelino. Outdoorsy, fun job in the entertainment industry, extroverted, and in love with his ultracool car, which he drives everywhere throughout the Los Angeles basin. A good friend of his mentioned a weeklong organized cycling trip through Oregon that happens each year. Jeff's first thought: *I'm a city guy who loves tennis and the beach. I enjoy my Peloton, but why would I want to be on a bike for a week?* His friend talked him into it. They biked through some of the most spectacular natural beauty Jeff had ever seen, but it was the towns that they biked through and stopped to visit along the way that made the greatest impression on Jeff. Most of the small towns rolled out the red carpet and welcomed the cyclists. At ten to fifteen miles an hour, alone with his thoughts for a good chunk of each day, he noticed things about these communities he would never have seen and experienced while driving. He met and learned things about some of the residents when they stopped and had conversations with people. The week left him feeling a sense of connectedness to himself and his fellow countrymen that he found difficult to describe in words other than to say it was a life-changing experience.

What we are suggesting here is that you need to create your own "biking through Oregon in September" experience and regularly repeat it over and over again in your life. At the very least, take interest in the lives of others and have empathy as you encounter their worlds, even if it's only a brief encounter. They aren't strangers if you are able to shift your view of things. Each community touches the next, sometimes literally, and making positive connections will spread outward and affect all the people around it.

You might ask yourself the following questions regarding each of the communities you touch and inhabit: *How might I offer support to this community, and how does being connected to others in that community support me? Can we support one another's interests and needs? How do my actions affect how other people think and feel, and vice versa? What helps to motivate and encourage me to increase my level of participation? Is my involvement welcomed or discouraged? Is the social fabric of the community tightly woven together, or does it appear frayed?* There are many communities today where the social fabric is fraying. Our participation and interest can make a difference—and again, what is often less apparent is how this benefits us.

Larger communities have particular gravitational forces all their own, often described as their *culture,* and some can pull you in directions that are inspiring and supportive while others may not necessarily be healthy or positive for you. Jonah, the aforementioned photographer, was drawn to spend more time in a community that inspired and supported him as an artist. As you consider your wider circles of association, question what you are experiencing.

You may realize that some communities might be pulling you in directions you don't wish to go. And just as we have to look at personal relationships that might be pulling us down, we should also look at communities that might be having the same effect.

Eve, a single mother of two, recognized that her young kids were being overwhelmed by the requirements of the school they attended. And the school's culture, which involved ungodly amounts of homework, had the kids buckling under the pressure of ever-longer projects and ever-shorter deadlines. To make matters worse, the *parents* had begun to make homework a kind of competitive sport. *Your son is only doing two hours of homework a night? My kids do four!*

Eve sensed something wasn't right. She caught an image of herself one day in the mirror and realized she wasn't looking her usual healthy self. She too was overwhelmed, worrying about her kids, having to drive them long distances to school on traffic-clogged roads, and helping manage their lengthy homework assignments.

When an opportunity arose to relocate to a different state with a forward-thinking public school–education model that bucked current competitive trends and refused to pile on homework or teach to tests, she jumped on it. Beyond less homework, an unexpected benefit emerged. "Instead of long commutes in the car," Eve explained, "I moved close to my new job and to the kids' new school. Before, my kids were buried in iPads while I fought the daily traffic. They never said a word to me or to each other unless it was to have a spat. Now, I walk them to school and we talk with each other along the way. We all feel happier and more relaxed. I really feel at home in our new community."

Where you live, where you work, and whom you socialize with during the course of your days all matter. We don't always have to end a friendship or relocate like the people we've met here, but we must always seek to connect with people who help us be the people we want to be.

Make Connections Within Your Community

Consider this question: *Are all the communities I am a part of healthy and supportive to me, or do they bring me down?* Start with the smallest circles of association and work your way outward. *Do my family and friends value and support me to be at my very best? What about my place of work and my colleagues? Am I learning, growing, and developing as part of my work? What about my neighbors and neighborhood? What about my physical location—do I live in a town and a state or province that offers opportunity and support for me to expand my personal agency?*

If the answer is no, what should you do? You don't necessarily need to leave your loved ones or immediately pack up and move. Instead, start exploring and participating in some groups and organizations around you. Or find a moment and connect with someone new. One woman we spoke with talked about a favorite corner grocer that she decided one day to break the ice with. That grew into a friendship. Her son, some years later, ended up working at the store.

Some people tell us that they see many of the same folks every day, like at their gym, but don't say hello or even nod. One man in his thirties told us, "It's weird, I see these guys at the gym more than most of my friends. We're within feet of each other, doing the same thing, but locked in our own worlds with our earbuds in place." He started chatting one day with someone he'd seen many times over the past few years and noticed that a few others nearby joined in for a few minutes. Those friendly faces and few minutes of social support is something he now values and looks forward to each day.

People have told us about forming social connections at delis, coffee shops, their favorite pubs, really anywhere a casual friendship can spring up. Societies are formed and improved by everyone's participation. The society you live in needs you and your input. Through your participation, you will feel less isolated, more engaged, you will get your ideas out into the world, and you will gain agency.

Who Is Your "Friend"? Associating Selectively in the Digital Age

In recent years, our social lives have rapidly been moving onto digital platforms. With advancing technology, we are spending less time interacting with one another in real time, face-to-face. Social media is fun, fast, and designed to keep us tuned in. It's also mostly free—but is it really cost-free? Companies make money by selling advertisements that interrupt our experience, and they track our online behavior for marketers and sell them our data. In this rapidly evolving landscape, we need to ask ourselves, *Are we using social media, or are we letting it use us?* The answer is probably some of both.

There are other hidden costs. The time we spend on social media is time we surrender from engaging in other activities, such as socializing in real time. We often make this trade-off unwittingly. As psychologists, we can't emphasize the point around *opportunity cost* enough. As Sherry Turkle of MIT notes, we all too willingly sacrifice conversation for mere "connection." Turkle adds, "Human relationships are rich, they are messy, and they are demanding, and we try to clean them up with technology."

Watching someone's body language, hearing their voice, mining the complexities of emotion in the subtle expressions of a human face, and engaging in real-time, fluid back-and-forth volleys in the same room cannot be replicated on screens. Humans have evolved to require being physically alongside one another to communicate, gather information, and, most importantly, to build and share intimacy. This is a primary building block of agency.

> **Use Your Agency:** Think about what you gain from spending time, in person, with friends versus interactions on social media. Don't allow online interactions to become a substitute for in-person time with the people you most care about.

We maintain that if the bulk of your socializing is being done through social media, you will have diminished agency. Our message, though, isn't one of anti-technology. Far from it. Technology and social media are useful and valuable tools. Our message instead is about awareness and balance. Digital platforms are absorbing more of our precious time. With only so many waking hours in our busy days, real human experiences are being swapped out for screen time. The trade-off is real, and it's not without risk. Heavy exposure to social media has been correlated in studies to a number of psychological problems, including depression and anxiety. Researchers also tell us that self-esteem may decline, and behaviors—what you buy, who you vote for, who you date, who you call a "friend"—are being influenced, persuaded, nudged along, and redirected click by click.

Anthony's Notes from the Office:
Hyper-Social Referencing

Jamal is a high school sophomore. You wouldn't know he's shy just by passing him on the sidewalk. He's tall and broad shouldered and

(continued)

moves with the fluidity of an athlete, but Jamal worries a lot about how he measures up. He constantly compares himself to others. His worries intensify at school because peers judge one another harshly. They trade jabs and make comments about social status constantly. Being attractive and a talented athlete have pulled Jamal into the "popular group," where many eyes track him through the hallways. He's expected to act relaxed and above it all.

The pressure gets to him. He confided in me one day that he's been escaping into the bathroom with his smartphone when the stress builds too high at school. There, away from the high expectations of others, he scrolls rapidly through Instagram and Twitter to distract himself. "It takes my mind off the stress," he told me.

What Jamal doesn't realize is that his worries of fitting in are only being amplified by the smartphone right in his hand—and he's exposing himself to more stress every time he swipes through the images or tweets. The phone unloads exaggerated images and messages into his mind that—intentional or not—make him question his worth. Is he attractive enough? Popular enough? Is he as good an athlete as everyone says? Is he smart enough to make it into a college? Is he going to be rich?

He opened his Instagram to show me what he's been looking at. "Check it out," he said while he scrolled through photos and video clips of laughing teens that captured moments of their days. To me, the kids looked a little too perfect, falsely confident, artificially poised and posed.

I explained a bit about agency to Jamal and how associating selectively works, and Jamal, to his credit, listened with great interest.

We came up with a simple plan. He agreed that he would try deep breathing rather than escaping to the bathroom with his phone at the first sign of feeling anxious. If that didn't work, he could go to the bathroom, and rather than scroll through social media, he could use apps to guide him on staying calm and simple meditation. We also arranged for him to shoot baskets in the gym a few times a day with one of his favorite gym teachers who makes him feel valued and lifts his spirits. Less social media will mean less exposure to exaggerated and ego-deflating social messages. More time in the company of supportive people who reflect back to Jamal his genuine worth will better help him build confidence and cope with social anxiety.

How Social Media Changes You

Social media is full of carefully selected images and messages. One teen we spoke with called it "the three Fs": *fun, fabulous, and famous* people. It's also full of shorthand conversations and, often, cutting and nasty quips that promote a culture of competition. Sometimes we feel envious of the places others visit and the things that others have. A lot of social media can be a numbers game. Many people tell us they've caught themselves reloading feeds over and over to see whether the number of "likes" and "retweets" on their posts are moving up, while they watch, over and over, how popular (or unpopular) the posts of other people are. For people on dating apps, there is a continual supply of information about whether people are looking at your profile and "swiping left" (meaning they don't find you attractive) or "swiping right" (meaning they're interested).

Be Wary of Social Media's Power to Manipulate Your Desires

Social media's power is changing us—or at least it has the power to as people take lifestyle cues from social media trends.

Rachel Monroe, writing in *The New Yorker*, explored the social media movement of so-called van life, where people document their lives on the road living out of vans, with days spent surfing and

(continued)

doing yoga and living outside of regular consumer culture. The #vanlife social media posts are extraordinarily popular, with millions of followers who gaze wistfully at the bucolic photos and dream of different selves. "God, I wish my life were that free and easy and amazing," is a typical comment.

The problem is that the digital world is full of people and organizations that are selling us something, and their pitches are often hidden. When door-to-door salesmen show up at our homes, we know we're being marketed to. Online, the enticements to buy things are often subtler and more disguised.

The van life article, for instance, pointed out that some of the most popular celebrities in the bohemian van life world are making money by including product placements in their images. What their followers are seeing as a life free from consumer culture is actually a life supported by branding partnerships.

Technology journalist Farhad Manjoo, writing in *The New York Times* in 2017, noted the power of these digital social signals. He cited a 2006 study from Microsoft researchers showing that music downloads were influenced by people being able to see how many times *other people* had downloaded a song. This tendency spiraled into a reinforcing "inequality" in media choices: "When people could see what others were downloading, popular songs became far more popular, and unpopular songs far less popular," Manjoo wrote.

Take this same idea and transfer it to Facebook or Twitter or Instagram. In the same way, we can see which of our friends have posts that are popular, and we can see our own posts by comparison. Having your post be less popular can be a gutting feeling, especially for teenagers, and adults are not immune to wanting the same affirmation. So we see both behaviors and emotions being driven by participation in social media. How deep and widespread are these effects? There's now experimental evidence based on millions of Facebook users (published in 2014 in *PNAS*) of massive-scale emotional contagion through social networks, where emotional states are transferred to others digitally. Being on your devices and the time you spend on them matter.

We are also seeing people change themselves to fit what's expected of them by others they don't even know or may never meet. Mia is a successful businesswoman in her early thirties. She uses social media to get control of her stressful, often excitingly fast-paced job, but she also began to feel unsettled by its role in her social life. Like most young people, she was using dating apps but caught herself refining her dating profile regularly for the women she was attracted to. "Changing myself on OkCupid, I started to become a person I no longer recognized," she said. "I slipped into thinking I should try adopting certain personas to see which got more responses." As Sherry Turkle's research at MIT suggests, not only does the technology change how we relate to others, it changes how we relate to ourselves. This can have a seriously negative affect on your level of agency.

Mia started feeling like her public persona was beginning to rewrite her real persona, and it was making her increasingly uncomfortable. She also said she realized that keeping up on activities she heard about through social media—from networking events to friends' invites to parties—was causing her to move away from the few people she was closest to. The realization that she was losing experiences of greater depth in her social interactions made her decide to take action. She's keeping a sharp eye on how much time she spends in the virtual world and making it a priority to stay connected with her oldest, closest friends.

Like any technology, the force of social media is something we must be wary of if we're to use it intelligently and positively. Without a careful awareness, the normal human activity of comparing yourself to others can go into hyperdrive and reach unhealthy levels on digitally driven social platforms designed to capture and keep your attention. Never lose sight of this basic reality: The lives presented by others online are typically highly glossed over, unreal versions of themselves. People aren't—and shouldn't be—always that perfect looking, happy, and well adjusted. Most people confess to taking up to ten selfies before getting the right "spontaneous" image that communicates a message that they are blissful, fit, and alluring. Taking cues from a false world of constant wonderfulness can set us up for all kinds of disappointment and self-obsession.

There's a much darker element to social media, too. It's changing how young people in particular view themselves. We have worked with teens who are drawn to online forums where people seek attention in more troubling ways, such as how many cuts they have made to their arms and other areas and how thin they have made their bodies. In addition, more and more people, both teens and adults, are trolled by scary, hostile online stalkers, sometimes anonymous and sometimes not. Some teens have gone as far as telling other teens, "Why don't you just kill yourself?" From digital martyrdom to dangerous bullying to simply high-drama conversations, the social media world can be as dangerous a place as anywhere else—sometimes more so due to its anonymity. It may not be "real" in the sense that it's only a snippet, an offhand nasty phrase, a picture or emoji, but these digital daggers cut deep. They enter our minds and have profound effects on emotions and behavior, especially for young people or those at a vulnerable place in their lives. Selective association in this instance involves both the recognition that this danger exists and being aware of early signs. Parents and educators need to coach young people to always know (and verify) who they are interacting with. While it is best to steer clear of these darker elements before becoming embroiled in them, they can catch any of us off guard. We frequently tell people to disengage at the first signs of negative and inappropriate behavior.

Associate Carefully: Rethinking Your First Impressions

It's difficult for many of our clients to grasp how vast the individual differences among people can be. Human beings are among the most diverse animals on the planet. Time and time again, we all make the assumption that other people are more similar to ourselves than they in fact are. While people obviously appear different on the outside, the differences on the inside are even greater because of the complexity of our brains. This holds true even among members of our own families. Many of us have a tough time fully appreciating this. It is the primary reason why it can be so difficult to recognize that associating with some individuals can actually be highly destructive to our personal agency and overall health and well-being.

There is a subset of people who are dangerously different from you—sociopathic, even—and they often do not appear so different on the surface because they can be adept at passing as normal. Chances are you will come in contact with some of these dangerous and manipulative people from time to time. It may be someone who on the surface seems to take an interest in you and seek your friendship but who in reality is poorly equipped to be a positive, supportive force in your life. Such people can put not just your psyche at risk but your physical safety as well.

The Danger of False Agency

Our world is replete with examples of people promising to use their agency for your benefit. Demagogues, charlatans, con artists, manipulators, despots, and sociopaths exist in all shapes and sizes. They include politicians such as Adolf Hitler (perpetrator of the Holocaust) and Joseph McCarthy (U.S. senator who led reckless public attacks on people he accused of being Communist sympathizers and homosexuals) as well as business executives Kenneth Lay (CEO of the energy company Enron during its enormous bankruptcy scandal) and Bernard Madoff (convicted of running the largest investment Ponzi scheme ever). These people often claim to have the answers to all your problems and to be able to give you all that you need.

They often are compelling personalities with good selling skills. They are adept at homing in on what they think you need and what they can provide. Cult organizations and their leaders often

(continued)

use false agency to lure people into their orbit by offering a similarly false sense of security.

And what do these people look like? For the most part, they look just like you or the person next door. They do not come with warning labels. What they have in common is that they sell themselves as uniquely able to provide you with something that only they can deliver, and they can be highly persuasive by appealing to your base emotions. But you will always see chinks in their armor if you are paying close attention. For this reason, it's best to exercise appropriate skepticism and cautiously steer clear of this type of person at the first sign that they are not what they appear.

It's not our intent to make you paranoid, but we do want to make it clear that *you need to be able to change your mind about people,* and you need to be aware of how your first impressions of and feelings about someone can cloud your judgment. From romantic prospects who turn out to have an underlying cruelty to work bosses who begin unloading passive-aggressive criticism on a regular basis, our circles of association can become speckled with people whom we need to get away from as soon as possible.

Failing to recognize this is common, and it's a real human failing. It's something many of us are not good at. Yes, in lots of ways you are better off trusting people initially, but you need to also be open to modifying your view about a person as you begin seeing their true behavior. You need to allow your intellect to overrule your emotions. This is where a lot of people make mistakes—they don't change their perspective on another person when they should.

Fortunately, most of the people who enter our lives are not out-and-out dangerous, but that's a pretty low bar for the company we choose to keep. You have to learn how to stop holding out hope that people will always remain exactly as you first imagined them to be or desire them to be. Sometimes you need to listen to the little voice in your head that says, "Run for the hills!"

Use Your Agency: Give yourself permission to reevaluate positive first impressions of people, from work colleagues to romantic prospects to parents of your kids' friends. The true character of most people takes time to emerge.

Don't Fool Yourself About Isolation

As you work to limit the people who have a negative pull on you, be careful about going too far. We believe that isolation is one of the most limiting factors on human agency.

How many times have you gone off into your thoughts alone, come up with a brilliant idea or a damning perspective on a situation, and then shared it with a friend—only to realize that your thinking was actually pretty muddled? Too much isolation can prevent us from realizing our full agency because we typically learn best while interacting with other people. Human contact provides necessary perspective. People who are isolated from other people for an extended time miss out on that. If you're outside the reach of other people too often, you're likely to become mentally, as well as biologically, vulnerable.

It's a tender balance. There's a big difference between spending time alone, which is healthy and facilitates introspection and reflection—both of which are critical to agency—and being dangerously alone. Silent retreats can be valuable, and social introversion is fine, but keeping yourself away from other people and isolating your thoughts will atrophy your social skills, can accentuate your neuroses, and will get you stuck in skewed thoughts and trapped in emotional rabbit holes.

There are forces at work in society that are causing more isolation. Many people bring work home with them or work two or more jobs. Many people spend hours of free time in front of computers or phones, zipping through social media channels, and find themselves becoming isolated without ever realizing it. They wouldn't call themselves cut off, but on important levels, they are socially starving. Over time, their social skills begin to decline as they use those skills less frequently.

Associating with people allows us to see ourselves more realistically.

It allows us to feel valued. It helps us to think, to reflect better, and to make better choices. And when it comes time to act, which happens with all people who are paying attention to their agency and taking charge of their lives, it ensures that we will be as effective as possible in dealing with other people; nine times out of ten, we have to associate with other people when we take action. We can't always do everything by ourselves, so we have to make sure that our thoughts aren't stuck, that our social skills are in tune, and that our self-absorption is in check.

Work to Build New Associations as You Age

Older adults may be better at associating selectively. A growing body of research suggests that older people are more satisfied with their social lives than younger adults. They stay connected with and invest in closer, more satisfying relationships. They don't invest as much time trying to meet new people or engaging in casual socializing; they're better at weeding their social garden. This, however, can be both a strength and a weakness. A ten-year study that followed people eighteen to ninety-four years of age (published 2014 in the *International Journal of Behavioral Development*) found that by midlife, people's social networks started to decline. Some of that decline was due to death, but mostly it was due to letting go of "peripheral" people. Further, older people in the study reported more positive emotions in their relationships despite having fewer relationships than younger adults. It's quality over quantity.

But older adults do face unique social isolation challenges by virtue of a declining social network, as described by Rook and Charles, two researchers from the University of California–Irvine. In a 2017 article in *American Psychologist*, they point out that having smaller networks can place older people at risk for getting stuck in negative relationships. Older people may have fewer options to associate selectively. They may not have the means or health to move away from people who aren't supportive or helping them to stay positive.

New Friendships Should
Blossom at Every Stage in Life

Renee is in her early seventies and is a busy, engaged, socially connected person we met on our travels to Texas. She had to remake her life when her husband, Grant, unexpectedly died from cancer fifteen years earlier. They didn't have children, and there weren't many relatives close by. Renee saw the writing on the wall.

"Grant," she said, "was the connector. He knew everyone. I didn't use my social muscles much in the thirty-eight years of our marriage. Now it's up to me to make that happen." Renee consciously invested in rebuilding her social life without Grant.

She was strategic, having worked as an organizational assistant for Elizabeth Arden in the 1960s in Manhattan, an experience that taught her how to handle stress and nearly anything thrown at her last minute. Renne loves animals, so she got a dog, a transition that wasn't easy for her possessive Siamese cat. Dog walks got her out and about the neighborhood, and she met other dog owners. That led to play dates at the dog park. Joining community organizations and serving on her condo board were also good ways for her to connect.

She makes it a priority to schedule visits with relatives and maintains friendships across the country. She also has found that she enjoys socializing with people of different ages. "It keeps me in the know," she said, laughing. Renne is also using digital technology to her advantage. She sends out a short list of interesting articles she finds to friends. "Sometimes when I'm traveling, I can't send my reading list out. But I hear about it—people have come to expect it!"

In our older years, those of us who are introverts are more at risk of becoming socially isolated than extroverts. People approaching retirement who have built remarkable professional careers are also at risk of losing their social support networks and sense of competence and mastery, and they need to think carefully about that transition beyond work life.

Are You an Introvert or an Extrovert? Seek to Be Flexible

Introversion-extroversion is a personality type for everyone. We tend to fall on one side or the other of this continuum. Which are you? Introverts prefer to spend time quietly, be more in the company of themselves, and avoid large groups. Extroverts are drawn to lots of socializing and prefer not to spend time alone. Both types, when extreme, have blind spots when it comes to building agency through associating selectively.

Strong extroverts risk seeking too many social connections and ending up with superficial relationships. Think of the social butterfly or the guy or girl who is the life of the party. Their connections, while plentiful, aren't typically deep or emotionally supportive. Strong introverts have the opposite issue; they are so socially selective, shy, or need so much downtime that they risk isolating themselves and cutting off opportunities to identify and socialize with positive, supportive people.

Neither personality type is all bad or good. Writer Susan Cain's wonderful book *Quiet: The Power of Introverts in a World That Can't Stop Talking* (Crown, 2012) reminds us of the value of a more introverted way of living, especially in these frenetic, high stimulation times. Likewise, being regularly social and connected to others has been linked by researchers to physical health and a positive mood. The problem comes if you're inflexible and stuck in either extreme.

Many working couples, especially those with children, tell us that their demanding and busy lives make expanding their social circles nearly impossible. But by the time they're empty nesters or approaching retirement, many find that their social circles have become quite narrow. Many tell us that as they age, they suddenly feel more isolated or alone, not having a place to work or responsibilities that have kept them engaged with others and the world. Some feel low confidence getting back out there to try to meet new people. "Out of practice," is how one woman described it to us.

It's for all these reasons that we strongly encourage people around midlife to start expanding their social circles. Associate selectively through pursuing opportunities to find new positive, interesting people to engage with. Choose people who are both older and younger than you are. Stretch the range of types of people you spend time with to invigorate your social life. In short, seek out greater diversity. Select one new place or group that appeals to you—maybe it's a neighborhood organization—that gets you out of your house, interacting with new people, helping you get the cobwebs out of your social skills. Continuing to work after retirement in some way that's enjoyable and not too stressful can be a great source of satisfaction. Push yourself out of your comfort zone.

The bottom line of *associating selectively* is to surround yourself at every stage of life with supportive, open-minded, optimistic people and minimize involvement with people who are not. Being aware of this and acting on it will have an enormous positive impact on your state of mind and your physical health, two critical building blocks of personal agency.

YOUR AGENCY TOOL KIT

SEEK THE POSITIVE: Find positive people who will lift your mood and increase your confidence and motivation.

GET DIVERSE: Seek a diverse circle of friends and associates to enrich the fabric of your life.

BUILD A COMMUNITY: Establish a healthy social support network and offer your time to others who are welcoming and cooperative.

ASSESS OTHERS: Read and interpret the deeper motivations of others, recognizing that your feelings can cloud your ability to see others accurately.

THINK INDEPENDENTLY: Distance yourself from groups or individuals when you register uncomfortable feelings.

AVOID THE NEGATIVE: Actively avoid sustained proximity to people who are hostile, negative, and aggressive.

KNOW THAT BODY LANGUAGE MATTERS: Be alert to physical and verbal cues that signal anxiety and negativity to guard against their contagion.

BE RELAXED: Transmit your ease to others to inwardly feel and project greater leadership presence.

SEE THE BIG PICTURE: Step back and reframe relationship issues to keep focused on what is at stake and what is possible.

BE A TRUTH TELLER: Be honest and think for yourself, especially around powerful people, and don't fall into automatic agreement.

DEFUSE TENSION: When interacting with irritable or stressed people, point tension out—with compassion—to defuse it.

SET HEALTHY BOUNDARIES: Let others know when you need some space, don't try to be all things to all people, and learn to say no at times.

PREPARE TO BE UNPOPULAR: Tolerate criticism when you move away from the pack and take an independent stand.

MAKE THE TOUGH CALLS: Insist that unhealthy relationships improve quickly, and if they don't, sever them.

RESPECT YOUR BODY

THE PRINCIPLE
Move

Physical movement, along with proper rest and nutrition, will put your body and mind into balance, giving you greater motivation, strength, and stamina to move forward in your life.

We all know what it feels like to sit around like a slug all day, not getting outdoors and moving about. But when we get some real movement in, it is a kind of agency in itself. It primes our minds and our senses to fully engage in the world.

When we say *Move*, we really mean this: Pay attention to your body so that you can provide it with what it requires to be healthy and in balance, because when your body is out of balance, your mind is out of balance. To achieve this, engage in physical movement in multiple ways, rest adequately, and eat nutritious food. Your agency depends on it. Without physical health and balance in your life, everything else will wobble and decline. Flexibility, strength, and stamina are the most obvious things that begin to deteriorate when you are physically out of balance. But likewise, your motivation, your ability to pay attention, and your ability to delay gratification are adversely affected. Most important to realize, without healthy amounts of movement, rest, and nutrition, your psychological state—your thinking skills and ability to manage your emotions—deteriorates, and along with it your personal agency.

The benefits of physical movement for mental health are well documented, and again not surprisingly, they extend to personal agency. We use the term *movement*, though, to refer to something beyond just exercise, though exercise is certainly an important part of it. Movement, as we use the term, is fundamentally about becoming more actively aware of your body, of engaging with it and reading its signals—particularly at times when you're feeling mentally stuck—and activating it in one way or another as a way of activating yourself.

Physical movement can spark the voluntary decision to change yourself in some way.

So what does movement include beyond exercise? Movement, when it comes to agency, is about making a decision to engage your body to *do* something.

It might start by just paying attention to your breathing. Or standing up. Or moving into a different room. It might be picking up a musical instrument, taking an improv class, painting, helping a friend do chores, or making dinner instead of having it delivered. And yes, it also includes traditional exercise like dancing or biking or taking a long run.

The Challenge: We've Taken Away Many Requirements to Move

When we're outdoors, we're more likely to move. We walk, run, hike, bike, and we're even more likely to stand because there are fewer places to sit for long time periods. Unfortunately, outdoor physical movement is becoming all too rare in many people's sedentary, stay-indoors world. The trends are telling:

- People spend enormous amounts of their daily time indoors—90 percent, according to one 2001 survey by the National Human Activity Pattern Survey and sponsored by the U.S. Environmental Protection Agency.

- Between 1975 and 2010, American homes grew from an average of 1,645 square feet to 2,392 square feet. With bigger houses come more cozy furniture and more screens—giving people more incentive to cocoon and stay inside and be sedentary.

- In 2010, the Kaiser Family Foundation reported that, on average, U.S. children were on their screens more than seven hours a day.

- Researchers from the University of Michigan reported that children's free outdoor time declined by 50 percent between 1981 and 2003, to only seven minutes per day on average.

Overall, Americans are heading in the wrong direction to acquire agency through movement—they are moving less and less.

> **Use Your Agency:** Moving primes the mind for agency. Move when you feel mentally stuck, need to jump-start creative thinking, or to pump up sagging motivation.

Monitor Your Mood

We know that our moods are directly linked to agency—when we feel down, it gets harder to take the steps necessary to change things and move forward. We counsel our clients to monitor their moods and take these down moments as a signal that it's time to take action by *moving*—the kind of movement is up to you, and ideally it will involve a change of location and scenery, but even standing up and stretching is powerful.

And the benefits don't just accrue when you're feeling down; moving can be a way to preempt distraction. Focus and concentration are better when the body gets movement throughout the day. Movement also helps combat the fatigue that builds up when we're working too long and hard. If you're in deep at work, preoccupied with multiple tasks, set a timer to go off every hour. Use this to remind yourself to check on your mood and tune in to your body signals. *Do my eyes feel sore? Are my muscles tired or aching? How's my digestive system? Am I hungry and need to eat? Or am I feeling too full and a brief walk would help my stomach feel less distressed?* Engage in some brief, healthy movement throughout your day. Feeling stuck on a task? Overwhelmed? Then literally get yourself up and move— any amount, no matter how small, is beneficial.

The psychiatrist John Ratey summarizes it well: "The real reason we feel so good when we get our blood pumping is that it makes the brain function at its best," he writes. In his view, "this benefit of physical activity is far more important—and fascinating—than what it does for the body."

Studies connect all types of movement, including standing, to improved cognitive functioning and better focus. EEG studies show blood flow to the brain changes for the better even when "just" taking a brisk walk. Children with attention and hyperactivity symptoms have been shown to stop showing symptoms after having as little as twenty-six minutes of good physical activity.

Better focus, creative-fluid thinking, and improved mood—the brain functions that, to borrow Ratey's term, "spark" our agency—have all recently been connected to movement.

And then there are studies showing a link between exercise and greater self-control. Self-control—the ability to defer gratification and control impulses—is a key part of agency. This is an issue for even some of our most achievement-driven clients who cite impulse control as a key source of why things don't get done as planned. For others who have a very serious ongoing struggle with impulsiveness, it holds them back from successfully pursuing the life they desire.

This link seems obvious to us. Exercise, particularly when you're new to it, is about doing something difficult without obvious immediate reward in the service of a longer-term goal, and if you can keep to a good exercise program, you are in effect practicing delayed gratification. Those who push themselves to stay in shape via regular movement, no matter how small, are already practicing self-control. And self-control, actively controlling oneself rather than letting oneself be controlled by outside forces, is at the heart of agency.

The Immobility Trap (and How to Break Out)

When people are immobilized—either in reality *or by their perceptions*—they start to lose agency through actual physical changes within the brain. And negative mind-sets follow.

For people who work in an office, immobility has traditionally been the default, but it doesn't have to be.

Our friend Sara described the before and after. Initially, her day went like this: She sat in front of her computer all day. After a high-calorie lunch, she noticed a considerable drop in energy and level of motivation. To stay alert, she turned to coffee and a sugary snack from the office vending machine. But this regimen led to battles with headaches, energy spikes and crashes, and extra padding around her waist. She also felt a general sense of malaise much of the time.

Tired of feeling this way, Sara started incorporating small amounts of physical movement into her workday. She took the stairs back up to her office after lunch. She stood at her desk when possible. She walked the perimeter of her office building every hour or so. The result after just the first week, she said, was improved focus and higher productivity and—as she put it—more time spent functioning as "the best version of herself." She also described simply feeling "better."

In a few small changes to her daily movement, Sara added productive time to her day, improved her health, felt better, and started working more creatively. Her increased activity level also affected her appetite. She had less of a taste for fast food at lunch, and it was easier to skip the midmorning and afternoon candy bar habit to lift her spirits. She also noticed that she started sleeping a bit better. What was happening on the inside to Sara? Her body, which had been out of balance due to prolonged inactivity, was beginning to rebalance itself via movement. Her challenge was to pay greater attention to these signals coming from inside herself and resist the temptations of french fries and candy bars.

> **Use Your Agency:** Walk. It's simple. If you're physically able to walk, your body and your mind *need* you to walk—walk briskly for at least twenty to thirty minutes at a time when possible.

If you're looking for an example of a simple program to follow, we like the seven rules of Chris Crowley and Henry S. Lodge, authors of *Younger Next Year: Live Strong, Fit, and Sexy—Until You're 80 and Beyond* (Workman Publishing Company, 2007). They have separate books targeted to men and to women. We like the simplicity of the rules for any age, and more than half of them aren't about exercise! They recommend a positive balance of staying fit, eating right, and connecting with and caring for others. You can also partner with and learn from someone you know who enjoys and adheres to a more healthy lifestyle. Have them guide you on their typical movement and exercise habits.

The more movement you use, the more dramatic its benefits. Don't be discouraged if you've been sedentary for long periods of time or struggling with your weight. Just get started.

> **Use Your Agency:** Start small. Use simple movement and exercise programs that you can easily integrate into your life.

What's at Stake

Your body is a system—a living system that is inextricably connected to your mind. If your body is out of balance, your mind responds in kind, and your thoughts and emotions follow suit. Not heeding the signals deep inside prompting you to move, to eat nutritious food at the right time, and to rest adequately throws your body system out of balance. Lisa Barrett, of Northeastern University and author of *How Emotions Are Made,* describes in great detail the way our emotions are affected by our bodies. More so, Barrett's research indicates that our bodies *are the source* of our emotions. When we keep our bodies in a healthy state of balance, the emotions that are produced are healthier. We feel better, think better, and everything just works better. Simply put, being able to accurately read and interpret all your body's signals will allow you to increase your level of agency.

Prolonged immobility often results in diminished motivation. When you fail to move for hours on end, when you aren't navigating and exploring the environment beyond the surface of your desk or computer screen, or when you're staying within the walls of your house or office most of the day, your brain is being sent signals that there's nothing to be motivated for. Sluggishness isn't always a sign that you need to rest; it may be coming from immobility. Being immobilized too long, your brain may think it's time to slow down and disengage, saving its energy for when something more important comes along. The result is physical *and mental* passivity. Passivity is the enemy of agency.

And the mental effects of low movement aren't just in the moment; they accrue over a lifetime. A twenty-five-year study looked at the connection between early adult patterns of physical activity and television viewing and the effect on cognitive function at midlife. The study first checked in with 3,247 adults aged eighteen to thirty years in 1985 and then looked at them again in 2011. Using three tests of cognitive function, "Compared with participants with low television viewing and high physical activity, the odds of poor performance were almost two times higher for adults with both high television viewing and low physical activity," concluded the report. Conclusion: "High television viewing and low physical activity in early adulthood were associated with worse midlife executive function and processing speed." In other words, lack of movement early in life led to a decreased ability to think for oneself, to think several steps ahead, and to make good, rational decisions. The good news is that starting to exercise seems to improve cognitive functioning throughout life—even seniors with dementia have been shown to gain significant improvements in thinking skills after six to twelve months of exercise.

The physical effects of immobility are serious as well, increasing your chances of developing a chronic illness or chronic pain. Back pain is a common problem associated with immobility. Over time, as muscle atrophy occurs, you are left more vulnerable to muscles tightening and tearing. This increases your chances of experiencing significant back pain, the second-most common cause of disability in U.S. adults. Americans at all income levels and education levels are also getting heavier, which is related to both inactivity and eating behavior. Data from a 2015 survey by the Centers for Disease Control and Prevention found that 30.4 percent of Americans ages twenty and older said they were not just overweight but actually *obese*. Diabetes is increasing, too, with 9.5 percent of adults reporting they had the disease in 2015. The bottom line is that your body being out of balance leads to poor physical health and a decline in well-being. When this happens, you won't feel good and won't be at your best, and your personal agency will be considerably compromised.

The Capacity to Move Is Always There

Some remarkable people have shown us that the involuntary loss of muscle movement didn't stop them from reaching goals that many of us can only dream of. Famed physicist Stephen Hawking had a form of amyotrophic lateral sclerosis (ALS) that began to paralyze him in college. He eventually had to speak using a speech-generating computer with his hand, and, after he lost the use of his hand, he learned to control the device with his cheek muscles. Artist Joni Mitchell developed polio as a child, and she later told *Rolling Stone* that it was during her recovery when confined in a full-body cast that she began composing songs in her mind and considered a singing career for the first time. One of the very first songs she ever wrote, she titled "Urge for Going." Lack of physical movement, although it made it more difficult, didn't keep these remarkable people from developing agency.

This tells us that the way one *perceives* immobility may be as important as a literal lack of movement. If you keep telling your brain that moving, changing your environment, or doing new things isn't possible or valuable, your brain is likely to give up trying. But if, as Hawking and Mitchell did, you keep moving in whatever ways possible, even mentally and through imagination, it appears that you keep creating and thinking and moving toward your full potential. We tie this into psychologist Carol Dweck's important work on maintaining a *growth mind-set*, covered in more detail by the principle *Position Yourself as a Learner* later in chapter 4. In short, it is crucial not to believe or see your potential as a fixed thing.

Every day, new technologies bring movement and communication assistance to people whose movement is compromised. Athletics and exercise programs are tailored to everyone. Find the way of movement that works for you.

Your Brain Needs Stillness, Too: Incorporate Mind-Body Practices into Your Daily Life

As much as we need movement to help ourselves achieve agency, our brains also need rest to process and use all the material they take in.

Writer Ferris Jabr details beautifully the decoding that goes on in our brains during rest in his *Scientific American* article "Why Your Brain Needs More Downtime":

> Downtime is an opportunity for the brain to make sense of what it has recently learned, to surface fundamental unresolved tensions in our lives and to swivel its powers of reflection away from the external world toward itself. While mind-wandering, we replay conversations we had earlier that day, rewriting our verbal blunders as a way of learning to avoid them in the future. We craft fictional dialogue to practice standing up to someone who intimidates us or to reap the satisfaction of an imaginary harangue against someone who wronged us. We shuffle through all those neglected mental post-it notes listing half-finished projects and we mull over the aspects of our lives with which we are most dissatisfied, searching for solutions. We sink into scenes from childhood and catapult ourselves into different hypothetical futures. And we subject ourselves to a kind of moral performance review, questioning how we have treated others lately. These

moments of introspection are also one way we form a sense of self, which is essentially a story we continually tell ourselves. When it has a moment to itself, the mind dips its quill into our memories, sensory experiences, disappointments and desires so that it may continue writing this ongoing first-person narrative of life.

Meditation, yoga, tai chi, rest, and overall mindfulness are all significantly different from immobility, even when practiced slowly or in stillness. Mindfulness practices are the most popular and are based on Buddhist meditation, well worth the effort to learn, but be open to all techniques and find the ones that feel best and work best for you.

The intention behind them puts the mind into a state of relaxed alertness, or deeper relaxation, which is drastically different from the stuck feeling of immobility. We like to recommend two techniques that don't take any formal training or tools and that can be done wherever you find a quiet space.

The first is *progressive muscle relaxation* (PMR). With this technique, you think about each muscle of your body, one by one, and intentionally let go of tension you are holding in them. Progress from head to toe, or start at the core of your body and move to your legs and arms until reaching your fingers and toes. Tune in to the pleasant, deeply relaxed sensation that takes over your body. This sensation tells you that you are on your way to diminishing cortisol, the stress hormone. Eyes closed works best. Do this every day, at least a few days in a row, to assure benefits.

The second technique that's simple to adopt is *mindful breathing*. This is the only way to slow your heart rate down relatively quickly without drugs. Breaths should be slow and not shallow or fast. Don't let your upper chest rise. If you're able to lie down, rest a hand on your waist and you'll feel breath rise and fall from that part of your stomach. Breathe in and out while listening to the peaceful, rhythmic sound of your breaths. With practice, some people can focus on the quiet beating of their hearts. As your heart rate lowers, you stem the accumulation of cortisol. Again, daily practice is recommended.

To Move Means to Break the Spell of "Learned Helplessness"

Many people we have spoken with see themselves in one of these ways: *I feel like I'm chained to my monitor and caught up in tasks all day.* Keeping up with email fills me with a sense of futility. *The longer I sit there, the more I lose interest in doing other things . . . When the kids were little, I was stuck at home most of the time. Now that they're grown, it's too late to start over and meet new people. Why bother? . . . This is the third terrible manager I've had, they're all terrible, so there's no sense looking for another position.*

People don't usually recognize when they're ensnared in a *helplessness* mind-set. Moreover, they rarely know what caused it. And often the last thing they recognize is that something as simple as physical movement, or lack thereof, is involved.

Martin Seligman, a psychologist best known for his pioneering work in positive psychology, conducted groundbreaking research many years ago highlighting how crucial movement is to maintaining mental health. Most people have forgotten these studies that started in 1967, but we've found that many of our clients can relate to what the learned helplessness research illustrates. That's why in our work, we often refer to these studies.

The studies went something like this: Animals received nonlethal but unpleasant electric shocks on the floor of their holding cages. At first, the animals willingly moved to escape from receiving the shock. Seligman then blocked their escape, and over time, the animals gave up even attempting to move out of harm's way. Later, when they were again given opportunities to avoid the shock, they remained in one spot, having completely given up trying. This proved true for dogs, rodents, and monkeys. Seligman called this giving-up behavior *learned helplessness.*

Now, learning about these studies, ask yourself if you have ever felt like one of those animals. Haven't we all been trapped in situations that dole out painful or stressful moments and our escape isn't possible, at least at the start? In time, even when our situations improved—and the door to the cage was open, so to speak—many of us stayed put. Why? Learned helplessness—it's the *Why bother?* attitude and a killer of agency.

The experiments offer us hope. Seligman's research showed that when the animals were prodded to physically move, they then began to avoid the negative experience once again—even after they had previously given up all attempts to escape. Yes, through physical movement, learned helplessness could be unlearned. That's why we tell people to stand at their desks, take frequent small breaks, stretch and move their bodies, and better yet, step outdoors whenever they detect early signals of frustration, anger, and stress. Get up and move to combat learned helplessness and access your agency! Tell yourself, *I'm not caged or tethered. I have agency . . . I can move, if only a small amount . . . I don't have to stay stuck in place and stew in a helpless, hopeless feeling.* I have agency.

Here's a simple example of how this all may work: Roll your shoulders and neck, right now, and stretch your arms above your head. These now repositioned muscles have sent messages to your brain that you're alive, engaged, and possibly getting ready for something new to happen. Lean back and look away from your book or screen, out a window if possible, even at a work of art or colorful object. Your brain will start to think in new ways once unlocked from a confined, two-dimensional, often repetitive visual field.

Better yet, get up and walk around. After you take a few steps, register how that simple motion frees you first physically, then mentally. The key is to move consciously. Tell yourself why you're doing it and what you hope to attain. *I'm getting out of this chair to shift my perspective. Sitting here too long isn't doing me any good. I'm not trapped. I can get up anytime and move about.*

The Healing Power of Movement

Moving reverses the buildup of your body's stress hormones and is instrumental to the healing process. Even the smallest physical act or change in body position, location (especially to natural settings), and routine can lessen stress, boost your mood, and give you the energy to lift yourself out of a rut. This is particularly true if you are recovering from a serious condition, such as anxiety, depression, or post-traumatic stress disorder.

Anthony's Notes from the Office: Motion Over Emotion

One patient particularly drives home the power of movement to increase motivation and balance emotions. Eight-year-old Jace came to me with his parents, who were concerned by their inability to get him into a bedtime routine, but only four days after our meeting, his father suffered a sudden fatal heart attack. A relationship that had started with a routine family problem would now confront a severe trauma.

In the first months after his father died, Jace came to my office for an hour each week and slumped passively, refusing to engage beyond small talk. School was *okay*, his soccer team was *okay*, the new video game he was playing was *fun, I guess*. He didn't make eye contact very long. He was still in shock. Using a talking therapy approach to help him express emotions and develop new coping skills wasn't likely to work well in the short run; I needed to try something different. Child therapy often involves using movement in the form of play, games, and nonverbal imaginative activities to build rapport with children, to earn their trust, and to dig for deeper feelings that children can't as yet vocalize. Anyone who works with kids in this way knows that movement is key—playing on the floor, drawing, staging a small play with puppets . . . almost the whole space of the therapy room gets used.

I started our next visit by giving him small fidget toys and puzzles. No explanation—I just handed them over. Next, I gestured to him to walk with me to the window, stopping along the way to look at a bookcase crowded with curios. He began to show a flicker of engagement. But what really broke the ice was when I tossed a soft squishy ball at him. He laughed, had a devious look in his eye, and tossed it back—pretty hard, in fact. As we played catch, we talked about what had happened. He started by telling me about how

(continued)

weird the funeral was. He said it was like a bad dream because it didn't seem real at the time. He caught himself talking about his dad in the present tense. I told him that was cool, to do it if he wanted to. He said he was sad and mad, often at his mom, although he didn't know why.

This would become our ritual. We invented competitive games. Can you catch the ball with your other hand? Can you catch with your eyes closed? He would try to catch two at a time. When a ball inconveniently rolled to the farthest corners of the office, we took turns retrieving it. His mood began to lift over time. This was motion over emotion.

Motion, I learned, empowered Jace—it made him feel strong and safe and able to cope with an incredibly difficult moment in his young life. And it would become a big part of who he became as a young adult—he took up karate and pursued his father's favorite sport, soccer. For him, and many boys I work with, words aren't what agency is about. It is about movement.

For kids growing up in urban areas with inadequately funded school systems and heightened stress due to violence, movement outdoors often performs a protective function and facilitates the development of agency. As author Onaje X. O. Woodbine writes in *Black Gods of the Asphalt: Religion, Hip-Hop, and Street Basketball* (Columbia University Press, 2016), which explores what he terms the sacred space that the basketball court provides to young black boys and men, "street basketball informed the confidence with which we walked and talked."

U.S. Army Delta Force captain Josh Collins suffered traumatic brain injury (TBI), PTSD, and depression following seven deployments to Bosnia, Afghanistan, and Iraq. In an interview he did with *Florida Today* on May 17, 2016, he explained that traditional therapies were ineffective for him, and he seriously contemplated suicide until he discovered a very special form of movement, paddleboarding, which involves both movement and control of external stimuli. For Josh, paddling on a board in the water involves a quiet, repetitive, and meditative movement in a natural setting that facilitates healing of his deep wounds. He said, "Paddling has now not only become my passion but a means of coping with the lingering mental and physical damages I continue to endure."

Some countries are considering the role of movement in promoting the physical and mental health of their citizens. Japan has been giving serious thought to the healing properties of movement, taking advantage of the natural settings that cover 67 percent of their country. It is one of the most population-dense, urban places on the planet, and one estimate shows they have the second-highest suicide rate among eight major industrialized nations. Over the past twenty years, they have been looking to solutions beyond drugs and talking therapies, and they believe that moving in natural settings will help.

Shinrin-yoku is "forest bathing" and was inspired by Shinto and Buddhist practices, according to Florence Williams, writing for *Outside* magazine in 2012. It's a full-sensory experience, an immersion in the primal smells of pine and earth, the sounds of cicadas and birdsong, the feel of wind on the body and of rough contours of bark across the fingers. It's the soothing, near-infinite shades of green and browns from countless varieties of flora that the eye can soak up. Walking paths are being constructed in Japan's ancient forests on a national scale to encourage people to move about in nature and "bathe" in a natural setting. A hundred "forest therapy" sites are being designated over the next several years. It's not a fad. Researchers have recorded significant biomedical changes in people while on these trails, including lowering of the stress hormone cortisol, lowering blood pressure, and calming the heart rate. According to the researchers who published their findings in the journal *Environmental Health and Preventive Medicine* in 2010, "measurements show that forest environments can relieve human psychological tension, depression, anger, fatigue, and confusion, and moreover, that they can enhance human psychological vigor." A 2008 study in the *International Journal of Immunopathology and Pharmacology* showed forest visits also had measurable immune system benefits that lasted beyond the time spent in the woods.

For most of us, there's been a substantial loss of connection to all things natural, and the closer we are to urban spaces, the more detached we are from the world that our minds actually evolved in. In the age of overwhelm, might we be missing an opportunity to heal what ails us and lower our stress with a dose of nature?

What if you're in the city and not close to conservation trails? There are parks, but many close at night, and most of us can't enjoy them during the daylight hours while we're working. The good news is that nature never sleeps. One young man who lives in downtown Boston waits until dusk, looks up at the apartment buildings around him, and watches the silhouettes of bats darting and diving. The moon, if you can see it from your vantage point, appears to rise and fall, changes in color and size, and can help to center you in a mindful way. Stargazing is difficult in the city because of light pollution, but there are great apps that use GPS to create—like a planetarium—the stars and planets that are above you at any time of day. Take a moment and look what's above you, and the busy, congested noise of the moment will fade into the background.

The Science Behind the Brain Benefits of Vigorous Movement

Running has significant benefits beyond muscle and bone strength and cardiovascular health. University of Arizona scientists who studied the effects of running on the brain found that running seems to help connect our many brain functions.

In a paper published in 2016, the researchers reported that through brain imaging, they found that "locomotion, especially at an elite level, likely engages multiple cognitive actions including planning, inhibition, monitoring, attentional switching and multitasking, and motor control." Running may "lead to altered brain connectivity, which in turn has implications for understanding the beneficial role of exercise for brain and cognitive function over the lifespan."

We see related effects of moving in people we call *super movers*. Their agency is very much tied to ongoing running or swimming, as one competitive college elite runner we know showed us. He regularly runs fifty miles a week for training, but two to three times a year he takes a break (recommended by trainers) for seven to ten days. Anxiety-like symptoms emerge each time he does so. He says he feels agitated and antsy, less focused, less centered, less productive. "I find myself sleeping too much, and I feel less sharp and less like my energetic self," he says. "When I get back into running after one of these breaks, it's like shaving, putting on a clean shirt, and gelling my hair!"

A study recently published in *Frontiers in Aging Neuroscience* pinpoints what's likely happening during the running break at the level of the brain. The study found that when a group of exceedingly fit older men and women, all competitive runners, were asked to stop exercising abruptly, they experienced a significant decline in blood flow to the brain, both the left and right lobes of the hippocampus. In other words, blood flow is tied to vigorous continued movement. Agency is enhanced by the improved cognitive functioning, which comes from maintaining a healthy active brain, which comes through ongoing, regular movement.

> **Use Your Agency:** Commit to moving—even if not vigorously, at least every thirty minutes. Set an alarm as a reminder. At the very least, roll your shoulders and do a quick stretch.

Know Your Numbers

Think of your body like a wonderful interconnected country of complex regions that, to work most effectively and efficiently, must have ongoing maintenance and frequent monitoring. That's how to feel your best, think your best, and move throughout the world as healthily and happily as possible. People with agency understand not to deny their biological needs. They accept their biological vulnerabilities. They make it their business to know their family histories.

Health statistics that should be regularly monitored include blood pressure, cholesterol, body mass index (BMI), resting heart rate, and blood sugar. Be forward thinking with your health and get preventative screenings.

Lives Out of Balance: Women Are at Risk

Naomi is a cardiologist at a Boston teaching hospital, and her friend Hanna is the administrative director for the group practice. Seated nearby at a restaurant, we struck up a conversation. They'd overheard us talking about people's agency declining in the age of overwhelm and were curious to learn more. It turned out that the conversation had unexpected significance for them. The serious expressions on their faces made more sense when we learned what had happened in their lives just hours earlier.

Their office manager, Camila, had not shown up for work that morning. She had collapsed and died of a massive heart attack just before heading off to work. A lively, forty-two-year-old, hardworking single mother of three, she possessed an outstanding ability to cheerfully keep everything and everyone organized. They were still in shock, finding it impossible to believe that Camila was gone, as they had all been working late together the very evening before. No one had thought it might be necessary to say a final goodbye or give one last hug.

"Overwhelm," Hanna repeated. "That's a good name for what we're seeing among the women in our cardiology practice." Naomi agreed and told us that many more younger women are dying suddenly of heart attacks, "the silent killer," than ever before. They are stressed in dual roles of being caretakers and breadwinners, they're not moving enough, they're not eating well, and their bodies are seriously out of balance. Data supports that this silent killer is a national trend. Cardiologists like Naomi are also seeing more frequent cases of something called *brain-induced cardiomyopathy*. It's a condition when the heart starts beating erratically and can be due to stress signals from the brain. It mimics a heart attack, but unlike a heart attack, there is no blockage, and patients sustain no lasting damage to the heart. The increase of this in Naomi's practice is something quite ominous, suggesting that our minds are being over-loaded to the point of physical malfunction.

Listen to all your body's signals, and certainly don't pass off intense signals of stress and anxiety as one-and-only fleeting moments of panic that are tied to some recent stressful event.

Welcome Your Interruptions

If we said that you'd live longer by sitting less, you'd probably think that advice, while good, would be hard to put into daily practice. Who remembers to move? Many of us don't, unless our bodies ache, we get hungry or thirsty, we need a bathroom break, or we get interrupted and have to get up out of the chair or off the couch. Normally, we hate interruptions, especially when we're at home working or grabbing some well-earned relaxation time. But if you interrupt yourself from prolonged sitting about every thirty minutes, that will, a recent study suggests, increase your chances of living longer.

Elaine is a professional writer, college professor, and mom of a six-year-old boy. Her opportunities to move are significantly stymied. With each new writing project, the hours of sitting per week increase dramatically. This is added to the time she needs to prepare her lectures and grade students' papers. But she decided something had to change. There's a history of cardiovascular problems in her extended family, and it's made Elaine and her husband, Mike, acutely aware of the importance of staying healthy. Mike has taken to running, and he gets lots of opportunities at work to move between meetings. Elaine enjoys going to their town pool for swims but still finds herself sitting long periods of time working at home.

She figured out a terrific simple solution: She interrupts herself every thirty minutes with a lighthearted chime that she's programmed on her laptop. When the chime goes off, she stands, stretches, walks to a window, sometimes steps out onto her enclosed porch for a breath of fresh air.

Elaine's technique of interrupting her sedentary behavior fits perfectly with findings from the above-mentioned study, which was published in 2017 in *Annals of Internal Medicine*. The study tracked the sedentary behaviors of nearly eight thousand adults ages forty-five and older using a hip-mounted accelerometer. Correlations between prolonged sitting and early mortality were found, as expected, but people who had interrupted their sitting, even very briefly, every thirty minutes had less of a risk of dying prematurely—even if their total time being sedentary was similar.

The Special Problem with the Workplace

Work easily tops the list of places that people feel most physically stuck. Think of the many workers who are assigned to manufacturing stations or find themselves penned up in cubicles in front of computer screens all day. Many of us are in jobs that require sitting at desks for hours or standing at long cashier lines or spending hours a day inside trucks or other vehicles. Most of us dread long commutes where we're confined on congested roads or packed into crowded trains and buses. As medical researchers have noted, this presents a dangerous tipping point. Prolonged sitting increases the risk of cardiovascular problems—even among people who get exercise at other times of the day.

Technology's false promise was that it would free workers by increasing their efficiency and giving them more time for leisure activities, but it's actually having the opposite effect. Many employers expect workers to be on call 24-7, in a kind of "digital overtime." If you bring your work home and take it on vacations because that's what is expected, that means more time working and less time moving.

Some progressive companies provide incentives to get their workers active. Employees are encouraged to go outdoors and walk around, sometimes through friendly competitions. Small groups get together to power walk at lunch. Some companies have gyms and health centers on-site. Some offer treadmill workstations.

At first, companies that encouraged employees to move more were targeting obesity, but there was an unexpected result. Physical movement boosts productivity and creativity. A recent study at Stanford University reports that walking, compared to sitting, "opens up the free flow of ideas." One financial company conducted a recent yearlong study on the effects of movement while at work on a treadmill and found that overall productivity, both in quality and quantity, increased for people while walking slowly, even at only two miles per hour.

Take a Stand at Work—Literally

Many people we've met who have figured out how to maintain agency in their lives often prefer to stand rather than sit. They tell us it keeps their metabolism going and their brains sharp. They avoid being sedentary as much as possible because they've realized it sends the wrong message to the brain: *I'm slowing down. I'm stuck. I can't move. Options are limited.*

Standing during a job where people usually sit is a simple, sensible, and effective way to invigorate your body and mind throughout the day. By standing, you engage the large muscles of your body, legs, and core. By contracting those large muscles, you use up fuel and decrease blood sugar.

Forward-thinking businesses have invested in desks designed to use standing up, but mobile technology and laptops make it possible to stand and work even without this progressive office furniture. Simple desktop computer stands cost twenty-five dollars or less, and you can even use just a sturdy cardboard box on a room table to raise a laptop high enough to work while standing.

> **Use Your Agency:** Bring some creativity to your daily routine. When (and how) can you stand if you usually sit? When can you move if you're usually stuck in place?

Try Out the Walking Meeting

Nilofer Merchant, a technology entrepreneur, CEO, and author, kick-started the national conversation about walking meetings, or "walk and talk," with a 2013 article in *Harvard Business Review*. Its provocative title: "Sitting Is the Smoking of Our Generation." Merchant is an evangelist for the idea:

> Four years ago, I made a simple change when I switched one meeting from a coffee meeting to a walking-meeting. I liked it so much it became a regular addition to my calendar; I now average four such meetings, and 20 to 30 miles each week. . . .
>
> After a few hundred of these meetings, I've started noticing some unanticipated side benefits. First, I can actually listen better when I am walking next to someone than when I'm across from them in some coffee shop. There's something about being side-by-side that puts the problem or ideas before us, and us working on it together. Second, the simple act of moving also means the mobile device mostly stays put away. Undivided attention is perhaps today's scarcest resource, and hiking meetings allow me to invest that resource very differently. And finally, we almost always end the hike joyful. The number one thing I've heard people say (especially if they've resisted this kind of meeting in the past) is "That was the most creative time I've had in a long time." And that could be because we're outside, or a result of walking.

Walking while talking appears to have a mitigating effect on conflict, too. A 2017 article in *American Psychologist* concludes that the process of walking together can help you to resolve conflict both inside yourself and between yourself and others. Walking side by side encourages creativity and brainstorming (known in psychology-speak as *divergent thinking*), which are necessary tools for resolving conflicts. Walking while talking also opens up new possibilities for empathy and close listening.

Paul's Notes from the Field
(or in This Case, the Stairwell)

A few minutes before our meeting, Anna found me standing by the fifth-floor company elevator. She suggested that, rather than wait for the elevator, we take the stairs up to the seventh floor to her office. It certainly got my blood pumping, and by the time we reached her office, my post-lunchtime mental fog had lifted. My mind felt razor sharp.

As a leader of others on her team, Anna is all about movement. "It's how I motivate people to move in the direction of a long-term strategic vision for the company," she explained. She holds hour-long "innovation meetings" while walking. "The movement—not staying in place—it sparks kinetic thinking and creativity and problem-solving," she told me.

A highly positive, quick-witted woman in her late thirties, Anna showed a moment of uncharacteristic seriousness when she confided in me that only a few years ago, she had a serious weight problem that was affecting her health. She'd developed sleep apnea. Her husband, Cory, had also found that dedication to his career was hurting his ability to stay fit and active.

Together, Anna and Cory started to take walks before dinner every night. Their five-year-old, CJ, loved the outings. They pushed each other to stick to it, and soon the ritual felt natural, like it had always been something they liked to do instead of something that they "needed to do." Anna told me, "The desire to move around grew, and I crave it now." She made movement a part of life more because of how it made her feel than about how it might make her look—although moving also helped her lose weight.

Embrace Physical Movement in All Its Forms

We need movement in our daily routine, and it can come in many forms, from formal workouts at a gym to brisk daily walks to using bikes or our feet as our transportation. Stretching is important, too; yoga practitioners know how moving into a squat is a good, simple way to stretch the muscles of the legs and back. You can literally walk, run, or swim the stress hormone cortisol out of your system.

Minnesotan minister Dr. Paul Hill knows about the power of all kinds of movement to build agency, both in himself and in his parishioners, and he uses more than just words to preach his message. Since the early 1980s, he has been leading young people by example, participating alongside them in adventure-based experiential education. A day's work for the rugged youth pastor can consist of rope courses, camping, or canoeing in the wilderness. Challenging muscle, mind, and soul is what he believes will help nurture a spiritual life both for himself and the thousands of troubled young men he's worked with.

Hill says he lacked faith in himself as a teenager. "I was paralyzed at times by low self-esteem and self-doubt," he says. His trip at age fourteen exploring the wilderness failed, but he decided to give it another try a year later. A grueling twenty-five-day canoe trip changed his life, he says. Traversing rivers and the wilderness somehow gave him a psychological strength he hadn't experienced before. In years to come, he challenged himself in different ways in the wilderness, even putting himself on an island with no food for three days and nights.

Hill credits movement as a key to creating the profound changes in himself and in the disadvantaged and sometimes desperate teens he's worked with for many years. It hasn't always been easy. On one canoe trip, a kid stabbed another through the hand during a fight. On another, a young man robbed another campsite. But Hill is full of positive energy, speaking in upbeat and enthusiastic tones, gesticulating with vigor. He isn't fearful or hesitant. There's nothing passive or quiet about this reverend!

He doesn't deliver long sermons or focus exclusively on the pages of scripture—that would keep him standing in one place for too long. He doesn't ask young people to experience God merely by sitting in houses of worship, with their bodies motionless. He believes in the body's capacity to transform the mind and soul through movement.

Even Fidgeting Has Value

We're pro-fidgeting! Fidgeting has a bad rap; when adults do it, they're often perceived as impatient, annoying, and rude, and when children do it, it's seen as a "symptom" used to justify a diagnosis of attention deficit hyperactivity disorder (ADHD). ADHD is the most common childhood disorder assigned to children in the United States, particularly boys. Imagine how many fewer diagnoses (and ADHD medications) would be given to children if that one "symptom" were taken off the diagnostic list?

Very recent research now indicates that fidgeting has necessary health benefits, including helping blood flow to our legs. "The muscular contractions associated with fidgeting are really quite small," Jaume Padilla, an assistant professor of nutrition and exercise physiology at the University of Missouri–Columbia, told *The New York Times*, "but it appears that they are sufficient" to fight the negative consequences of sitting. Padilla led the study, whose results were published in 2016. Another study, by the University of British Columbia–Kelowna, found that a three-hour period of uninterrupted sitting caused a "profound (33 percent) reduction in vascular function in young girls. Importantly, we also demonstrate that breaking up sitting with regular exercise breaks can prevent this."

We, the authors, are going on record here to ask the American Psychiatric Association to remove fidgeting from their ADHD symptom list and to ask all allied professionals who work with children to not use this as a criteria for ADHD. It's time that all of us professionals join in this movement to stop demanding healthy motion be suppressed (or worse, medicated) out of childhood.

Bottom line: Many of us *need* to fidget. So please, fidget at will! It can prolong your life.

Our Schools Need More Movement, Not Less

When Anthony visits schools in different parts of the country, he's astonished to find that recess and in-school breaks for movement vary considerably from one school to the next, even within the same town or city. Movement facilitates learning, but many children aren't afforded the options and freedoms to move about in classrooms, to stand at their desks, to take a quick mind or body break, to stretch, or even to go to the bathroom.

The trend toward less movement is harming the bodies and cognitive capacities of children and teenagers. An in-depth 2011 review article in the journal *Obesity Reviews* said it best: "Ironically, too much work with no play may be weakening those cognitive abilities that we are so eager to test."

Over the years, more time has been devoted to preparing kids for standardized tests. Kids are indoors and sitting at tables and their desks longer. Recess and other opportunities for healthy physical movement have been drastically reduced and sometimes completely eliminated from the school day.

Many parents and educators are crying foul, and with good reason. We know movement is essential for healthy living, but it is now being shown to improve children's self-control and learning. In a 2014 study, 221 children, seven to nine years old, either attended a nine-month afterschool exercise program or were part of a wait-list control group. The exercise program group did markedly better on brain and behavior measures after exercise. They were notably better at executive functions and showed more flexible thinking. The researchers also recorded EEG brain wave patterns and found more brain activity in the minds of kids in the exercise group.

We strongly urge educators and policy makers to do the right thing. Movement throughout the school day should be a biological right, practiced and integrated into the schoolwork itself whenever possible. The emphasis on tests and test preparations that keep children sedentary must be curtailed. Let's follow the model of best practices for medicine, where tests are considered when really needed, with potential risks considered up front, keeping in mind a *first, do no harm* mentality.

The Importance of Rest and Sleep: Maintaining Balance Is Key

You need to modulate expending physical energy with taking time to rest, reflect, and recharge. *Scientific American* noted that research published in 2012 by researchers from the University of Southern California and MIT argued that "when we are resting the brain is anything but idle and that, far from being purposeless or unproductive, downtime is in fact essential to mental processes that affirm our identities, develop our understanding of human behavior and instill an internal code of ethics."

These processes may depend on the brain circuit that kicks in when people are in a kind of daydreaming, resting state—a circuit brain researchers call the *default mode network*.

You might be surprised to read that we think napping is an important part of the *Move* principle. Of course, as both the Mayo Clinic and any parent of a toddler will tell you, napping too much or at the wrong time of the day is counterproductive; it can leave you foggy if you nap too long and make it harder for you to sleep at night if you nap too close to bedtime. But the upsides are significant: You'll have less fatigue, be more relaxed, be more alert, have quicker reaction times, have better memory, and be in a better mood. All these benefits are directly associated with being able to access and act with greater agency.

There may be no better way to assure your mental and physical well-being than assuring yourself consistent sleep. Your agency depends on it, as experts in circadian rhythms will tell you that interfering with your wake-sleep cycles, a common occurrence of modern living, is dangerous to your physical and mental well-being. Disturbance of our natural biological rhythms has been linked to problems with cognitive function and memory formation, along with a range of mental and medical problems, such as depression, neurological disease, heart failure, stroke, and diabetes.

Sometimes the sources of stimuli are obscured. Vince Warren, a civil rights attorney in New York City and executive director of the Center for Constitutional Rights, told us he realized one day that he wasn't sleeping well because he was worried that he might miss some important detail in his work. "It didn't make sense," Vince told us. "I've been at this for a long time and know my work is solid." Where was this anxiety coming from? He finally figured out its most unusual source. Vince is an avid reader, and he realized that the nonfiction he loves was overstimulating his mind when he read late into the evening before retiring. He found himself jumping up constantly to jot down notes. His brain wanted to make certain there was no detail or point that he'd missed. The more he read, the more new ideas crowded his downtime and infused him with unhealthy worry. "I switched to fiction in the evening," he said. "It was an incredible change for me once I realized that I wasn't giving my mind a rest." His sleep improved, and the worrying stopped.

Nutrition Matters

We have focused primarily on movement in this chapter, but poor nutrition may underlie why many of us don't move enough. If nutrition is lacking, you'll be tired, lethargic, and more inclined toward sedentary habits, hence less inclined to move. Nutrition, independent of movement, is also linked to improved brain functions, including memory, attention, and overall thinking skills, all of which are agency enhancing.

It's not only what we eat but *when* we eat that matters. If we were better able to read and interpret our bodies' signals in terms of when we are truly hungry—and able to better identify the food that our bodies actually need—many diseases that interfere with our functioning would be drastically reduced.

Perhaps not surprisingly, what you eat is often driven by the emotion you are feeling at the moment. According to research published in the *Journal of Consumer Psychology* in 2014, when you feel stressed or feel down, you are more inclined to reach for fats, salts, sugars, and refined carbs. *Comfort eating* or *emotional eating* are the common terms for this. Learn to recognize the emotions that can drive you to make unhealthy food choices. Next time you catch yourself craving comfort food, step back and ask yourself, *Am I upset or in a negative mood, or am I really hungry and this is a healthy time to eat?*

To bolster agency, retrain yourself to eat and enjoy healthy food. Educate yourself about nutrition; learn the basics, the differences between fats, complex and simple carbohydrates, proteins, and the various sugars often added to what we eat. Learn how your body feels after eating mostly proteins versus sugars versus complex carbs, for example. Which foods or food groups give you the most energy over the day? Which foods or food groups spike your energy or take away your energy?

Don't follow fad diets; they throw your body out of whack. Establish and follow a healthy "diet" for life. The Mediterranean diet, according to the Mayo Clinic, is highly recommended for lowering cardiac illness, various cancers, and premature mortality. This diet emphasizes fruits and vegetables, whole grains, legumes, and nuts. It recommends olive oil and canola oil instead of butter, herbs and spices instead of salt, low alcohol consumption, and less red meat. The simplest rule to remember is to eat a variety of fresher, more locally sourced, minimally processed foods. In other words, eat more *real food* whenever possible.

Make Movement an Intentional Practice

What is most helpful is incorporating physical movement throughout each of our days as an *intentional practice.* This helps decrease the amount of stress hormones circulating within our bodies.

Robert Pozen, formerly the vice chairman of Fidelity Investments and now a lecturer at the MIT Sloan School of Management, notes in his book *Extreme Productivity: Boost Your Results, Reduce Your Hours* (Harper-Business, 2012) that making movement part of your life often requires a proactive decision to *just do it.* "It is up to you to make time," he writes. "Choose a time of day that makes sense for you, such as early in the morning, around lunchtime, or after work. Being busy or lacking equipment is no excuse for missing exercise: a friend of mine blocks off forty-five minutes in the middle of the day to walk up and down the stairs of our office building."

At the same time don't overdo it. Don't push yourself to sign up for an overly challenging exercise program you are not ready for or view exercise solely as an achievement. Start wherever you are most comfortable and feather more movement into your day—and by all means find a way to enjoy it!

YOUR AGENCY TOOL KIT

USE YOUR BODY: Use walking and exercise, progressive muscle relaxation, and deep breathing to combat the buildup of cortisol and to trigger a sense of possibility and options in life.

READ THE SIGNALS: Listen and learn to accurately interpret the signals coming from your body.

ESTABLISH A CYCLE: Alternate between expending energy and taking moments of reflection to recharge and improve focus.

FIND OUTSIDE TIME: A dose of nature sparks the brain and encourages healthy movement.

STAND: Sitting slows your body and mind.

EMPLOY A THIRTY-MINUTE/TWO-HOUR RULE: Move at least every thirty minutes, if only briefly, and never stay seated for more than two hours.

INVITE THE NEW: One way to get moving is to seek new experiences and visit new places.

EAT SMART: Pay attention to what you eat and how you eat to keep your body and mind nourished and in balance.

REST: Tune in to your body's signals that it needs rest, take breaks and naps, and make sleep a priority.

LEARN ALWAYS
AND IN ALL WAYS

THE PRINCIPLE
Position Yourself as a Learner

Actively positioning yourself to learn from a wide range of people and trustworthy resources will serve to continuously expand your knowledge and capabilities.

We were both living in Boston in 2013 when two brothers detonated bombs at the finish line of the Boston Marathon. All of us Bostonians were tremendously impressed by the quick action of police and first responders to help the wounded and bring the perpetrators to justice. What we didn't know was that other of our fellow citizens were preparing to deal with a collateral crisis related to the attack.

As nineteen thousand National Guard troops began pouring into the Boston area immediately after the terrorist bombing, Carol Rose, a human rights lawyer and executive director of the American Civil Liberties Union (ACLU) in Massachusetts, was tasked with monitoring law-enforcement activities. There hadn't been a police occupation on this scale in a major American city since the Watts riots of 1965 in Los Angeles, and the group was justifiably worried that the civil liberties of some of the city's residents could be at risk.

"I got word immediately about the bombing," Rose said. "We were all huddled around screens in the office. We had to put our anxieties and sadness on hold because we all had a job to do. The press was reporting a total lockdown of the city. That had obvious implications for civil liberties." Rose had the job of monitoring how ordinary people were being treated during this uncertain time.

"I put together a team and set it up as a collective process so I could hear other voices," Rose explained. "I called the governor's office, the Boston mayor's office, and senior law-enforcement officials. I needed to tell them what we were hearing and open up channels to get information from them firsthand. They were in crisis mode, too—I respected that by not pouncing on them with threats or ultimatums. Things were moving very fast."

The ACLU has often had an adversarial relationship with the police, but Rose recognized that her influence and impact wouldn't be diminished by seeking input and help from others, even potential adversaries. In fact, she said, the opposite is usually true.

"I always talk and meet with the police, hear them out. You'd be surprised how often that's worked in everyone's favor." Being an engaged listener and open to hearing others' ideas strengthens Rose's impact as a leader and her effectiveness to ensure the rights of everyday citizens are protected.

Why Learning Is Essential to Agency

Agency helps us to adapt to the demands placed on us by our environment; anything that expands our ability to learn expands our personal agency.

People with high levels of agency are continually learning more, and, as importantly, they are also expanding their *capacity to learn*. There is a self-reinforcing quality to it—as you benefit from learning, you strengthen the skill and develop an ever-stronger hunger to learn more.

Keeping yourself receptive to new ideas, both your own and those of other people, not only increases your accumulation of knowledge but makes you a better learner by increasing your ability to make sense of new information. Taking on a project to learn something new—from learning to speak a different language or play an instrument to understanding a complicated political problem or even redecorating—shapes your mind. You become more alert to all things around you, more inquisitive about what you don't know, and more confident about handling future situations you might be unfamiliar with. As one biology teacher told us, "I tell my students that you're not here only to learn more stuff but to learn how to be better learners."

What We Mean by "Being a Learner"

Being a learner involves adopting a more open, collaborative approach to everything in life. Part of this is acknowledging that as much as you may think you know about a given situation or problem, there is always the possibility that someone else knows something that you don't. Part of this is acknowledging that many people won't bother to share their knowledge with us if they're worried about being attacked or cut off— hence the emphasis on collaboration.

Depending on your personality, this may require shifting some of your behaviors and thinking. For some, it means not trying to always be the smartest person in the room. It means sometimes being less opinionated or quick to judge. For others, it means summoning the courage to ask questions even when you feel you might look foolish. It means adopting new routines, allowing yourself to feel awkward and unsure at times, and loosening up so that you move away from the safety of your usual comfort zone.

Like every other principle taught in this book, learning is about being active rather than passive. Positioning yourself as a learner requires *active questioning*. That means moving beyond the surface of things, pushing past what's easy or simple to dig a bit deeper. As you ask questions, new and deeper questions typically emerge. This process, which we all have the ability to develop, can be fun and invigorating (admittedly, it can be exhausting sometimes, too!). As you learn more, you accumulate a richer base of knowledge about the world around you. You can build on this to make more nuanced assessments of the challenging situations that you face. This questioning process, extolled by Socrates (whose Socratic method involves asking question after question), facilitates effective critical thinking that enriches the quality of all your judgments and future actions.

This is at the heart of building and maintaining agency. You cannot engage in deep critical thinking unless you open yourself to new learning.

Much has been written lately about the importance of critical-thinking skills. Two scholars, Michael Scriven and Richard Paul, provided a helpful definition back in 1987: Critical thinking can be formally defined as *the process of actively and skillfully conceptualizing, applying, analyzing, synthesizing, and/or evaluating information gathered from, or generated by, observation, experience, reflection, reasoning, or communication.*

More and more jobs list it as a required skill. The overall goal of this ability is to see more clearly into situations by being able to discern what is real and at stake versus what is not. On a personal level, this allows you to make informed decisions in all areas of your life. In essence, it's a system that allows you to fully utilize your mind's reasoning ability to learn and comprehend what's happening around you. You may hear it referred to in other ways, such as *higher-order thinking, analytical reasoning,* or *using your frontal cortex* (logical, planful) versus your limbic system (reactive, emotional).

Research is being done on how human beings form opinions and beliefs and how these influence our behaviors and can hinder our ability to learn. We discuss this more fully in the next chapter, which focuses on the principle *Manage Your Emotions and Beliefs.* For now, simply keep in mind that to be an effective learner, you need to adjust or at times suspend your opinions and personal beliefs, sometimes even deeply held ones, to position yourself to truly learn.

Pursuit of "Answers" Often Leads to New Questions

U.S. politician Al Gore—vice president during the Clinton administration, presidential candidate in 2000, and current climate change thought leader—came to politics by way of the military and divinity school. He enrolled in Vanderbilt University Divinity School shortly after his return from Vietnam in 1971.

In 2017, he told radio host Terry Gross that he had volunteered for the army because he grew up in a small town in Tennessee and didn't think it was right to avoid military service. He said that after returning from the war, he experienced a personal crisis of sorts.

"When I came back from the army, I would devote some serious time investigating the questions that were really looming large for me at the time," Gore remembered. "How do you reconcile your duty as a citizen with a moral conviction that the war your country was waging was based on false premises and triggered by a lie?"

His struggles led him to a divinity school program for people pursuing secular careers.

"When you're twenty-one years old, those kinds of questions can really take hold of you," he said. "I wanted to really immerse myself in the ethical systems that might give me some answers—what I found were better questions."

Don't Be Smart, Be Curious

In his book *Why? What Makes Us Curious* (Simon & Schuster, 2017), astrophysicist Mario Livio tackles some of the complex and interesting questions about curiosity. For example, what drives some people toward one primary interest, while others, like Leonardo da Vinci, the definitive Renaissance man, are interested in nearly everything? Curiosity involves not just the love of gaining knowledge but seeking to know more when confronted by the unknown and ambiguous things. That conflict, the unpleasant and perplexed feeling that we all have experienced in the face of something new that we don't quite understand, is the driver inside us to learn more. We want resolution. We want the reward of an answer. But there are many people who turn away from that feeling and simply ignore it.

Journalist and biographer Walter Isaacson has said, "Smart people are a dime a dozen." The trait that elevated many of the people he wrote about—Benjamin Franklin, Albert Einstein, Leonardo da Vinci, and

Steve Jobs—Isaacson says, was that they were driven by curiosity and "a desire to observe things carefully."

Why doesn't everyone strive to learn about the world in this way? Impatience can get in the way, particularly among those who are used to constant stimulation.

But we have found that practice in sustaining attention builds the curiosity muscle. The next time you find yourself puzzled or uncomfortable about not knowing how something works or why someone is the way they are, don't simply dismiss that moment or allow yourself to get distracted. It's a signal that you *want* to know more.

You can also practice curiosity by challenging yourself to accurately observe what's around you right now, no matter how small or large. Maybe it's the room you're in or something on the table in front of you. Allow your mind to observe with all your senses and think about what you're seeing, hearing, smelling, touching, perhaps even tasting.

The Value of Open Inquiry

Open inquiry involves active questioning and careful observation. People who practice this successfully *avoid rushing to judgment*. They don't shut down the learning process prematurely by rushing to conclusions or by force-fitting data into an existing paradigm. They stay open to the flow of information, and they are willing to expand and adjust their existing paradigms to accommodate new information. Rigid adherence to an ideological framework reduces agency if it limits the scope of inquiry.

George Will, conservative U.S. political analyst, writer, and commentator, embodies the practice of open inquiry. A longtime member of the Republican Party, he is committed to the principle of small government, low taxes, and fiscal responsibility (low deficits). He pays close attention to facts, analysis, and results rather than just to politicians' words. When he witnessed his party enact a significant tax cut without the means to pay for it, he did the math and called the leaders out for exploding the deficit and thereby weakening the future financial health of the nation.

By looking more deeply into the particulars of the tax cut, which was highly popular within his party, he demonstrated commitment to his most important principle—protecting the fundamental best interest of the nation. Through open inquiry, he determined he could not in good conscience support the policy, confronted the issue publicly, and let the chips fall where they may.

Open inquirers also *take in other perspectives*. This allows for gathering critical information that can't come from one's own limited field of perception. As psychologists often note, we all engage in selective perception to some degree or another. Considering a situation from other perspectives arms you with more possibilities and choices and protects you from arriving at rash, narrow-minded, and potentially self-defeating judgments. It also offers the potential to increase empathy. As Arthur C. Brooks noted in a 2016 TED Talk on the perils of polarization, "We need innovative thinking. . . . We need a new day in flexible ideology."

We Can Learn Every Day from Everyone We Meet, as Long as We're Open

When you see things from another vantage point—or, as the old expression says, *walk a mile in someone else's shoes*—you bring yourself closer to others through increased understanding. It also gives you more leverage in addressing the challenges you face by strengthening your connections with others, ultimately empowering you further by recruiting their interest and their resources to help you to handle tough situations.

Of course, when asking others to share their opinion or advice with you, you are free to use it fully, use it partially, or to ignore it. The general idea is to combine it with your own thinking when it is additive. Soliciting others to share their perspectives helps you to arrive at good common-sense solutions. As a colleague often says, "By definition, it is not 'common' if it is not shared." Don't reject an outside perspective just because it doesn't fit with your own view—you may need to expand your view.

Use Your Agency: Be careful about selective perception, focusing just on what you want to hear and ignoring opposing viewpoints. Don't be so arrogant that you dismiss out of hand the point of view of others.

Consider Paul's client Brent, a thirty-six-year-old manager within the investment management business, who was experiencing a troubling career setback. He knew he was viewed by most of his colleagues as extremely bright and full of promise, and yet one day his boss delivered some difficult feedback: He had alienated a great many people within the company, including many of the company's senior leaders. This came as a complete surprise to him, and he struggled to make sense of it. *Was there something wrong with him or wrong with everyone else?* But as Brent thought back to his interactions with colleagues over the past months, he realized that he had a tendency to react impatiently or dismissively to colleagues who disagreed with or challenged him. He knew he was strong-willed, but he thought that was because most of his ideas were the best ones out there and that once people saw this, they would be grateful. But of course, they weren't grateful at all; they resented his lack of openness, which some described as arrogance.

Brent's confidence in his own judgment was, at times, blinding him, and in the highly collegial, team-oriented culture of his company, this dynamic, unless interrupted, was about to derail his career. Perhaps equally devastating, his behavior preempted the possibility of collaboration and the learning that inevitably comes with it.

Paul suggested that Brent work on suspending his judgment temporarily to position himself more fully as a learner in his interactions with his colleagues. Initially irritated at the idea of practicing this (*Why should I when I really don't need their advice and it will only slow things down?*), he agreed to try. In the initial weeks as he attempted to put the idea into practice, the process was two steps forward, one step back. He felt awkward and forced. He said he hated it.

But to his surprise, when he took the time to ask people probing questions, he found he sometimes received useful information and advice.

And Brent noticed that the back-and-forth conversations that he was starting to have sometimes generated new ideas, both from himself and from others, that had never occurred to him before. Furthermore, he started noticing an ancillary benefit: Others seemed more interested in helping him to succeed, and he found he was actually enjoying working with others in a way he hadn't before.

While Brent still struggles at times to remember to position himself this way, he has come to recognize that it has added to the quality of his business judgment and his overall effectiveness as a leader.

The Many Benefits of Positioning Yourself as a Learner

Many benefits are derived from positioning yourself as a learner. They include:

- Improved listening skills
- Better control of strong reactions that lead to impulsive decisions and actions
- Staying more levelheaded during conflict
- Stronger aptitude for empathy

These skills are critical to developing agency, especially when you are attempting to share your own ideas and influence people, because this requires learning where other people are coming from—appreciating and considering what they need, expect, and believe. This principle sets the groundwork for developing better interpersonal negotiation skills. Positioning yourself in this way also sets the stage for effective critical thinking, an enormously important aspect of agency discussed in depth in the principle *Deliberate, Then Act* in chapter 7.

At the outset, learning involves gathering information—basic data, facts, statistics, and real-time observations as well as the thoughts and perceptions of others. Being a deeper and more independent thinker requires understanding the vast difference that separates information from true knowledge. Think of information as the building blocks that can create something larger. For information to lead to actionable knowledge, you have to become very familiar with that information and come to understand it on a deeper level and ideally see it from multiple perspectives.

Nurture a *Growth* Mind-Set

According to Stanford University psychologist Carol Dweck, adopting a belief that your *true potential is unknown,* not fixed, encourages you to continually learn and grow. Adopting this mind-set, you will be forgiving of yourself as you make mistakes along the way and likely will persist when challenged. If you believe that your potential is set or limited, you have what Dweck describes as a *fixed mind-set,* and you will likely close yourself off to new learning opportunities. Dweck has decades of research to back up this powerful observation. We, too, have seen this play out in our work over the years. It applies to a CEO navigating through a complex business situation as much as to a fifth grader struggling with drills on the soccer field.

Pinpointing your actual mind-set may sound somewhat elusive. If, at times, you have felt discouraged or highly anxious when faced with something new—*Why bother trying? What's the point?*—that's a fixed mind-set moment. With a fixed mind-set, your effort, persistence, and tolerance for the errors inherent in learning new things will plummet and opportunities to learn will be lost.

Failure Really Is Part of Life
(and Necessary in Learning)

Many young people have been raised in an era of hypercompetitiveness, to be not only their best but to try to be perfect in every way. When young people reach college or their first jobs, they quickly learn they are just like everyone else—good at some things and not good at others. Accepting their fallibility can be a shock.

Many get discouraged or give up, while others spend their energies demonstrating only on what they're good at.

A Smith College initiative called Failing Well is one of a crop of university programs that aims to help high achievers cope with inevitable setbacks. Smith students were asked to create a "failure résumé"—something any of us could do by jotting down a few setbacks and any lessons learned—and then sharing it with others who have done the same. In short, students realized how important making mistakes or having setbacks was to their growth and future learning. Resilience was the goal here, not getting pulled down by the errors and misfortunes—the teachable moments—we all experience while learning.

Staying the Course in the Face of Mistakes and Failures

When errors, missteps, and mistakes occur in your life—as they inevitably will—what you believe about yourself at that moment matters. A growth mind-set means accepting that mistakes are part of the learning process and that achieving success takes time and trial and error. People with agency face failures and even welcome them as a sign that they are actively learning.

Levi, a bright, charismatic twenty-nine-year-old native Californian, had a "personal learning story" to tell. We interviewed him to understand some of the key learning and decision points he experienced during his twenties—what psychologist Meg Jay describes as *the most defining decade in life.*

Committed to pursuing a career in medicine, Levi, at twenty-five, was living his dream. After a year in Kenya working in a clinic, he moved to Chicago and enrolled in a premed program at the University of Chicago, tending bar at night, living a go-go life, experiencing the best of all worlds. Offered a position on an organ transplant team at the University of Chicago—an amazing, almost unheard-of opportunity for a young premed student—he felt he'd won the lottery. Suddenly, his go-go life began moving even faster—now flying all over the country whenever a transplant organ became available. He also had a full social life, with a new girlfriend and long nights partying in his few free hours.

But of course, a pace like that is sustainable for only so long before it becomes impossible to do everything well.

Sleep deprived while switching gears fast and furiously each day began to take a toll on his level of attentiveness to detail and his attitude. His supervisor at the university, unhappy with his performance, fired him from his plum job on the transplant team. Soon things at his bartending job weren't going so well either. Tension with his roommate escalated due to spats over basic housekeeping, leaving Levi to find both a new job and a place to live—a serious string of challenges in a short span. The only good thing was that he was nearing completion of his premed studies. Levi didn't pause for long—he kept going. He quickly landed a high-paying job at a five-star hotel, "which I really wasn't qualified for," working there two years before getting fired. "During this time, I got totally swept up in working and partying with no infrastructure or plan at all," Levi reflected. "It was all improvised. I was completely ungrounded. After losing the hotel job, I found myself biking around the city for two full days trying to gather myself, wondering, *Where to now?*"

Returning from the second full day of biking, he was ambushed as he entered his apartment. Pistol-whipped by a hooded man and an accomplice, his head cracked open and bleeding, he lay on the floor hog-tied alongside his roommate and watched the men ransack their apartment. Later, the roommate confessed he'd been dealing pot out of their apartment. The thieves had likely targeted them.

"Everything came crashing down," Levi said. "It woke me up." He needed a "hard reset" to regain his physical and emotional health. He decided to take a deep look inward to assess and open himself to new learning to get back onto a healthy life path. He rented a cottage back in California and found a simple restaurant job in a small town. Getting away from the intense stimulation to create space for reflection, he was able, painfully, to question himself on why and how he had veered so far off the path he'd most wanted to follow. Reconnecting with an old friend who was an effective sounding board, reading, long walks with his new dog, and focusing on physical fitness, Levi steadily put his life back together. He met a woman pursuing a career in medicine who would later become his wife. Now in medical school and beginning the decade of his thirties, he looks back. "I learned from all my mistakes and successes," Levi said. "Somehow through it all, with help from my friends, I never fully lost sight of my potential."

The twenties are an important time to experiment, to try new things. A critical part of developing greater agency is making meaning of and learning from our mistakes—maintaining a growth mind-set through setbacks and failures facilitates this.

> Make New Mistakes. Make glorious, amazing mistakes. Make mistakes nobody's ever made before. Don't freeze, don't stop, don't worry that it isn't good enough, or it isn't perfect, whatever it is: art, or love, or work or family or life.
>
> —Neil Gaiman, author, in a post on his website, December 2011

Recovery from Setbacks

Recovering from setbacks, both large and small, isn't easy but is essential to personal agency. Do you have a particular approach that you can rely on? Do you recover quickly when you swing and you miss, whether it's a baseball bat or tennis racket—or when you don't get the promotion, the callback, the invite to the party, or whatever it is you were expecting?

Keep in mind that setbacks always create an opportunity for recovery, and *the act of recovery builds confidence and agency*. To use a baseball analogy, immediately following any setback, your focus should be on getting ready for the next ball to come sailing across the plate. What you do in that moment—recognizing and seizing upon the next opportunity—is paramount to building agency. By virtue of being able to say to yourself, *I can overcome a difficult setback,* you develop confidence that you'll be able to handle other future setbacks.

The best athletes understand this. They have much to teach us about how to recover from setbacks because they confront setbacks continually while practicing and competing. The most successful athletes don't ruminate over mistakes because they've learned that their performance will surely suffer. An incomplete pass, a missed free throw, or a bad stroke must be seen as a separate event that is disconnected from the next potentially positive action. Imagine the power it gives a person to see himself or herself that way and to see the whole world operating that way! Each moment is fresh and untainted by what just happened. It generates a sense that new possibilities are always within reach.

Use Mindfulness to Stop Ruminating and Move Forward

"It's history—why bother thinking about it?" one college wrestler named Sam said. Alongside strength training and perfecting his techniques in duck-unders and takedowns, Sam rehearses that phrase in his head in the days and hours leading up to an important match. During a match, he doesn't want any setbacks to linger in his mind, not for a second. He's got to endure a grueling seven minutes of intense physical and mental battle against a strong opponent, and he can't afford to let negative thoughts intrude because it would be like letting a psychological gremlin into his system. If he does so, he'll become distracted, his reaction time will slow, his hand-eye coordination will be off, his balance will lessen. Becoming overly self-conscious and hesitant allows an opening for his opponent to rush in and take him down. Instead, Sam needs to be in a state of mind that athletes call *being in the zone*. He needs to be squarely in the present moment, automatic and fluid in his motions, and in a nonthinking mental space. This is nothing more than the sports version of *mindfulness*.

Mindfulness helps you to stop judging and appraising each action you have. It allows you to experience life more as a constant flow of experiences. Setbacks are acknowledged and let go of. There's not always a need to stop, to consciously evaluate, and to fix. That can come later if necessary.

Practice mindfulness and related techniques, such as meditation, focused breathing, or positive imagery to help you stay more in the present moment and focused on pleasant thoughts, feelings, and body sensations. You'll find that each moment can be slowed down, disconnected from the previous (or the next) if you allow yourself to see it that way. An intense, pleasing focus will ensue. Time will seem to slow down as you enjoy being lost in whatever is happening or whatever you are doing. A deeper, richer, and more fulfilling experience can be had once you let go of moments that are, as Sam says, "history."

Many top athletes insert a positive emotion into their minds immediately after a failure or mistake. They wedge it in there fast. Try this yourself: Tell yourself after a misstep that you're doing great. Sounds strange to congratulate yourself even after a setback, but we've all seen players bumping fists when their teammates miss a free throw or penalty shot. They know the power of inserting a positive emotion into a negative moment. It neutralizes the negative, unhelpful emotion that a bad play or missed shot brings about. "Shake it off," many athletes say as if setbacks are like invisible parasites trying to cling to them. Next time you experience the negative emotions of a setback, immediately remind yourself of your worth. *That wasn't a big deal . . . move on . . . it's history . . . the next opportunity to show my stuff is on its way.*

Susan is an experienced executive in her fifties who has learned to practice letting go of bad moments in her high-stress job. Self-possessed and self-assured in her role as a chief financial officer for a large business, it's hard to believe she wasn't always so poised and confident. "I used to be the kid who never raised her hand in class," she told us. Her biggest fear was making a mistake in front of her teacher and the other students and feeling like a failure. Years of hiding like this and worrying about what others thought of her held her back socially, too.

Fast-forward. Susan regularly gives important presentations—her quarterly meetings typically have over fifty people in attendance. "Mistakes? Errors?" She laughed. "Are you kidding? They happen all the time." Susan told us about a problem she experienced during one of her most important meetings for the company's senior executive team and a group of outside investors where she was presenting the company's strategy and financials. Many of them had flown in for the day for the offsite meeting. "I was one slide into my crucial presentation when my computer crashed," she explained. "I was standing there flooded in blinding light. The room went dead quiet. The anxiety in the room was palpable. Some of my senior colleagues got nervous, looking like deer caught in the headlights. I quickly realized it would take too much time to send for a backup computer. I decided to just keep moving. Instead of breaking momentum, I went with the moment, didn't fight it or react to it. I walked over to the projector, turned it off, and not missing a beat, I said, 'Well, fortunately, I'm a better CFO and strategist than I am a slide projector operator.' Everyone laughed. The tension in the room disappeared. I just continued to talk about what I knew, assuring them they would receive copies of the slides. We had one of the best back-and-forth exchanges we'd ever had at one of these presentations. The slides weren't why they were there."

Take a moment and let Susan's confidence sink in. Confidence is as contagious as anxiety. She isn't any different from many of us who have felt shy, experienced awkward moments, and have worried about making mistakes in front of others. She's learned how not to beat herself up and obsess when the mistakes come. She accepts that mistakes are normal, part of life, part of what makes us grow. "Never put your faith into a machine! Assume it's going to mess you up," Susan joked. Her confidence was contagious in that boardroom at that critical moment just as it can be now hearing her story. Let her confidence find its way into you.

If this is hard for you to do, give it a name so you understand why you have a hard time letting go of errors or missteps. In psychology, we often warn people not to *catastrophize*—imagining worst-case scenarios and worrying that you will never be able to fix a mistake you've just made. Catastrophizing is particularly risky immediately after a setback. If you catch yourself falling prey to this way of thinking, don't buy into it. It's history. Move on. Get ready to take another swing.

Recognize the Four Modes of Learning— and Which Work Best for You

There are many ways to learn, and we highlight this variety in our work with clients. People with agency maximize the opportunity to learn by being flexible and using more than one method. They also consider which mode is best employed in any given set of circumstances. For example, you might call someone for a quick consult on a topic you know they are well versed in rather than spend fifteen minutes googling an answer or trying to fix something on your own.

These four modes we present below are not an exhaustive list, nor are they airtight categories since they frequently overlap.

Most of us learn by using some combination of the four, but each of us usually has one method that we gravitate to. As you read about each of these modes, ask yourself:

What kind of learner am I?
Do I prefer to learn alone, by, say, reading or watching
    instructional videos?
Do I like to learn in groups?
Do I need to daydream about an opportunity first before
    I approach it? Do I learn by jumping right into doing and
    then picking up what I need to know along the way?
Or by being tutored one-on-one, or working in collaboration?
How averse am I to failing or experiencing embarrassment?

LEARNING MODE #1:

Learning Through Classroom-Based Study and Self-Study

Early in our lives, the expectation in school settings is that we all learn from books and in classrooms. Once we're out of school, reading books and studying become optional. In our experience, people with strong agency never outgrow books or other means of trying to educate themselves.

Reading offers terrific, deeper learning opportunities. Many people with agency we interviewed told us they regularly read both fiction and nonfiction to take them into worlds they don't know or want to explore more deeply. Reading takes time and requires the control of external stimuli. Podcasts and narrated books may appeal to more auditory-inclined learners and can be useful, but there is great value derived from creating the quiet and developing the patience for reading—quiet and patience are two things that are always required to go mentally deeper into whatever interests you.

Beyond high school or college, classroom-based study can take many forms. Adult education programs at community colleges and local universities, workshops at libraries, and retreats sponsored by health centers are all great opportunities to expand yourself, and many are inexpensive or free. And don't be afraid to think outside the box. People we've worked with sometimes sign up for a class in something completely unexpected, like the Boston cop who learned improv and acting skills at a local adult education center. In terms of self-study, some people we know keep journals of everything from dreams to creative ideas that pop up unexpectedly. Seventy-two-year-old Bobbie Gates told *The Wall Street Journal* that playing the flute, which she began studying when she turned sixty, "fills my body with love and with peace." The article noted that "a growing body of research suggests that playing an instrument or singing in a choir can enhance emotional well-being, brain health, cognition and hearing function."

Many people make it a point to take trips to places they've never been to. One retired couple we spoke with travel by car to small towns and villages along the New England coastline, researching landmarks before they head out for the day, while another couple who are craft beer fanatics visit new breweries. The unfamiliar environments these people experience fuel their learning. These adventures keep them in a state of constant exploration.

Gerald Chertavian, the founder and CEO of Year Up, an organization that helps disadvantaged young people succeed and reach their potential, has figured out strategies to promote learning in himself, too. "I spend an hour a day purely educating myself on things," Chertavian told us. "Just today, before speaking to you, I ran through the business cards I collected from people who I met this week. I went online to learn more about them. I also download and assemble things to read when I'm traveling, which is several hours a week at this point. I make it a point to keep exposing myself to things I don't know and should know. It's a strong driving force in me. I bump into many things, and if I'm not actively inquisitive and learning, how will I possibly know I'm doing things right?"

Learning from (and with) Machines

Technology is a great tool for (virtual) class study and self-study, but as yet it's not a full-fledged teacher in and of itself. According to a 2017 article in *The Economist*, it remains a challenge for machines to calculate our learning style and tutor us accordingly. Artificial intelligence (AI) is paving the way with the development of software that can customize instruction by adapting to the individual's knowledge level and rate of learning. Many promising developments are under way. Meanwhile, here are three forums that technology offers that can help you position yourself as a learner.

- **Information searches.** Researching facts and getting helpful information and resources is by far the most common way many people try to learn from machines. Search engines and online encyclopedias are great examples of this. Always double-check what you read, though, by fact-checking and double sourcing. Don't accept what you're being told as truth without considering the source.

- **Virtual classrooms/workshops.** Webinars and online courses offer the potential for learning with others, either in real time or at your own pace, whenever you choose. Research is mixed on whether virtual educational experiences match the quality of real-life learning. It may be a matter of your learning style. If you learn best alongside other people, sharing the same physical space, having opportunities to easily ask questions, and engaging in exploratory

(continued)

back-and-forth dialogue, in-person class settings make the most sense. Still, online learning from organizations such as edX, founded by the Massachusetts Institute of Technology and Harvard University, are helping many people gain access to top-level knowledge and experienced educators.

- **Social media.** These platforms connect us to people, organizations, and news outlets, but they shouldn't be seen as a primary way to learn about complex ideas. Social media is designed to help us socialize in the moment, share experiences, and communicate basic information. Interactions are usually truncated, such as texting to find a location, asking a friend to lunch, or offering a supportive word for a friend going through a hard time. While learning new things can certainly be a part of the mix, beware of how much of your daily "knowledge" you are getting from these quick-hit digital sources.

  With technology, to position yourself as a learner, you also have to position yourself as your own teacher.

  Technology is very seductive, and on the surface, it can deliver learning experiences with remarkable efficiency and convenience (and potential low cost), but it can lead us to overestimate what we think we know.

  To learn through technology tools, keep these general tips in mind:

- **Prepare to be your own teacher.** In the real world, where we're not as autonomous as we can be when we're interacting with a computer or other technology, teachers evaluate us, grade us, track our true learning, and keep us honest. You'll have to take on that role to get the most out of the learning you do with machines.

- **Actively manage what you learn.** Participate in the process. Don't let yourself passively sit back and allow screens and algorithms to dictate what you learn and what you'll experience next. Don't let programs automatically load new videos or modules for you to

consume unless you specifically plan for that. Pay attention to opportunities you have to control the flow of information.

• **Apply what you've learned from virtual learning to real-life
experiences.** Supplement online learning with, for example, groups
or classes that address the same topic. Have get-togethers with
other learners to explore more, and try putting into practice what
you've learned online. Otherwise, the information you get on screens
will fade from your memory quickly.

LEARNING MODE #2:
Learning by Doing

We all learn how to talk, walk, and many other things at the beginning
of our lives not through being explicitly taught but through our motivation and persistence. As adults, many times we learn by doing while
on the job. Beginning waiters, for example, are typically novices thrown
into the task. First-time parents figure out how to calm a crying baby.
Entrepreneurs quickly learn to be business savvy, considering cash flow
and revenues in addition to developing creative projects and products.

Other times, learning is cultivated by doing things over a long
period of time. A love for something or a hobby can blossom into a career.
John is a forty-six-year-old living in southwest Florida. His love of an-
tique clocks started with an old broken clock his grandfather gave him
in his youth. Taking it apart and seeing how it was designed gave him
many joyful hours spent in exploration. He became fascinated by the old,
delicate analog mechanisms and got good enough to fix other people's
clocks. Today, he runs a small clock repair business and says he loves what
he does.

Learning many, if not most, complex things is enhanced by actually
doing them. In medical school, students often perform basic medical
examination procedures on each other, which teaches them not only
how to get better at their medical skills but also what the experience

feels like for the patient on the other side. Through this training, they can develop empathy for people undergoing exams.

We've visited very interesting places to observe how tinkering with technology can facilitate great learning. Anyone who has seen a maker-space or an iLab (information lab) in action immediately sees how young people become animated and engaged standing around large worktables, creatively combining bins of materials into complex, novel objects. Using everything from Lego to wires to transistors to popsicle sticks, and sometimes aided by 3-D printers and other technologies, participants in these spaces solve problems jointly. Interestingly, there often are no "teachers" per se but helpful educators guiding students to use their thinking skills to solve problems more on their own. This type of learning by doing is highly collaborative and fits very well with our view of how agency is often best achieved when working alongside others.

When we visited the MIT Media Lab in Cambridge, Massachusetts, we expected lots of computers and robotics, which there were, but there was just as much cloth, styrofoam, glass, paint, and cardboard. Each area was busy with researchers in their unique territories, devoted to invention and solving complex problems. One researcher, Tal, showed us a remarkable project that he described as computer-mediated expressions in paint. It would, among other possibilities, allow people who had lost nearly all muscle movement to create paintings using eye-tracking technology. It was evident that hands-on experimentation with many different materials was as much a part of these sophisticated projects as formal learning and planning.

People learn by doing when they take apprenticeships, both formal and informal, when they take on internships or temporary work, or when they volunteer for an organization or event. All these activities provide opportunities to try out new skills, watch others at work, and put one's interests into action. And while some of these activities, such as becoming a member of the Peace Corps, for example, demand large time commitments, most others do not. Habitat for Humanity, local libraries, animal shelters, food kitchens—all of these organizations depend on volunteer help and offer unexpected ways to learn new skills and develop inner talents outside of traditional classrooms.

Use Your Agency: Try a new skill, a new volunteer role, or any new way of interacting with the world to cultivate some of your underutilized talents.

Working farms near suburban and urban areas provide wonderful opportunities for both adults and children who don't live in rural communities to work with outdoor materials and see nature up close. One of them we know well. Drumlin Farm Wildlife Sanctuary, part of the Mass Audubon network, is located in Lincoln, Massachusetts, and is an example of this in action. At a preschool program there, kids collect samples from small ponds to study, identify birds, and draw pictures of everything they get to experience, touch, and collect. They watch honey being harvested from a beehive, and they later use it along with milk they've churned into butter to bake cakes. They plant vegetables they will later eat.

Vocational education is getting more attention in the United States these days. Like apprenticeships, these learn-by-doing education programs provide direct laboratory application of real-life work, from hospitality services to automotive techs to medical office assistants.

We've also seen some very unexpected examples of learning by doing, such as when businesses bring professional actors into their companies to help executives become better leaders. Especially for introverted managers, acting programs can help them become more relaxed and personable. They learn, in a tangible way, the value of stepping outside of themselves and the strictures of social roles. They get practice at the old adage "Fake it until you make it," practicing in a safe way how to be confident and outgoing.

LEARNING MODE #3:
Learning Through Imagination and Play

When young children play, they often pretend. They may become different people or animals so that they can develop and practice new social skills. They use their imaginations to solve problems, and they're constantly mastering how things around them go together and function—whether the end product is a Star Wars Millennium Falcon Lego model or a meal of plastic food made in a toy oven.

From the outside, this kind of play can look, to us adults, like a frivolous activity. But it is, in fact, very serious. The amount of gained knowledge and thinking skills that come from this type of play is extraordinary. The cognitive connections that children forge when learning through imaginative processes are nearly unparalleled at any other time of their lives.

Many people we know in their twenties have turned the delight of play into new learning opportunities. As the Harry Potter generation, they grew up reading the book series (which debuted in 1997) and many are unapologetic about their continued love for the Harry Potter world and YA (young adult) fiction overall. Many join the thousands of children and adults who turn out for cosplay (costumed play) events and conventions to dress up as their favorite comic book characters or anime action figures. They get to be creative in a joyful, exuberant way. They also learn the value of being nonjudgmental as they interact with others in their subculture. They explore different parts of their personalities and assume new roles of behavior, all in a playful atmosphere.

Being open to play is very much connected to being open to new ideas and approaches. "If you haven't thought that thought before, you don't even know how that [brain] pattern feels," says Barbara Oakley, a professor at Oakland University in Michigan, in her online course Learning How to Learn. She highlights the need for "diffuse" thinking, rather than just focused thinking, to be able to look at challenges and tasks broadly and from a big-picture perspective.

Unfortunately, somewhere along the way while growing up, most others of us stopped approaching the world playfully. We don't fiddle, putter, whittle, tinker, or imagine as much as we should.

But this can be brought back. Cam was leaving his first job in New York City as a financial analyst on Wall Street. Those three years had been great. He'd made good friends and loved living in Brooklyn, but he was pretty sure he wouldn't be happy staying in the financial business. He didn't have another job lined up, mainly because he was unsure what direction in life he wanted to take next. "I don't really let myself mentally explore and consider all options," he told us. "I pretty quickly shut them down one by one. I don't want to make a mistake and choose the wrong job."

We asked Cam to practice thinking like a kid, not as someone weighing serious issues like viable career paths, student debt, and future mortgages. We asked, "What would you do if you could pretend anything was possible?"

His answers showed that he had many passions beneath the surface that were going unmet: "Ski instructor for a year . . . maybe teach English abroad . . . I've always wanted to learn competitive sailing . . . or maybe get time on one of those tall ships."

By parking his adult expectations to the side and adopting a child's freer imaginative explorations, Cam tried on different options and personas without feeling trapped by the strong messages (*Don't be silly . . . come on, be realistic*) that keep most of us from playful wandering. Given some freedom, our minds can come up with creative options. We can solve problems if we give ourselves permission to imagine. For Cam, it led to the realization that there didn't need to be a single best path at this time for him to follow. Being flexible and adapting to opportunities as they arose made the most sense.

The Challenge of Continuous Change

This is your time and it feels normal to you, but really there is no normal. There's only change, and resistance to it, and then more change.

Actress Meryl Streep, in a commencement address to Barnard College

Meryl Streep understands the power of change as well as anyone; to be a good actor, after all, means to make yourself "new" in some way for every role. And Streep is right that becoming new isn't just

(continued)

a tool for actors in theater or film. Change, and adapting to it, is a part of life for everyone.

To the extent that you resist change, you will limit new experiences and won't be able to learn much, and you will suffer the consequences. Learning facilitates adaptation, and if you're not learning, you will struggle coping with change. It is useful to keep a close eye on your attitude toward change; some resistance is to be expected, but if you notice yourself becoming angry or frustrated, you might want to give further thought to identifying the source of your resistance.

People with high levels of agency work hard to keep open to change and update their ideas as things around them change and as they learn more. In high-change periods where things are moving quickly, you need to update your point of view and opinions more frequently as you take in new information. This serves to promote self-renewal, which is healthy change.

Interestingly, in times of significant stress, most people tend to do the opposite. They often keep a tight grasp on their beliefs to anchor them because they're feeling unsettled and unmoored. While this is an understandable human tendency, it also is a major inhibitor to new learning.

LEARNING MODE #4:

Learning from Other People

"For an entrepreneur, 90 percent of what you need to know is in somebody else's head," Waverly Deutsch, a University of Chicago Booth School of Business professor of entrepreneurship, has said. "And you learn faster by talking to somebody than by googling all day long. Because you can ask questions, you can interact."

Deutsch is right. There's a special kind of learning that can only happen while you're in the company of others, debating a challenging topic, brainstorming creative ideas, practicing athletic skills alongside competitors. The whole becomes greater than the sum of its parts. This kind of human synergy needs to be practiced, and many things we hope to achieve can't be learned if we are alone.

In our work, learning from other people seems to be the biggest opportunity for learning that many people neglect or need to develop. Modern work habits have us more separated, in cubicles, or working off-site or at home. We easily become isolated many hours a day on screens, and for these reasons, many people simply miss the full leverage of learning that can be gained through positioning themselves alongside others.

Vince Warren is the civil rights attorney in New York City we met in the previous chapter. Vince is also an avid jazz drummer. "Any opportunity I can put myself into musical spaces is when I'm my best," he told us. He noted that playing jazz in a group feels very connected to his work, as it helps him be a better listener and stay more connected to others, forcing him to see things in novel ways. "The learning when I'm playing is so much beyond what I can do or what I'd learn as a drummer alone," he says.

Millennials are known for being especially comfortable with learning through digital collaboration, and in this sense, many don't get as isolated being on screens. They grew up with the internet and social media, so they're adept at crowdsourcing—looking for answers from a wide variety of people—and at hashing out ideas in online forums. That's one of the reasons that digital business tools such as Slack have proven so popular; they allow for real-time discussion on any and every topic, even from the distance of a screen and keyboard.

People in high-precision jobs often see particular value in using the skill of being open and listening to and learning from others. Pilots and surgeons, for example, use reliability checks on the job, encouraging subordinates to question them routinely. Allowing subordinates or experts to step in to confirm or challenge decisions decreases serious, potentially fatal errors. Surgeon and author Atul Gawande captured the essence of this in a *New Yorker* article on the value of listening to the direction of others, whether it's in the surgical operating theater or on the tennis court. "I watched Rafael Nadal play a tournament match on the Tennis Channel," he wrote. "The camera flashed to his coach, and the obvious struck me as interesting: even Rafael Nadal has a coach. Nearly every élite tennis player in the world does. Professional athletes use coaches to make sure they are as good as they can be. But doctors don't." Gawande decided to break with tradition by asking a surgeon he had trained under to be his coach, and he brought him in to observe a surgery and give him feedback.

> **Use Your Agency:** Ask people to provide you with their *thought chain*. Ask them how they came to their conclusion. Ask them what their reasoning steps were.

The key is being selective about who you listen to and learn from. People you solicit advice from should be vetted—that is, trustworthy and experienced. You should know they have no agenda other than offering their helpful guidance and that they've been around enough to know something about what they are talking about. There is great value in finding mentors either in a formal sense as part of a mentoring program or informally on your own. We encourage clients to consider setting up their own personal "board of advisors" composed of people with different skills and backgrounds.

Again, keep in mind that these four modes of learning aren't airtight and there's no single right way to learn. Many artists, entrepreneurs, mechanics, writers, cooks, and gardeners started by taking up a hobby, practicing on their own, apprenticing, volunteering, or just dabbling enough for something to spark. Visual artist Paul Gauguin was a thirty-five-year-old stockbroker in Paris before committing himself to painting in the late 1800s. Respected chef Ina Garten (host of *Barefoot Contessa* on the Food Network) wasn't formally trained in the culinary arts and previously worked at the White House Office of Management and Budget writing nuclear energy budgets. The point is that you shouldn't think twice about picking up a paintbrush or a whisk. Go ahead and take on anything you desire. Have fun and see where it goes. One woman told us that learning, for her, is a lot like hiking, which she loves. "I keep going and going; it's not always just to get to some end spot," she explains. "It's the unexpected things along the way that keep me wanting to move."

Pursue the Learning Approach and the Topics That Are Best for You

Developmental psychologist Howard Gardner describes humans as having "multiple intelligences," and he highlights eight, such as *spatial intelligence* (the ability to conceptualize how things move about and work in physical space, in the way a pilot or a chess player might) or *interpersonal intelligence* (the ability to accurately read other people's emotions and motivations as a psychotherapist or negotiator might). Gardner tells us there are intelligences pertaining to music and sound, use of body and movement, even an intelligence related to concepts of nature.

The eight intelligence types remind us there are multiple ways that people express intelligence and navigate their worlds. Given this, it logically follows that teaching and learning should ideally not be one-dimensional. Most people, through trial and error, gravitate toward topics and learning approaches that feel right and suit them best, but some people can get turned off to learning through bad experiences. Learning, while sometimes challenging and tiring, should ultimately be rewarding, even enjoyable. If it's not, take a step back. Consider what you are learning and if the learning approach is best for you. Don't give up too early, but know that if learning feels like a constant fight or is complete drudgery, you may be going against your natural grain. Try a different method. Consider learning about other topics or learning through a different approach.

Remember: We're all equipped to learn, but we need to seek the best way for ourselves.

Multisensory Learning with Simple Tools

Robert works in sales with an energy company based in California. We met him recently while traveling, striking up a conversation while waiting to board a plane. Robert told us about a simple technique he uses during meetings to prevent his attention from straying. He carries a small paper notebook with him at all times and makes himself jot down notes by hand.

Writing notes helps him recall a meeting's details, but that's not the main reason he does it. He explained that the physical touch of the paper and holding a pen in his hand—and the freedom from distracting screens—help him slow his mind down, help him focus, and help him benefit as much as possible from each meeting he attends. Otherwise, he says, his eyes and mind roam.

Simple note-taking like this engages more parts of the brain. Fingers move to capture the words, hands experience the texture of the paper, and eyes scan to stay within the boundaries of real pages. The physical act of moving the muscles of your fingers and hand in fluid, real ways does increase concentration. Compared to clicking keys and tapping glass, the senses must work together rather than process separate stimuli. This, in turn, reinforces memory.

Neurologically, activities like taking notes on real paper encourage what's called *multisensory learning*. The more your various senses are engaged when trying to learn something, the better chance you have of getting the right information into your brain accurately, and the better chance that information has of staying there.

Move to Learn

From our last chapter, "Respect Your Body," we know that getting regular healthy movement improves learning and fosters creative thinking. But what about movement *during* learning?

One study suggests that movement while learning a new language is beneficial. The study, published in *PLOS ONE*, involved college students in China who were learning English. Half learned while seated, and the other half learned while cycling in place. According to the researchers, "The results of the study are clear-cut: learning a foreign vocabulary while performing a concurrent physical activity yields better performance than learning the same vocabulary while being in a static situation."

Now, this is not to say that all learning is enhanced in this way or that it is reasonable to set up most learning environments with tread-mills and exercise bikes. Further, more intense movement may actually detract from learning, as the exertion can pull resources and energy from the brain. But this is an intriguing finding that future studies can build upon. Anecdotally, many offices are using treadmills and standing desks to keep muscles engaged, and there have been positive anecdotal findings that these practices are enhancing performance.

Learn Without Being Led Astray

There is an important challenge when learning from other people, and that's the risk of being *unduly influenced* through our interactions. Groups are particularly powerful at influencing individuals. Engaging with the media we consume, the talk shows we watch or listen to, and the social groups we interact with all provide opportunities to learn from people, but they all come with this risk. How do you position yourself as a learner without getting misled in the process?

We explored in chapter 2 the principle *Associate Selectively* and how mirror neurons can make us experience other people's emotions. We also explored how social comparison happens constantly—to some degree, we're continually sizing each other up—and may realign our thoughts and behaviors. In fact, whenever we affiliate, we are suscepti-ble to being persuaded by others' beliefs, agendas, and needs. We've all had this experience; if a few people in a group start looking upward or in one particular direction, chances are we do, too. When people start to applaud or laugh at a joke, we tend to follow. In short, most of us are strongly wired to follow the herd as it functions from an evolutionary standpoint and as a survival skill.

Anthony's Notes from the Office: Coach?

Who we listen to and take cues from are critical. We went into detail about this in the principle *Associate Selectively*. That principle can make all the difference when we are seeking specific information or guidance.

Max was a twenty-three-year-old recent college graduate when I met him. He was confused over his love life. His girlfriend of two years wasn't committing to anything long term. She wanted to explore other relationships because she was only twenty, but when Max leaned toward a breakup, she wanted to spend more time together. This was Max's first serious relationship, and he said he had never been this much in love, but the emotional drama of the relationship was wreaking havoc. Some nights, Max couldn't sleep.

Max came to my office looking for help with "the direction of his life." After talking for a while, it became apparent that one of the main reasons he was so confused and distressed was because he was seeking advice from many close friends and getting wildly contradictory advice. "Break up," said one friend. "Take her on a romantic trip," said another. Another advised that if he loves her he should "go for it" and propose. Another said to unfriend her on Facebook.

What helped Max most was guiding him to assess which friends he should listen to and which he shouldn't. Who among his friends had the most relationship experience? Who had relationships that to him seemed positive and healthy? Once he did this assessment, he was able to easily zero in on who would be the best source of advice and whose advice was better off ignored.

Be Smart About How You Get News

Max's story makes an important point about considering the sources of information that you're using to help you make decisions. Whatever the context, agency involves considering the source of information. Nowhere has the threat to agency posed by bad information become more clear recently than in the world of news, where the specter of "fake news" has left many paralyzed about whom to believe.

Access to reliable information about current events and society's trends and challenges is vital. Without accurate and reliable information, how can you make good decisions? You simply can't. For example, if you're misinformed, you can't make good decisions in terms of supporting leaders who will best represent your values and needs. Choosing to vote for a particular leader directly impacts the community you are part of. When you participate as an informed member of your neighborhood, your town, your state, your country—you ensure that better decisions will be made on issues that impact your personal agency—such as funding for training and education, cultural and arts programs, infrastructure, and of course economic opportunities.

In the information age, the explosion of new delivery vehicles has created a voracious hunger for content. The twenty-four-hour news cycle means that news cable shows, websites, Twitter feeds, and Facebook updates are always on and always churning out something. Unfortunately, there are unreliable "content providers" who dole out inaccurate, biased content designed to appeal to specific market demographics. It's become a commercially viable industry to produce "news" that isn't designed to reliably inform but rather to entertain and build emotional reactions—to *attract eyeballs*, in industry parlance. It can be dangerous to rely on this type of information.

It has become necessary to exercise great caution in terms of where you get your information. Tim Cook, CEO of Apple, delivered a groundbreaking speech in October 2018 critiquing the "data industrial complex" of big tech. "Our own information, from the everyday to the deeply personal, is being weaponized against us with military efficiency. . . . Platforms and algorithms that promised to improve our lives can actually magnify our worst human tendencies. Rogue actors and even governments have taken advantage of user trust to deepen divisions, incite violence, and even undermine our shared sense of what is true and what is false." We live in high-stakes times where pivotal issues regarding standards around privacy and even what constitutes "news" need to be addressed. Until this is addressed on a societal level it is crucial for you to be as aware as possible of the personal risks and benefits of the massive intersection of technology and media. It has a direct bearing on your level of personal agency.

Beware of Deceptive "News"

Just because a website looks like news, with well-designed graphics and authoritative journalistic language, doesn't make it news. It's vital to know the difference between proper news organizations that follow journalistic procedures and organizations (and dubious individuals) passing off untruths and their ideologies as news.

One of the best-known recent examples comes from Facebook. It was revealed in the fall of 2017 that leading up to the 2016 presidential election, Facebook sold more than $100,000 worth of ads to Russian agents tied to the Kremlin. Some three thousand ads went out over several months targeting Facebook users in specific voting districts. Many of these posts were made to look like news, when in fact they were a mixture of fact and fiction designed to provoke dissension. Facebook says that these misleading posts reached about ten million people. Similar online ads were placed with Twitter and Google as well. The purpose was to manipulate the presidential election and undermine American democracy.

When you hear people say, "I read it on my Facebook news feed," remind them that Facebook was never intended to be a news organization. It's a social media company that makes money by selling ad space. It tracks the demographics and online behavior of its users. This allows marketers and companies to target their ads and products most effectively. All of us must think critically about the source of our information in the digital age.

Studies in the United States have found that a large percentage of people think all news is biased and that they may as well just pick the source that *feels* best to them. Problem is, it just isn't true that all news sources are crassly biased. Just as scientists welcome critiques of their work and they seek alternate explanations for their findings, good journalists and news organizations work to be impartial and strive to get the most accurate information out to the public.

So, what news to watch, read, or listen to? Our first advice is to not get discouraged. Don't throw up your hands in surrender because there's too much information coming at you (even though there is) or because you're being told that all news is false or misleading. Don't stop seeking the accurate information that you need to make better life choices for yourself. Here are a few specific recommendations:

Use the power of the internet in savvy ways. At your fingertips, you potentially have access to all the information you need to be properly and accurately informed, but you can just as easily be misled.

- Pay attention to the source that's listed before you click on a link. For instance, if you're looking for medical information, click on pages from the Mayo Clinic or nih.gov, the website of the National Institutes of Health, a U.S. government body. Both will provide information that's factual and without a hidden commercial bias.
- Don't stop at the first search hit. Instead, check out those below it and on the next pages.
- Don't accept what's on Wikipedia without verifying the sources. Most entries have accurate information, but because it's an evolving digital encyclopedia with a reported twelve million edits a month, many are bound to have inaccuracies, and most are bound to be incomplete. Go the extra step and check the original sources listed at the bottom of the entry. Visit other encyclopedia resources to verify.

Select Professional News Outlets That Employ and Value Journalism

Many of the best news organizations use fact-checkers, people trained to verify details going into an article before it gets published or broadcasted.

This is similar to reliability checks done by surgeons and pilots to decrease serious errors, and it is similar to conducting reliability studies so that researchers know if their results are by chance or if they will hold up over time.

- Start with traditional media, such as established newspapers, magazines, and noncommercial sources, such as public radio and television. These sources follow established standards of journalism. Many require that you become a subscriber to read more than a handful of articles. This is money well spent. If you immediately reject news sources because they are "too liberal," you've just lost agency.

- Consider sources such as the American Enterprise Institute and organizations such as PIMCO and McKinsey & Company. If you immediately reject these news sources because you think they are "too conservative," you've just lost agency.

- Remember that professional information gatherers value discourse, research, and logic. No matter what ideological end of the spectrum you fall on, you can find reputable sources that will engage your critical-thinking skills, pose important questions that you aren't likely to think of, and challenge your assumptions.

Separate Entertainment from News

Over the past few decades, this line has blurred. To stay informed, you generally want less flash and more facts. We strongly suggest you do not get your news from social media sites that use algorithms to curate your news feed. This will only magnify your blind spots and reinforce preexisting bias. If tuning in to cable news, notice whether the newscasters are chatting more than reporting verifiable information? Are they trying to play to your emotions by peddling a particular ideology in hard-sell fashion (if you find yourself shaking your head in agreement, you may not actually be getting real news)? Are they giving you room to think for yourself?

Are their featured experts legitimate experts providing fact-based analysis? Know the difference between news and theater. If you want to be indulged and entertained, Netflix is great.

Learn from Authority Figures Without Blindly Following Them

We're more likely to follow and be influenced by people who project authority or are authority figures. These include politicians, police, judges, business leaders, military personnel, doctors, and teachers. Just how far does obedience go? Almost anyone wearing a uniform gets our undivided attention or is seen as having greater knowledge or skill. Desks and furnishings in offices are often positioned to communicate power. We're also unconsciously susceptible based on physical characteristics, such as people who are tall or physically fit, attractive, dress elegantly or stylishly, or simply because they speak with a confident voice and manner. We need to pay attention to our human herd instincts! It's best to look beyond the nameplate and the suit. Look beyond the setting or situation, too, such as when in a large, imposing building or posh store, if you sense that someone is expecting you to accept what they say without a reasonable explanation.

> **Use Your Agency:** Respect authority figures, but be open to second-guessing their ideas and looking for additional ideas and opinions.

When we're working with clients, we tell people to be on the lookout for "talking points." These are phrases that are just a little too smooth and rehearsed. They're phrases that have been designed ahead of time to sway. Talking points are built into product packaging, many consumer situations, and, of course, political messaging. Years back, Anthony noticed that the price of iced coffee had suddenly increased at a café he regularly visited. Why the price bump? "We take time to shake it after pouring it over ice," the barista answered with a steady smile.

Anthony asked, "What is the benefit of having my iced coffee shaken?" The answer came fast and well-rehearsed: "It unlocks the flavor!"

Use your critical thinking when trying to learn from others. And of course this applies to authority figures as well. Take in information as objectively as possible (*Does shaking my coffee really unlock its flavor?*) to reach your own conclusions. Watch for social sleights of hand that are intended not so much to teach you something but to get you to move more in someone else's direction. Ask yourself, *Is this person trustworthy, reliable?* And don't stop there. Consider all sources and ways that people try to influence you.

Don't Completely Outsource Your Decision-Making

There is fascinating research on how people literally shut down the part of their brains that otherwise helps them make independent decisions when they are listening to an expert. A recent study by Emory University, for instance, looked at brain MRIs as people were listening to advice from a financial expert.

"Results showed that brain regions consistent with decision-making were active in participants when making choices on their own; however, there occurred an offloading of the decision-making process in the presence of expert advice," said Jan B. Engelmann, a research fellow in Emory's Department of Psychiatry and Behavioral Sciences and a coauthor of the study, in an Emory news release.

This abdication of focus in the face of an expert happened even when experts weren't delivering advice that led to the best outcomes. "The expert provided very conservative advice, which in our experiment did not lead to the highest earnings. But the brain activation results suggested that the offloading of decision-making was driven by trust in the expert," said C. Monica Capra, an economist in Emory's Department of Economics and another coauthor of the study.

The brain essentially gave up responsibility when an authority figure was providing advice. That's dangerous, obviously. As Emory professor of neuroeconomics and psychiatry Gregory Berns, another coauthor of the study, put it, "The problem with this tendency is that it can work to a person's detriment if the trusted source turns out to be incompetent or corrupt."

We all do this to varying degrees, and we do it in many situations. We tend to trust others with seniority or with more experience. On the surface, this seems logical, but we have to be careful that we don't fully shut down our logical decision-making apparatus, no matter how much we want to trust others. Learning is inhibited when we reflexively give ourselves over to expert opinion.

Critical thinking, a term loaded with agency, is crucial to us in important situations, especially at times when our health is on the line. Research has indicated about 15 percent of medical diagnoses we or our loved ones receive can be flat-out wrong. Medical errors are the third-leading cause of death in the United States, a Johns Hopkins research team reported in 2016. And yet, how often do we question our medical providers or the procedures and therapies they've recommended? How often do we seek out a second opinion? Before taking a trip to the pharmacy or agreeing to surgery, or before ignoring symptoms because an expert tells you you're fine and not to worry, call up your inquisitive skills. Ask reasonable, respectful questions. Reach out to another expert you trust to see if the diagnosis or treatment makes sense. The bottom line is to be a learner in all aspects of your life, *especially when speaking with experts*. Healthy skepticism increases accuracy and better outcomes.

What Inhibits Learning (Hint: Stress Is a Factor)

Few of us find it easy to always listen to others with a completely open mind. This is especially true when we're under stress, when conversations get personal, or when the topic being discussed is one that inspires extreme passion or anger. Few of us find it easy to listen to others when we're convinced that the other person is misleading us, is uninformed, is highly biased, is condescending, or is professing views we find abhorrent.

The tension that results from encounters like these produces something akin to white noise that drowns out everything else. It is difficult to feel calm and balanced and to truly hear what is being said when someone you are engaging with disappoints or offends you or when that person hurts your feelings. Typically, your protective emotional shields go up. You either shut down or counter with strong suspicion or hostility of your own. This is a remnant of the animal instinct to play dead or show teeth when threatened. Your brain thinks you may be in some kind of danger and reroutes its activities to move you into a defensive mode.

Remember that the goal in many conversations, even if they're incredibly stressful, is often not to "be right" or "win the argument" or to completely shut the other person down. More often, it's to expand the capacity for dialogue in a relationship to get to a better place. Think about the bigger picture. Would it be useful to form some sort of understanding or alliance, or at least to understand how the other person arrived at their opinion, to build a communication channel? If your answer is yes, then you need to do the work necessary to open a flow of valuable information.

> **Use Your Agency:** Remember that it can be easy to win the argument but lose the battle. The next time you're having a stressful conversation, remind yourself of your end goal. Are you looking for an alliance? If yes, then it might make sense to back off.

The best strategy in situations like this is to take the perspective of the other person. To do this, you first need to get yourself calm. Whether you're discussing sensitive matters with your spouse or dealing with a difficult neighbor or trying to keep your cool during a heated work meeting, you effectively position yourself as a learner only when you are able to *lower your defenses, take a few breaths, try to keep an open mind, and stay relaxed.*

Other inhibitors to your learning include fear of failure, perfectionism, limited or no interaction with people different from yourself, closed-mindedness, and rushing to judgment.

If You Want to Encourage Learning, Don't Kill the Messenger

Interacting only with like-minded people or exposing yourself to the same routines and situations will limit your learning options. Even people you find uncomfortable to be around may provide valuable learning opportunities that will help you grow as a person and maybe help you understand a problem from a new angle. (There are limits to this, as people who aren't ever respectful of you should be avoided.)

Guy experienced a variation of this firsthand when roofers had just finished installing a new gutter system on his home. While they were packing tools into their truck, Guy asked how the job went. One of them said in a hostile and exasperated voice, "Well, I don't know why you're putting up fancy new copper gutters when your roof is in a state of failure!"

Guy was shocked. Why hadn't anyone said anything while they were working up there? Why hadn't the other supervising contractors on-site been told?

To Guy's credit, at a moment of high stress, he practiced positioning himself as a learner. He didn't show anger outwardly, although he was very upset. He stood his ground and demanded the workers remain on-site so he could ask questions. He got more details about the condition of his roof. The more calm he was, the more information he got.

The next day, the owner of the roofing company came and apologized. "Look, I don't want an apology," said Guy. "And I don't want this guy to get in trouble, either. He spoke up, and I want to hear what he saw and why he came to that conclusion. He was up there on my roof getting his hands dirty while the rest of us weren't."

Fortunately, the roof turned out to not be in as disastrous a state

(continued)

as that one roofer implied, but his outburst did lead to a more thorough assessment of the roof's conditions, and it spurred several repairs that would extend the roof's life.

The "Alpha Personality" Type Inhibits Learning

Those with the so-called alpha personality type often believe it's a sign of weakness to position themselves to learn from others. Many people with this personality style focus on projecting a strong outward façade of power and of appearing firm, steady, and unwavering. Being open to the perspectives of others is viewed as a passive—and thus a weak—behavior. They often react emotionally to bad news, serving to discourage others from bringing it to them. These kinds of alphas prefer to be dominant and to tightly control the flow of information—top down and doled out to subordinates on a need-to-know basis. Learning, for them, is generally secondary to being perceived as tough and commanding.

How can he remember well his ignorance—which his growth requires—who has so often to use his knowledge?
—Henry David Thoreau, *Walden*

Alphas run the risk of being misinformed but, at the same time, are invested in always being right. Research psychologists have a name for this. It's called the Dunning-Kruger effect, named after psychologists David Dunning and Justin Kruger. In short, it's when a person is ignorant of his or her own ignorance. In fancier terms, it's a cognitive bias where people with low abilities have an illusory superiority. They think that their knowledge and competence is much greater than it is.

Compare this to people with agency. People with true power and genuine confidence don't need to keep proving it or to act superior. They know that listening to others gives them significantly more leverage in assessing the real nature of a particular situation or challenge. This, in turn, typically opens up more options for them to consider in terms of actions to take. People with agency frequently describe this principle of positioning oneself as a learner as a fundamental skill. It enhances their personal power and effectiveness, particularly in more complex situations.

Positioning yourself as a learner takes self-control. Muster the confidence to set your ego aside, keep your emotions in check, and just listen. Many people don't realize that they increase their level of influence by strategically ceding power at times. Giving others the opportunity to exert their control can reduce tension and conflict. It can also set the stage for more learning in both directions. People open up more when they perceive you as fair-minded, and they may respect your viewpoint more. In the end, you may get, as negotiators hope to do, more of what you want.

Adam, a senior HR leader for a major corporation in a new role, was responsible for dealing with seasoned union leaders during challenging contract negotiations. This represented his greatest professional challenge yet. When he began strategically positioning himself more as a learner and an active listener by asking questions, not interrupting, and using more open body language and relaxed facial expressions, his negotiating adversaries responded in kind and became a bit more like partners. Seeing how present he was to the concerns and opinions of others, the union representatives were more willing to work with him and reach effective compromises. Adam's influence increased when he stopped always trying to appear tough and unmovable.

Find Your Way to Being a Better Listener

Sometimes we're happy to be listening and learning. Other times, listening is a struggle. Here are six strategies for trying to learn from people you might normally shut yourself off from:

1. Imagine yourself in the role of a journalist, interviewing a knowledgeable expert.

(continued)

2. Give the other person physical space and encourage them to talk. Keep an open posture and maintain good eye contact.

3. Demonstrate that you're really listening by not interrupting and by restating the other person's viewpoints. Acknowledge their value. Occasionally nod to affirm that you're understanding what they are saying.

4. Resist the impulse to challenge or defend. Don't come at the person you're talking to as an opponent or, worse, an enemy. Breathe.

5. Don't one-up the person you've decided to learn from. Don't talk about yourself.

6. Don't make up your mind too quickly. Suspend judgment to prevent yourself from reaching conclusions preemptively.

7. Keep conversations time limited, and steer them back on track. Say, "We're off course here; let's stick to what we can be productive on."

8. Consider taking a walk so you're side by side rather than facing each other in an adversarial way. The movement also helps lower stress and the buildup of adrenaline.

Learning About Yourself Is an Important Dimension of Learning

How do others see you? What's their experience when they're in your presence?

These are hard questions to answer. Consider how often the people you come in contact with don't know what informs your perspective. Consider how much—or how little—you know about what informs theirs. There's often remarkably little data on either side of the interaction.

The business world uses "360-degree" assessments to help executives and managers gain a better perspective on what personality traits and leadership skills they project and how they are received. The assessment often looks at competencies such as how clear you are in communicating, how open you are to feedback, and whether people find working with you to be inspiring. It finds out whether you are seen as nurturing or abrasive, supportive or condescending, encouraging or overly critical. It can help you understand if people trust your decision-making or simply grin and bear it and try to work around it.

The process typically takes the form of anonymous feedback (often coordinated by a third party) from a representative sample of people at different levels who work with the person. These people can include executives, managers, peers, direct reports, and clients. Properly conducted, these reviews can help people become better leaders and managers through increasing their self-awareness, nudging them to develop new skills, and helping them blossom in new ways after being given boosts of confidence to their self-esteem.

"Your own perception of yourself is rarely accurate or predictive," consultants Jack Zenger and Joseph Folkman have written in *Harvard Business Review*. "We are heartened when we see the process done well because we know that virtually every time that happens, someone's life will indeed be transformed in a positive way. In a very real sense, it can be one of the rare activities that truly does influence careers and change lives."

Use Your Agency: Undergo a 360 process or simply ask respected, trustworthy colleagues and friends who know you well for honest feedback to find out what skills you need to work on.

Gerald, the Year Up CEO we met earlier, uses the 360 process in his organization. "It's the ultimate way to position yourself as learner," he says. "We do a lot of 360 reviews and get deep and valuable feedback.

With 450 people working in twelve different cities, I absolutely must get multiple viewpoints for me to be at my best."

If it were easy to do, we would learn and integrate the perspectives of everyone around us all the time. We could use this increased awareness to help us increase our good qualities and decrease the negative ones. It would open the door to all sorts of learning. But it's not easy. It requires that you seek out and embrace the views of others without overpersonalizing what you hear.

In many ways, doing this kind of self-investigation is the ultimate example of positioning yourself as a learner. It requires orienting yourself to receive information and subjective views that may go deep and intimate, not getting swayed by outlying negative comments or petty observations, and then reflecting on the new information to update your beliefs about yourself. Done with openness and some modesty, it will help you to become your best self.

Preparing Yourself for Success in the Twenty-First Century

Will you be prepared as things change? Should you pursue a broad-based, general education, or should you learn highly specific skills? How can you learn to learn better?

We look to educators who are on the front lines of teaching for answers. After all, educators are preparing the upcoming generation of young people to effectively learn, grow, and adapt to a rapidly changing, evermore tech-driven world. It has become crucial today to consider not only what we learn but to consider how we learn—continuous change requires continuous learning.

In short, acquiring knowledge and skills alone isn't enough.

One helpful framework to consider and guide you can be found in the book *Four-Dimensional Education* by Charles Fadel, Maya Bialik, and Bernie Trilling. The authors explain, "Educational success is no longer mainly about reproducing content knowledge, but about extrapolating from what we know and applying that knowledge in novel situations." In their model for twenty-first-century learning, the first two dimensions may sound familiar: *Knowledge* (what we know and understand) and *Skills* (how we use what we know). The next two dimensions are less familiar for most of us who have been taught in traditional education settings. They are *Character* (how we behave and engage in the world), and *Meta-Learning* (how we reflect and adapt).

What are the main differentiators? Critical thinking, collaboration, and creativity, among other uniquely human attributes. As Fadel, Bialik, and Trilling remind us, "The world no longer rewards people just for what they know—search engines know everything— but for what they can do with what they know, how they behave in the world, and how they adapt."

Bottom Line: Positioning Yourself as a Learner Reinforces Other Agency Principles

Keep in mind that the principles in this book interrelate and build on each other. *Control Stimuli* and *Associate Selectively* provide a valuable boost when you put them together with *Position Yourself as a Learner.* Controlling the heavy daily volume of stimulation that comes at you is critical for keeping your mind primed to learn, and it widens your bandwidth to take in the important things. Associating selectively gets you to the right people who can provide the information and knowledge you need. It also can get you to people who will challenge you to expand your thinking by helping you see things from different points of view.

In general, you want to seek out quality time with others who also value positioning themselves as learners. Learning works best when it's a two-way street.

Most important, positioning yourself as a learner is central to developing a critical-thinking self because using your brain's frontal cortex for logical thought requires that you obtain good information for it to do its job. Your brain is designed to help you, but it needs factual, reliable data. It also needs discipline to stay on course. You can't just be on autopilot all the time and assume that things will work out. Surprising to most of our clients is the fact that, left to its own devices, the human brain doesn't think very logically. As we'll see in the next chapter, "Stable and Grounded," the human brain loves shortcuts and quick ways to size things up. Biases are the norm, not the exception.

> The beautiful thing about learning is that nobody can take it away from you.
>
> —American bluesman B.B. King, speaking to Texas high school students in 1992

YOUR AGENCY TOOL KIT

SEEK KNOWLEDGE AND INDULGE YOUR CURIOSITY: Pursue new information and ideas as a way to open your mind to learning and as a first step toward effective critical thinking.

LEARN TO FAIL: Embrace mistakes as a key aspect of learning. Focus on recovery, and figure out what you need to improve.

GO WIDE: Take in a wide range of information and viewpoints to expand your learning.

KNOW YOUR MODES: Employ the learning mode that best fits your situational need.

IF YOU'RE AN EXTROVERT, SPEAK LESS, LISTEN MORE: Don't dominate conversations, open up space for others to fill, and let uncomfortable silences exist, which facilitates the emergence of deeper thinking.

IF YOU'RE AN INTROVERT, SPEAK UP: Force yourself to ask questions, and don't fear looking stupid for not knowing the answer. The more you do this, the easier it gets.

BE MORE OPEN, LESS JUDGMENTAL: Cultivate an open mind to allow you to truly hear what others are thinking and saying.

PROJECT CALM: Consciously focus on relaxing your muscles and projecting calmness and neutrality to encourage a higher-quality dialogue and knowledge flow from others to you.

GET FEEDBACK: Ask colleagues and friends to provide their views on your traits and skills to gain fuller access to how others experience you.

SEEK THE CHAIN: Request that others walk you through their thought chain to better understand how they arrived at their positions or judgments.

GO FOR THE FACTS: Use reliable data to inform your ideas and to make good decisions.

TAKE PERSPECTIVE: Practice seeing things from other people's vantage points.

DON'T OUTSOURCE 100 PERCENT: Embrace your power as a prudent person by taking time to consider more critically the ideas and recommendations of experts.

STABLE AND GROUNDED

Manage Your Emotions and Beliefs

Increasing your awareness of how your emotions and beliefs drive your thinking, influence your behavior, and affect your judgment will help you navigate life with confidence.

How you perceive and define reality is largely based on your emotions and your beliefs. Like GPS, these are helpful navigation tools for you, but they need to be monitored and calibrated to best guide you. That's because they operate mostly behind the scenes and exert such a powerful effect in determining what you experience. This is the core of what the *Manage Your Emotions and Beliefs* principle is about, and your capability in this regard determines to a large extent your level of agency as it impacts the quality of all the decisions, large and small, that you make.

Emotions 101

Emotions aren't always easy to recognize.

At times of heightened emotions, your body signals arrive quickly and automatically, and they provide clues to help you to identify what you are feeling. Is your breathing fast or shallow? Are your muscles tight, especially around the forehead, neck, shoulders, back, and chest? These signals indicate fear, anxiety, and anger.

Other emotions, like guilt, envy, doubt, ambivalence, or nostalgia, are more complex, and require some reflection. Sometimes we have a nagging sense that something is wrong without being able to pinpoint the precise emotion in play. A neighbor tells us that they're sending their kids to an expensive summer camp program. Are we jealous that they have the resources to do it or guilty that we aren't giving our kids the same opportunity? These are complex feelings, but underneath is likely fear and worry.

To identify your emotions accurately and use them productively, you must assign them a proper name. The name you assign is a best guess, an interpretation of what you are experiencing. The goal is to recognize and label emotions in the moment and not allow them to overcome you, muddle your judgment, or go unaddressed.

Identifying your emotions, and their interplay with your sometimes unreasonable expectations for how you believe things should be, is absolutely central to agency. Until you can identify how a person, situation, or idea influences how you feel, why it makes you feel that way, and how it relates to the way you believe things should be in an ideal world, it's difficult to decide how to act.

What's at Stake: Why Managing Beliefs Is Critical to Agency

To have full agency, you need to adjust and update your beliefs periodically, and that requires a willingness to differentiate what's real from what's not real. John Maynard Keynes, one of the most influential economists of all time, said it quite plainly: "I change my mind when the facts change. What do you do?" At times, strong emotions can distract and exhaust you, but it's inaccurate, unexamined beliefs that truly can dominate and cloud your better judgment. That's because beliefs, like road maps, are referenced constantly to help you direct yourself and move ahead. If they're outdated or distorted, you won't get to where you really want to go.

Your brain is a predictive organ. It is on a mission to predict all possible next situations, to anticipate what may happen, and to offer up next-best choices and actions. The latest research on brain science by people like Lisa Barrett, a professor of psychology and neuroscience at Northeastern University, tell us that the brain isn't sitting there passively waiting for the environment to give it something to see, hear, taste, touch, or smell but rather actively interpreting these signals and making predictions based on them. It isn't waiting around to calculate or solve problems only when you summon it. It's many steps ahead of you all the time and is actually leading you more often than you are leading it. And at times, your brain's perceptions and predictions can be distorted or misled by your emotions—and even more so by your beliefs.

This chapter will teach you how to stay on top of your emotions and beliefs so that your brain can perform its mission better and more accurately. This will help you build an *inner agency voice* that guards against highly reactive emotions and distorted beliefs undermining what you want to do and where you want to go in your life.

> **Use Your Agency:** Your *agency voice* is tied to an optimistic mind-set: *I'm capable, it's worth a try.* A non-agency voice tends to be negative and self-critical: *I'm too old, my résumé isn't right, life isn't fair.*

Your Starting Point: Beliefs Aren't Reality

What are beliefs? The *Merriam-Webster* dictionary defines a belief as "a state or habit of mind in which trust or confidence is placed in some person or thing" or "something that is accepted, considered to be true, or held as an opinion."

For the purposes of agency, we focus on beliefs as a place from where many of our self-defeating behaviors emanate. Beliefs are often overly simplistic, all encompassing, and used as shortcuts to thinking. For example, holding the belief *Investing in stocks is speculative and dangerous* could lead one to rule out considering something that could be important to one's future retirement needs. Or, *One must have one's career pinned down by thirty because after that it is impossible to change* could result in professional inertia that's hard to break through. The formation of our personal beliefs typically occurs outside the rules of logic. This leads to the common experience that our beliefs, and the expectations that accompany them, are often contradicted by reality. At those times, agency is required to take a step back and reflect on the accuracy and the validity of the belief.

The problem is that we simply have a hard time stepping outside of our beliefs to question them. Anytime you have felt held back by doubt, chances are high that a belief was to blame. *She's wonderful and she makes me very happy, but I've been down that road before and don't think a serious relationship is for me.* Or, *Everything's about having the right connections—there's no sense in me applying for that job.* Sometimes these kind of locked beliefs are expressed in "nobody else" or "everybody else" statements, along the line of *Nobody else believes I am difficult to understand* or *Everybody else knows she's a bad person.* Our beliefs end up being wrong much more often than we realize because we don't stop long enough to look at them. They become simply a habit of mind. Furthermore, when a belief we hold is disconfirmed by what we actually observe, we often choose to ignore it. Updating beliefs isn't easy, as it can feel unsettling, but it's the only way to stay grounded and grow as a person—and develop greater agency.

Paul's Notes from the Field: Childhood Beliefs Can Simmer for Decades

Shortly after Bob's oldest son, Matt, turned nine, Bob found himself fighting with him a lot. Up to then, the two had been, in Bob's words, "thick as thieves." Bob was not an overly strict father. Standing at an imposing six feet three inches tall, he was known to everyone as a gentle giant. His wife, Marla, noticed something suddenly change in Bob. He was yelling at Matt nightly about his homework and criticizing him for being sloppy at the breakfast table. He complained when Matt didn't put 100 percent into his soccer practice. Matt

(continued)

started to avoid being around his father, sometimes cried at bedtime when Marla tucked him in, and within a few weeks, his teacher was emailing that Matt seemed distracted in class and was falling behind.

The weeks that ensued got worse, and Bob suffered what his wife described as a slow motion nervous breakdown as he became difficult with everyone. Everything felt off, like the family was coming apart at the seams. Marla, a seasoned mental health professional in the Chicago area, had the wherewithal to know that the problem wasn't their son. She convinced Bob to get into therapy. He was reluctant, as many men are to seek help from a stranger, but smartly agreed. Bob was fortunate to see a very experienced psychotherapist who was also near his work in Hyde Park, a more psychodynamically oriented clinician who encouraged Bob to explore earlier memories for clues as to why his life might suddenly derail. What was uncovered during the therapy was illuminating.

Many years back, not coincidentally when Bob was also nine, there was a tectonic shift in his family. His sister Gretchen was born with profound cognitive and physical delays. Bob's father had to work even more hours to keep the family financially secure, while Bob, being the oldest son, was suddenly thrust into adult responsibilities. Most of the day, he was in charge of caring for his other younger siblings. He stepped up to the challenge. He helped out as needed without complaint. He got his younger siblings to school and did chores, and he even served as a source of comfort and emotional support for his mother.

In his therapy, Bob uncovered beliefs that were driving the dysfunction and emotional pain. Interestingly, these beliefs didn't emerge until his own son turned nine. What were these destructive beliefs? *By nine years old, terrible and unexpected things are likely to happen. You need to be a man and grow up fast. You can never fail those around you.*

There's a hidden potency to many of our deepest-held beliefs. We often adopt beliefs without conscious scrutiny. Some can poison us with untruths and kick up destructive fear and aggression. They can lead us down unhealthy paths of behaviors. Some beliefs, like Bob's, lie dormant for years. They're like land mines that get set off when we step on similar life terrain.

Why we apply such outdated and often untrue beliefs years, even decades, later to our current lives makes no sense. It's illogical, but we do it anyway. The mind is trying to guide us by linking current experiences to similar past experiences, but it doesn't know if those experiences are still helpful years later. Beliefs that were helpful at one point in our lives may not be helpful at other points and may even be destructive. Stated differently, sometimes the coping skills we had as children were necessary in the context of what was going on then but are no longer adaptive in adulthood.

Understanding his beliefs and getting them into the daylight was a game changer for Bob. He set to work figuring how to flag his strong emotions early, labeling them as likely caused by his outdated underlying beliefs. He began channeling his fear and anger into physical outlets, making certain he got a daily dose of healthy exercise, like a good workout or a long run. Bob developed greater empathy for the boy he was at nine years of age as well as greater empathy for Matt. Matt fell back into being a nine-year-old and regained his close relationship with his father, receiving his understanding and support. Marla maintains a watchful eye, as many partners and parents do, to monitor when unhealthy beliefs might be driving up emotions. The two of them have developed a signal between them: When Marla senses Bob is too stressed or heading into being critical of Matt, she gives him one of her looks—an empathetic smile with eyebrows raised. It helps Bob catch himself early, stopping strong beliefs from reappearing again where they're no longer useful or helpful.

Self-Awareness Is Key to Managing Your Emotions and Beliefs

Of the seven principles laid out in this book, *Manage Your Emotions and Beliefs* may be the one that requires the most effort. That's because emotions and beliefs often operate beneath our awareness. It takes considerable mental effort to identify your emotions and beliefs and to see yourself more objectively. But this increased self-awareness can be learned and becomes easier as you do so. Being more aware of yourself through self-reflection helps to keep you grounded by slowing down your thinking process—highly beneficial in an age of overwhelm. We're all swimming in a hyperstimulated sea of digital information and rapid change that drives up anxiety and emotion. In short, the more amped-up emotion you are feeling, the less grounded and logical you likely will be—and that means the less agency you will have. You won't be as effective at thinking critically and making good decisions for yourself.

Practicing Self-Awareness Can Dissipate Overwhelm

When you're feeling overwhelmed, one of the best steps to take is to identify what is making you feel that way. Lots of times you think you know, when it turns out you were focused on the wrong thing.

To develop your self-awareness, start small. Practice becoming more conscious of what's going on inside your mind one situation at a time. It's best to choose a time when you register stress, strong emotion, or find yourself falling easily into the mind-set and following the actions of the herd.

For example, become more self-aware at lunch when your colleagues are drawing you into unkind gossip, or at home when a relative or friend dominates a conversation. When you're on a bus or train or driving in traffic, see if you note a rise in aggressive or fearful thoughts inside yourself. In such situations, adrenaline rises and, with it, irrational thoughts like everyone in the world is rude, all drivers are terrible, and they're all hell-bent on making you late for work. When you're sitting at your desk watching emails pile up and feeling overwhelmed, that's a good time to practice being more self-aware.

Ask yourself: *How am I feeling right now? What am I thinking? What emotional signals have just been launched?* Some people tell us they take a break from what they're doing as soon as they start feeling overwhelmed. They may stand or walk a few steps or simply look out a window and focus on something else. One woman we know looks in a mirror when she realizes she is feeling highly stressed. This focuses her full attention onto herself and helps her figure out what's going on inside. Some people close their eyes when they feel overwhelmed and breathe in and out slowly, another technique to become more self-aware. After getting yourself to a more relaxed state, next attempt to tie your emotion, and any distorted beliefs that emerged, to the situation taking place. Try to see the original emotion as simply a signal. Don't allow the strong feeling to dominate or take root. Recognize the ensuing belief as a provisional construct caused by that strong feeling and likely not very accurate.

By doing this, you won't be a passive recipient of what your mind is doing behind the scenes. You will become more aware of the thousands of automatic daily messages, signals, beliefs, expectations, or other thoughts in your head. Some of what your brain is sending you is helpful, well-intentioned, and maybe necessary, but a lot of it is biased, exaggerated, and trimmed to fit your desire or habit of seeing the world a certain way. Much of it can be flat-out wrong.

A key way to both more precisely define and work through your emotions is to communicate them to others. Talking about your feelings with supportive others helps you to better interpret and articulate more complex feelings. *I'm not comfortable with that guy* can turn into *That guy doesn't respect my privacy, which leaves me feeling vulnerable and embarrassed.*

We often recommend to clients books and articles written by psychologist Daniel Goleman on *emotional intelligence,* also known as EQ, which involves developing personal skills that help you better identify your emotions and communicate on an emotional level. Psychologist Lisa Barrett recommends, among other things, that you work to improve your *emotional granularity,* which is making finer distinctions among your feelings. Developing a larger *emotional vocabulary* to describe the true complexity of your feelings helps you to be more precise. For example, it is less helpful to lump all your negative feelings into a simple phrase like "I feel bad." Instead, being more precise, "I feel angry when my girlfriend expects too much from me," gets you much further. People with higher EQ and emotional granularity have more agency. This is because the ability to identify and express our emotions more accurately helps us to avoid common traps that get in the way of good decision-making and greater intimacy in our relationships.

The family dynamics in Anthony's office presented by Julie and her kids provide a good example of the role of self-awareness in managing emotions and beliefs. Julie worked as a manager in a health-care software business. She recently left her position to become a stay-at-home mother. She has two young children and a husband who travels a lot for his job. Julie has an MBA and is used to being independent, and she prides herself on being good at solving problems.

She and her two children had just arrived in Anthony's office, and her husband was calling in to attend the session on his cell phone while driving to a work meeting. Julie was explaining that she *loses it* a lot with her kids. There was too much yelling at their house, with everyone ratcheting up reactions to each other. Even there on the couch in the office, the kids were getting testy. "Please! Settle down and focus, and please don't interrupt me when I'm talking; it's my turn, not yours," Julie said with pressured speech and a raised voice. Her youngest son started whining and thrashing. Her husband was trying to say something, but the connection was going in and out. Julie looked at Anthony, eyes wide, eyebrows raised, hands gesturing in exasperation. *You see what I'm dealing with?* her face seemed to say.

Here's what Anthony said to Julie:

"This . . . is how . . . we talk . . . to our children . . ." The youngest child locked eyes with Anthony, fascinated. Anthony continued in a rhythmic, exaggeratedly slow, singsong way. "That's how . . . teachers talk . . . when they are . . . calming down . . . their classrooms . . . with lots of kids." The youngest child, mesmerized, settled back, nestled against his mom, his thumb finding its way into his mouth. He began to slightly nod off. His sensory systems were no longer being overwhelmed, and his emotions were starting to settle down. Once everyone was calm, Anthony could ask Julie about some of her beliefs about parenting. She looked at him, a bit confused. She said she was a good communicator, she was effective in her job, people listened to what she told them to do at work, so it must be something going on with the kids. She assumed it was likely a problem with their development.

Anthony helped Julie to recognize she was operating with a core personal belief that was setting her parenting up to fail. With some discussion, Anthony got Julie to pinpoint this belief: *I'm smart and competent at work. People listen to me and readily do what I say. I believe it should go similarly at home.* This led to an unrealistic expectation: *I expect my skills at work to translate directly to the job of raising my children.* It's an easy error to make unless a person slows down and thinks things through.

Another point: You must manage your own emotions and beliefs first if you want to help another person to manage their own. Without doing this, you can't be a highly effective parent. You also can't effectively lead and manage others at work. As they say on an airplane flight, in the event of an emergency, put on your own oxygen mask first.

Further conversations with Julie got her to appreciate that the demands of being a mom are not the same as managing adults in a business (in fact, they're often harder). She readily acknowledged that there's something about how she thinks and feels that's related to the stress she experiences. She was willing to delve deeper to better understand this. She connected a few important data points from her own history. She told Anthony that she was from a perfectionistic family that talked about success this way: *Every problem can be solved . . . the harder you try, the more quickly problems get solved . . . and when problems don't get solved, you alone are to blame.* "That way of thinking doesn't work with a five-year-old," she reminded herself during one of our meetings.

Managing her emotions and beliefs is an ongoing effort that helps Julie move her feelings and thoughts more into the light. She now asks herself, *What are reasonable goals for the morning, the day, the evening with my two young, active boys? What constitutes success with a five-year-old?* By doing so, she's recalibrating the unrealistic expectations for success that she picked up from her childhood, which her underlying beliefs had been reinforcing. This principle is helping her regain her confidence as a parent and to feel calmer, and that's helping her kids stay calm. She's enjoying time with her kids more.

Where Do Our Beliefs Come From?

We "inherit" many beliefs from our parents, from our families and relatives, from friends and coworkers, schools, religious institutions, and the neighborhoods we were raised in. Affiliation is a very powerful human trait—through being social, bonding, dating, falling in love, and choosing a career path, we continually strive to be connected and close to others. Along the way, we also develop a tendency to think similarly to the people we find attractive, powerful, and helpful to us, and to those whom we wish to emulate. We often unwittingly adopt the beliefs of those people we admire and sometimes those whom we fear.

Some of our beliefs aren't formed from the particulars of our upbringing but are absorbed from the wider culture around us. These are ways of thinking that are broadly held and go unquestioned within society, and many can be incorrect and stubbornly hard to update. *The world is flat* and *The sun revolves around the earth* have—we would hope by now—been put to rest, but you can find some people who still insist that those beliefs hold true. *Women's brains are not as good as men's at science* or *People of different skin colors have distinctly different intellectual potentials* or *Gay people can't parent as effectively as straight people* are similarly entrenched beliefs for some people. You may be a person who still thinks some of these beliefs are accurate and valid despite mountains of evidence to the contrary. You may find that when you hear others use research to (falsely) back up untrue beliefs, it appeals to what you already believe. These ideas may resonate with what you learned growing up in your family, your town, your house of worship, or from the geographic region you live in. Or, it may appeal to you because it's simply how you wish things to be.

Strong, unexamined beliefs can hinder our growth and put us at serious risk of not adapting as our life circumstances change. Think of the belief *Never trust anyone outside of family*, which, if fully adhered to, would prevent you from learning broadly by severely limiting your access to resources. Or the old saying *Spare the rod, spoil the child*, which could result in a visit from child protective services. Or the belief *Immigrants are prone to criminal activity*, which would result in any number of unfortunate, potentially ugly outcomes, not least of which would be the avoidance of many good people. Or a woman we know from England who believed it "selfish" to negotiate the initial salary offer she received from an employer—resulting in her colleagues getting higher salaries—consequently her salary, many years later, has never caught up with those of her peers.

You may stay stuck, trying to mold everything in your surroundings to your way of thinking rather than expanding your range by learning and thereby bettering yourself. Strong beliefs, left unchecked, reduce agency.

> **Use Your Agency:** Are you holding on to outdated beliefs? Some of the beliefs that we inherit from our parents or early life experiences may no longer adequately fit as we find out more about the world.

Just as Beliefs Aren't Entirely Real, Emotions Aren't "Real" Either

As adaptive mechanisms, our emotions are there to protect us from perceived threats. Fear, driven by the well-known *fight-or-flight response*, arose at a time when human beings had to struggle for existence on a daily basis. For those of us living in relatively modern societies, many of the problems we face are not best handled with fight or flight, even if our bodies trigger that response.

When your emotional signals fire, you experience feelings as real. These are real signals, after all, that are happening in your mind and body and are not easy to ignore. But remember that most emotions are mostly misfires—false alarms. For that reason, you don't benefit from grasping hold of one feeling, obsessing over it, nursing it, and making all your decisions based on it. To maintain agency, you have to learn how to monitor, interpret, and regulate your emotions. For example, you can easily go into high alert while standing in a long line at the bank, or waiting on a crowded subway platform with screeching trains, or viewing news containing a fear-provoking segment with negative images. Adrenaline levels can rise, and blood pressure can elevate just while waiting for a file to download. Consider how often during your day you see something on social media that interrupts your train of thought—and suddenly you are feeling an unexpected, strong emotion you weren't feeling a second earlier.

This is why we tell people that feelings are intended to be ephemeral, and that, in a healthy state, they should come and go. It's often when we grab hold of an emotion and don't let it go, feeding it by giving it a lot of attention, that it becomes problematic. At the same time, welcome feelings when they help you feel more alive and connected with the world around you. Paul recalls a TV producer in Los Angeles saying to him, "If a day goes by and I don't have a hearty laugh, I kind of think that it wasn't a great day—and by same token, if I don't shed a tear or two, it wasn't a full day."

Let Your Feelings Come, and Then Let Them Go

Getting caught up in feelings and obsessing over them will hurt you. Don't talk about them incessantly unless you have a strategy to understand and ameliorate them. If you want to vent, fine, but many people often can get tangled up in this. They think they're releasing the emotion, and instead, by talking and talking about it, they're reexposing themselves to more emotion.

When you're encumbered by strong negative emotions, try this instead: Picture that you're stopped at a railroad crossing, and you are watching a slow train pass by. Envision that each car is a feeling. Watch it come, and watch it go. Watch the next one come, and let it go. Practice "seeing" your feelings as train cars that pass in front of you, coming and going.

If you're more movement oriented, you can cleanse your mind and body with healthy, strong physical activity. Tell yourself you are channeling the feeling out of your mind and the adrenaline out of your body. Many people talk about sweating out their toxins, and you can similarly sweat out strong emotions.

Anything can trip your mind and body to start signaling you, and your threshold for keeping these signals in check is lowered when you are tired, stressed, rushed, and when your mind is crowded by incoming information. Surrounded now by so many digital devices, we can expect more emotional (and largely false) bursts of fear, worry, anger, hostility, and aggression.

Bear in mind, humans are not digital. We're not designed to process the information coming at us at such high volume and speed. We're not unfeeling machines that can simply be programmed or upgraded to a faster processor. We're highly vulnerable, thinking creatures. We're constantly absorbing everything around us, including a stream of messages and signals being generated inside our brains. It's a lot of influence, noise, and nudging to try to process, and the brain is constantly trying to make sense of it all. The entire ecosystem of our bodies is doing its best to adapt, process, stay balanced, and guide us onto next steps.

A Major-League Example of Managing Emotions and Beliefs—In Action

Major League Baseball legend Derek Jeter was always a cool customer on the playing field. In the fall of 2014, during the final games of his last season on the New York Yankees, people watched him stoically study the field as he watched his team lose again and again. This was, in many ways, an unfamiliar situation for him and for his fans—the Yankees are one of the winningest teams in baseball, and Jeter, the team captain, had been one of the solidest players of the modern baseball era. Jeter's fans desperately wanted to see him express a frustration and an anger to match their own.

In the final inning of his storied career and in the final minutes at play in Yankee Stadium, Jeter concentrated all his passion into his game and hit a walk-off single, resulting in a 6–5 win against the Baltimore Orioles.

After a tough game and a challenging season for the team, the moment was poetic. Watching the team captain waving to the cheering fans, smiling and tearing up, was enthralling. Only then, when the game was over, did Jeter give expression to the bittersweet mixture of joy, gratitude, love, and sadness he felt during this incredible moment in baseball history.

Jeter is an example of how people who demonstrate agency manage the emotional and thought centers of their brains. In general, the people we've met who have the most agency grasp the difference between feelings and facts. Many identify their worries and obsessions early, naming them in order to keep them at bay so they don't unduly cloud their judgment—or in the case of this elite athlete, interfere with his performance under extreme pressure. They exercise traits of being open-minded, philosophical, and thoughtful. They adopt a big-picture view rather than getting caught up in passing, distracting details. When they express sentiments, they make sure it's the right time and situation so that it is helpful to themselves and others.

How do the Jeters of the world do this? How do they maintain their control and composure, unlike volatile athletes such as John McEnroe, who was infamous for his explosive antics on the tennis court?

Let's look again at Jeter himself. There were clues seven months earlier, at the press conference where he announced his retirement from the game that he so loved and from the team that he'd been with for twenty-six years, since he was drafted out of high school. The room was packed with reporters. "Why aren't you showing any emotion?" they baited. What they got instead was a brief insight into his self-control.

> **Use Your Agency:** Guard against emotional inflation. Emotions can take over and become a runaway train. Use rational, slower thinking skills to keep these fast, incendiary emotions in check.

Jeter leaned into the microphone. "I have feelings," he acknowledged. "I'm not emotionally stunted. I've just been pretty good at trying to hide my emotions throughout the years. I try to have the same demeanor each and every day. It's not the end of season yet—we still got a long season to go."

To us, that press conference was another example of the same control Jeter has consistently shown on the field. If you ever watched him play, you would have seen none of the chest-beating self-congratulations, anger, or inflated sense of self that is typical of many pro athletes. He stood at the plate waiting for pitches, focused on the moment with a Buddha-like expression. Packed stadiums. A raucous, often obscenity-laced roar. Millions watching on television. Such stimuli are beyond what most people ever face. Yet none of it ever seemed to shake him. It's a model for agency-managed behavior that is worth studying and emulating.

Anthony's Notes from the Office: The Dueling Styles of Jeter and McEnroe

Not long after the broadcast of Derek Jeter's last game as a New York Yankee, I met with an aggressive ninth grader who was in the habit of picking fights. Scott seemed to relish opportunities where he could show his strength. That got him labeled a bully, mostly while playing sports like basketball and lacrosse. His younger brothers, who often sat patiently in my waiting area with their mother, confided in me that they were afraid of Scott's outbursts.

But Scott had everyone fooled. Below the surface—in the quiet of my office—I could hear his self-doubt and vulnerability. He was

(continued)

using aggression to cover up how helpless and insecure he actually felt about not being as good an athlete as his peers. He also struggled academically, and that piled onto a growing self-hate.

Scott, like a lot of fifteen-year-olds, was also stubborn and unlikely to benefit from my telling him directly what he should and shouldn't do, so I showed him some YouTube videos of Jeter. After watching a few minutes, he shrugged. Then I played another clip, for contrast, of another talented athlete: John McEnroe. His tantrums on the tennis court during his most successful years in the 1970s and '80s are legendary. If Jeter was Buddha behind the plate, McEnroe was Godzilla on the court. I clicked between Jeter and McEnroe.

"Which one would you want to have as your coach or teammate?" I asked him. "Who's the cooler guy? Who is likely to be the more consistent performer?"

Scott laughed. He found McEnroe "a bit out there and funny—maybe a little cool," but he also admitted he was way over the top. Scott saw Jeter as the model of self-control he preferred. Scott was also surprised to learn that sportswriters have said that given McEnroe's great athletic talent, he could have had a more winning record and a longer career had he been less inclined to throw tantrums.

Scott seemed to get my message. He was on the road to building his agency. It would take time and work to teach him to use better behaviors when his emotions flared—when he felt overly angry and worried—based on irrational beliefs that he wasn't measuring up, was physically weak, and was not very smart. Adding to this, testosterone in his young, developing body was building up, and he needed regular, vigorous, positive movement to channel aggression. Along with the agency principle of movement, managing his emotions and beliefs were critical tools to help him through his teen years.

The Hidden Ways Our Beliefs
Empower or Discourage Us

Our beliefs drive our emotions both positively and negatively. Having a strong sense of our worth and abilities is crucial to our sense of agency. When we have a positive belief in our capabilities and ability to act on a situation, it gives us emotional fuel to make a positive difference.

Paul met a woman, Lenka, who was a successful entrepreneur in Michigan. She had grown up in Romania, where she had been trained as an engineer but where her possibilities were quite limited. After she moved to the United States, she started a new life and completely reinvented herself.

"Here I can do anything if I put energy and time into it," she told Paul. "I can experience myself differently here." Although she wouldn't have put it this way, Lenka was speaking with a strong *agency voice.* She was acutely aware of the possibilities open to her (and ready to seize upon them) after moving to a country with more economic opportunity.

To be clear, there are certainly going to be times when Lenka feels discouraged. That's when a negative belief can rise up and sabotage how she feels about herself. Everyone experiences these moments. Think of the last time you felt unempowered—maybe depressed, anxious, or just somewhat stuck—chances are there was a trail of negative thoughts and feelings that got you to that state. And behind that were beliefs. If you had put some energy into reflecting on it, you may have been able to figure out what that negative belief was . . . *I've just never been good with numbers . . . Opportunity never comes my way.*

Buzz Luttrell, an Emmy Award–winning television talk-show host, has wrestled with some very powerful negative beliefs, but it wasn't always like that. He was born in 1944 and grew up in western Michigan. He told us that in high school, he was a star: class president, a member of the National Honor Society, a trumpet player in a dance band. On top of all that, he lettered in six sports—football, basketball, baseball, track, cross-country, and golf. Buzz was the whole package. "I expected that I would succeed and that doors would open for me," he said.

But one harsh, damaging experience destroyed that belief and instilled another—and that new belief ended up keeping him off-kilter for many years. His high school gave out an annual award for the school's top athlete, and at the awards ceremony his senior year, Buzz sat ready, expecting his name to be called. Everyone else seemed to expect it, too. But Buzz is black, and this was 1962, and when the name was called, it wasn't his—it was a white student's, someone who didn't have anywhere near Buzz's record of accomplishments. For the first time in his life, Buzz felt the punch of raw racism as the award he thought was his fell out of his grasp. It was a belief crash—there was no way he could fit this reality into his belief system, which up to that moment had felt like life offered a fair playing field.

The results of that single moment can't be overstated. Buzz told us he went off to college with a chip on his shoulder. He closed down socially, grew defensive and angry, and became a heavy secret drinker. Anger permeated the early adult years of his life. That's the power a belief system can exert—it affects how we feel about ourselves and our possibilities. While his belief system was based on a formative event that had occurred long ago in his past—something very real and not exaggerated—the strong negative feelings associated with it persisted. It would have continued causing Buzz problems had he not examined it and, with the help and support of his wife, Marva, come to see himself and his possibilities anew, allowing him to actualize the many talents he possessed. Now retired from television, Buzz has become a teacher of young black men, teaching them how to succeed and manage themselves through the racism that persists. "The anger still is there," he said. "I still get surges of adrenaline, but I've learned how to channel it."

Anxiety, the Emotion That Frequently Leads the Charge

A central premise of our book is that there's an epidemic of anxiety in the United States, which is eroding our agency. The reason we bring up anxiety again is that, in our view, it is the primary emotion that many people have to deal with. Exposure to anxiety from which you cannot escape—or perceive you cannot escape—leads to giving up, giving in, not trying, and accepting negative fates. That's the crux of learned helplessness, which we discussed in the agency principle *Move*.

Take a few minutes and ask yourself, *Do I even know when I am feeling anxious?* (Most people do not.) *What's my relationship with anxiety? How does it affect me?* Knowing the answers to these types of questions will help you better understand and address how this primary emotion may be significantly undermining your agency.

- How do feelings of anxiety show up in your life, in your family's routines, while you are at work?
- Can you recognize when anxious feelings arise?
- How do you respond to feeling anxious?
- Do you have a self-management approach to it?
- How dysfunctional do you become when you're feeling very anxious?
- What are the most common unhealthy (and healthy) habits and behaviors you engage in when you are feeling anxious?

To be clear, anxiety is a normal human emotion. It warns us of threats, makes us slow things down in case we might be getting into the wrong situation. It can sometimes prevent us from taking rash action. But when it's creating obsessive worry about the future—causing you to believe you are facing a set of circumstances that haven't yet happened—anxiety becomes a hindrance rather than a help.

Managing your emotions and beliefs means managing adrenaline. Adrenaline, also known as epinephrine, is a hormone that surges through our bodies when we are feeling stressed and anxious. The physical effects are increased rates of blood circulation, faster breathing, and sometimes a kind of white-noise breakdown in your ability to think straight. Adrenaline is crucial in allowing your body to go into a fight-or-flight response, but too much adrenaline over the long haul is damaging to your physical health.

Adrenaline exerts a powerful effect, either enhancing quick decision-making or making people freeze up altogether. In short, it's something you want in your body rarely, only when true threats are imminent. The bottom line is that adrenaline, beyond its longer-term health consequences, is often a catalyst for negative responses and can lead to over-reaction and bad choices. In today's stressful, overstimulated world, its influence on our mental state and decision-making cannot be overstated.

The Importance of Emotional Self-Control

Self-control is about regulating your emotions and matching emotions appropriately to the situation. If emotions appear like they are coming out of nowhere, it's a problem. When adults scream, whine, stomp, or unnecessarily withdraw, they look immature or, worse, unstable. Others recoil or simply move away in disgust. People with agency have emotional self-control, and it's a quality that others find attractive. Being around people who are capable of regulating their emotions facilitates greater cooperation, calm, and a sense of emotional safety. People who are capable of regulating their emotions are safer to become attached to as they engender trust.

The Moments After You Lose Control

What do you do after an outburst or significant loss of self-control? You probably feel a bit embarrassed, exhausted, and wish you had used a better approach to deal with your emotions. If someone was on the receiving end of your anger, you may wonder how best to fix the situation. If it happens regularly, you may wonder how you are perceived by others who witness such outbursts.

- **Acknowledge that you lost control.** Acknowledge it to yourself, and then acknowledge it either verbally or in a note to the person who directly experienced your emotional outburst. Don't procrastinate—do it as soon as possible.

• **Apologize.** Apologizing helps you take ownership (you can start by apologizing to yourself). It also helps you to regroup with yourself and the people you interacted with. Think of an Etch A Sketch. Sometimes you need to shake things off and try for a fresh start. But don't pretend it didn't happen, and don't avoid the people you lost it in front of.

• **Come up with strategies to manage yourself better next time.** A few examples: Pay attention to physical signs that your body is gearing up for a fight. Breathe to reduce muscle tension. Slow down your speech. If you're about to yell, stop the moment you recognize what you're about to do—stop midsentence if you have to. Lower your head a few degrees, for a moment, to signal to others you aren't a threat. Check your arms and hands to see if they look tense. Unball your fists and let your shoulders down. If you're still tense, change location. Walk away for a few moments, but tell others why: "I need to collect my thoughts. Give me a few minutes."

The Gullibility Factor

We are all influenced by emotionally appealing, strongly worded messaging. As discussed, many of us readily adopt the views of people we see as attractive, strong, decisive, and confident. Such charismatic people are adept at reading other people's needs and wants, and they know what buttons to push to nudge others in their direction. Groups we identify with have a particularly powerful influence over us as well. When exposed to these strong influences, you need to keep yourself calm and centered; otherwise, you can't think logically and independently. Heightened emotions move you from slower logical thinking to thinking that is reactionary and impulsive. Think of what happens when a mob of people is engaged—is there much independent thinking occurring? Keeping your head at such moments is essential to agency. It requires you to critically evaluate the powerful, emotionally appealing messages coming at you that can forestall independent judgment.

Mike is a tall man in his early fifties who maintains the athletic build of his college days. People gravitate toward Mike. He's friendly and funny, and he projects confidence in himself. He's assertive about his viewpoints, for which many people view him as smart. Mike has never seen himself as gullible, but that changed on a cruise ship in the Caribbean a few years ago.

"A hypnotist got me," Mike admitted a bit sheepishly. "It was a nightclub show we went to after dinner. Maybe way deep down, I wanted to get up on the stage with the others, and somehow I just let go of thinking for myself. The hypnotist started by telling the audience that only some of us could be hypnotized. Before long, I was up there, my wife later said, acting like a robot or something and, honestly, I don't recall much of it."

That cruise ship experience led Mike to wonder if maybe he wasn't always the strong-minded, independent guy he'd thought he was. Examining himself deeper led to some interesting insights. As a boy, he recalled seeking out strong, confident male role models. Fortunately, he had good people to model, like his football coaches. He recalled trying hard to impress male teachers that he admired. After college, Mike sought out successful men to be business mentors who could guide him in his career. Looking back, this desire to connect with other men and get their approval makes sense. Mike's dad walked out on his family when Mike was very young. Most of the male relationships Mike has found since have been positive, except for one. Ten years ago, Mike was led into some bad financial investments. "I trusted this guy too fast. He was senior, accomplished, sounded smart. I followed everything he told me to do, but he may have been a bit of a con artist. I wanted to believe he would help me. Men who sound powerful and talk a good game, well, it can be a bit of a blind spot for me."

People with agency acknowledge they are no less susceptible to gullibility than anyone else. In other words, they acknowledge their gullibility. They regularly examine themselves to figure out where their potential blind spots are. *What physical state leaves me most vulnerable to being easily influenced (tired, hungry, physically unwell)? Who am I most likely to be influenced by? What situations? Groups? Men? Women? Attractive? Smart?*

Socially aggressive? Hard to get to know and aloof, or people who are gregarious? People with agency also work at flagging when an idea or message sounds powerful or seductive, and they try to hold it at arm's length. They try to adjust for the persuasive marketing that ideas and messages often are packaged in. These are some of the ways they maintain healthy skepticism. And yet they aren't closed-minded or oppositional. They know it's important to be open to new ideas, products, and ways of thinking. They know it's valuable to join in with groups, but they do so with their eyes open, knowingly, not unthinkingly.

Here are a few tactical approaches for you to consider:

- Hit the Pause button as soon as you sense someone is trying hard to sell you an idea or a product or if you feel pressured to go along with the pull of a group.
- Consider what you've just heard. Mull it over in your head. Does it still sound like it fits with how you see things? Your beliefs?
- Compare what you're being told with what you already know. Try to be factual. Fact-check, like a journalist. Google it, and ask others you trust. Get a few independent sources.
- Along similar lines, seek out more information as needed before signing on to anyone else's beliefs or adopting a group's viewpoints. You should feel comfortable and calm when you adopt another person's or group's viewpoints or behaviors.
- Ask reasonable and probing questions anytime you want. Act like an investigative reporter or a good talk-show host. One of the best questions we ask in our work when we're evaluating the beliefs and ideas of others is: "That's interesting. Can you tell me how you arrived at that way of thinking? Can you walk me through the steps?" There should be a process they can identify. The steps should sound logical. If not, they're regifting a belief. It isn't theirs, and it wasn't thought through. If they balk at answering you or they double-down on a hard-sell message, be wary.
- Keep your emotions in check. When you're in a highly emotional state—angry at someone, attracted to someone, scared, moved by a poignant speech or passionate sermon—you are

more susceptible to losing control of your logic and making poor decisions.

• Finally, know that if you have the personality type of being a pleaser or a "harmonizer," you are especially at risk for conforming quickly, although, as we saw with Mike above, even strong, assertive people can be gullible at times.

Depending on the situation, our current mood, the internal physical state of our bodies, and our social needs at the moment, any of us can fall prey to gullibility. We all have the potential to lose a bit of our capacity to think independently around attractive, powerful, persuasive people. And again, groups have a strong gravitational pull all their own. Balance is key. We want to learn and grow from engaging with the world around us. We need to be part of the social fabric to be happy and healthy. And we all need the admiration and acceptance of others, but we must balance this with the need to hold on to the core parts of ourselves through not abdicating our commitment to think independently.

Managing Beliefs—A Crucial Dimension of Leadership

When Paul is conducting an executive assessment, a critical component is determining the role that beliefs play in the executive's thinking process. Assessing the degree to which a leader's belief system influences their ability to think logically and engage in situation analysis is essential given its importance to managerial success. Is the leader's belief system well examined? Is there an appropriate level of intellectual humility present? Does this person have the ability to exercise flexibility in their beliefs, or are they rigidly and defensively held? Do they demonstrate a capacity to question their assumptions? Are they comfortable with ambiguity? Executives who are able to separate themselves from their beliefs and see them as "objects" outside of themselves are more likely to be flexible and objective thinkers and better leaders.

Paul's Notes: Leader as Alienator

I asked my client, a CEO named Gary, to recount his initial meeting with his new team. He had retained me to help him improve the team's morale, which at the time was quite negative. A high-energy, former college athlete now in his fifties, Gary's leadership style ties directly to a set of beliefs about how best to motivate people. In particular, he believes that people perform best when under considerable tension and that it's important to project strength and avoid any sign of caring too much about his direct reports. And so at that first meeting, he arrived a bit late, took a seat, opened his laptop, and started typing on the keyboard. People looked at one another in silence. They waited.

"Go ahead and start," he instructed, lifting one hand from the keyboard and motioning but not looking up. "I can attend to this while listening to what you have to say."

Gary was aware that the tension in the room had increased as his team reacted to his behavior. The unfortunate first impression he conveyed to his team was that they were not worth much, as he expressed so little interest in them. Although he intended to demonstrate how capable, tough, and independent he was—"There's a new sheriff in town"—his actions instead communicated that he didn't value them. Not surprisingly, morale plummeted.

This may seem like cartoonishly bad behavior, a sign of Gary's total self-absorption and lack of EQ. But the reality is, we are all capable at times of being out of touch with what others require from us.

Beliefs and a defensive attitude were behind Jeff's issues at work as well. Jeff, a high-octane executive with a first-rate analytical mind, was struggling mightily in his role with a large, highly successful technology company. The senior-most leaders who had embraced him when he joined the company four years earlier had begun to see him as difficult to work with. Puzzled by this turn of events, Jeff reached out for help from an executive coach. It came out in the initial assessment and subsequent meetings that Jeff carried around a rigidly held set of unreasonable beliefs regarding his expectations of the company's senior leaders. In his view, most were falling seriously short of meeting these standards. This generated a lot of strong feelings on Jeff's part, chief among them anger and resentment, which occasionally seeped out in dramatic ways in his interactions with them. The group of senior leaders, in turn, found Jeff to be preachy, self-preoccupied, highly judgmental, and even, on occasion, arrogant—hence the "difficult" label that was attached to him.

As Jeff continued to talk and reflect about his situation, some insights began to emerge. First, he realized that his beliefs about this group of leaders were largely untested, as he had not tried to get to know any of them on a deeper level. Second, he was able to see that his own extreme competitiveness led him to compare himself to them at every turn and overemphasize their shortcomings. Ironically, he was able to acknowledge, with some prodding, that he wanted more than anything to be regarded highly enough by this group to become a member of the senior team! In taking corrective action, he made the decision to deepen his connection to several members within this group by becoming more curious about their thoughts on the business and what they were most concerned about. Focusing on this helped him keep his competitiveness in check and to more fully enter into their world. While still a work in progress, Jeff has developed closer working relationships with a few of the senior leaders, and they have become more supportive of him and his efforts. He is feeling more supported and optimistic about his future prospects with the organization.

Be Tough-Minded and Transparent as You Adopt Your Own Beliefs

If left unchecked, erroneous beliefs can misinform and lead us down destructive paths.

The scientific evidence is strong. More than fifty years of psychological research tells us that rational, reasonable thought is not our default way of thinking—we must work to achieve it. We're more emotionally driven and must question our beliefs and regulate strong emotions to ensure we are thinking clearly. It can be mentally fatiguing to do this, as it takes time and requires significant energy.

Consider this analogy—it's as if we keep reaching for and wearing whatever beliefs we have hanging in our mental closets, through every season and for all occasions, no matter how they fit, no matter how odd they may look to others or out of date they've become. Think of this analogy the next time you balk at updating your point of view or challenging your beliefs!

Some suggestions:

- **Listen to other people's beliefs, but be skeptical** when they're presented as self-evident truths, absolutes, or are abstractions wrapped in powerful emotions that feel difficult to question.

- **Be aware of manipulation.** Sophisticated media delivery systems pitch to the emotional centers of our brains routinely. While people always have been manipulated, today it's much more frequent and powerful.

- **Be aware of the physical state of your body.** When feeling tired or stressed, you can be more apt to adopt prevailing views uncritically. Recognize this as a point of vulnerability.

- **Be aware of beliefs pitched and pushed on you.** Propaganda works this way, and it can be seductively powerful. Mixing truth and fiction and charging up your emotions can influence you to abandon independent thinking and act against your own interests.

(continued)

- **Adopt beliefs only after thought and reflection.** Don't fall into the trap of copying and downloading other people's beliefs (even if you admire these people). Instead, while keeping an open mind and listening to others, build and update your opinions and beliefs.

The Blame Game

Throughout your waking day, you're constantly assembling perceptions and judgments of other people's behavior—provisional constructs to help you make sense of your world and guide your actions. Some of these beliefs are more accurate than others, many are distorted, and most are incomplete and not well-considered. If you are unaware of this, your level of agency is reduced.

Among the many places you can run into trouble with this is when something goes wrong, when a mistake is made—particularly when it is you who made the mistake. When this occurs, there is a marked human tendency to point the finger elsewhere—to justify one's actions and avoid taking responsibility, sometimes at all costs. According to social psychologists Carol Tavris and Elliot Aronson, in their book appropriately titled *Mistakes Were Made (But Not by Me),* "We each draw our own moral lines and *justify them* (emphasis added)." This should give us all pause. Knowing that we're in the right isn't as obvious and easy to determine as we may think.

This is where the capacity to step back and reflect can be of tremendous help to you. Keep a watchful eye on the biases that lead to blaming others and relinquishing personal accountability. Take responsibility, own up to your errors, and apologize when it's called for. And commit yourself to learning from these mistakes. It enhances agency. Tavris and Aronson give a great historical example, noting that after the disastrous Cuban Bay of Pigs invasion in the early 1960s, President John F. Kennedy said to the American people, "The final responsibility for the Bay of Pigs invasion was mine and mine alone."

On a more personal level, think for a moment if you could remove the weight of all the blame and malign motives you assign to people around you. There is genuine freedom and, yes, agency in reminding yourself to do this whenever possible.

Managing Your Beliefs Will Help You Manage Emotions

Erik is a young man from Seattle in his early thirties who describes himself as a true romantic. A part-time musician and full-time graphic artist, he uses his rich emotional inner life to create. He's sensitive, empathetic, and imaginative—all wonderful qualities—but strong emotions are sabotaging what he wants most in life: to fall in love and settle down. Attractive and highly social, he has no trouble meeting women to date, but his high emotions often cause him to overthink even the smallest of social interactions. *Why didn't she text me back right away? Maybe I should ask my friend what I should do next. I'll be alone forever if I don't find the right one soon.* In his personal life, Erik is insecure and indecisive, while professionally he can get on a stage, appear in front of an audience, and play music with confidence. On the outside, he looks like he's got it all. Inside, he's secretly suffering.

The reason? Erik carries around an underlying belief that generates ongoing anxiety. Erik believes he won't be happy until he finds his perfect soul mate, his one and only life partner. This is a belief that doesn't provide Erik much perceived control.

As soon as he meets a woman he would like to ask out, Erik unconsciously starts working to fit her into his rigid, unrealistic, one-and-only ideal of what love is supposed to be. He spends a lot of time analyzing and worrying about everything that could go wrong rather than living in the moment, exploring, enjoying where the new relationship might lead. His belief that he must find his one and only soul mate generates so much anxiety that Erik often moves in too quickly at times and pulls back suddenly at others. It causes him to send very mixed signals to women, that he's either not interested, ambivalent, judgmental, or desperate. Most women stop wanting to see him after a short time.

Until Erik acknowledges and updates his belief, he's unlikely to better regulate his feelings and get his anxiety under control. He goes through frequent periods where he smokes pot to reduce his anxiety. This works in the short term, but symptom management accomplishes little because he soon repeats the same pattern. What would work better for him is to attack the belief head-on. Challenge it, stop it when it surfaces, and replace it with a more accurate belief, something like, *There are many great people out there who could be a potential match for me. There's no one person who determines my happiness.* Adopting a more realistic belief would help Erik feel more in control of his life. It would help him keep his anxiety at bay so that when he meets someone he's attracted to, he can be more himself by allowing his natural, fun-loving, romantic nature to shine through.

Adopting an Internal Locus of Control Builds Agency

Having just heard about Erik, ask yourself how much control you believe you have over your world and over your happiness. Is it realistic to believe that you are, more than not, the master of your destiny and your well-being? How much control should you attempt to exert through your actions and in what circumstances?

Generally, people who have a sense that their actions have the power to change their lives for the better have more agency.

Psychologists employ a useful term called *locus of control* (LOC), basically a concept that defines whether an individual operates with the belief that their fate is largely determined by outside forces or whether they believe they personally have the wherewithal to create their own fate.

Do you know where you fall? Read the two statements below and select the one that you agree with most. Try not to overthink this simple exercise.

I have often found that what is going to happen will happen. Trusting to fate has never turned out as well for me as making a decision to take a definite course of action.

If you agree with the first statement, it suggests you may have an external LOC. The second statement suggests an internal LOC. People with an internal LOC operate with a stronger, more positive agency voice. They believe they can effect change in their lives and are more willing to exert effort to move themselves forward.

People who assume leadership roles generally have more internal LOC. They tend to see themselves as capable of acting on their environment. They tend to believe they have the right set of skills to do whatever their situation requires. Obviously, this doesn't mean minimizing significant hurdles, but rather having the confidence to believe that, with thought and work, they can be overcome. It also means recognizing situations where ceding control is the best approach but doing so in a thoughtful way with a strategic purpose in mind.

While having an internal LOC promotes personal agency, there is a point of diminishing returns—think *control freak*. If you have a super-high internal LOC, you may not cede control when it makes best sense to do so. In short, don't attempt to overcontrol; simply lead with a belief that much is within your means to influence and it is worth the effort to try.

Staying flexible with your locus of control is key. If you have an extremely high internal LOC and are rigid and overcontrolling, you can practice giving up control in small increments. See how it feels. This teaches your brain that the world doesn't come to an end if you trust others more or relax and trust a process to work itself out. It is not useful to try to manage things that are truly beyond your reach. If you have an extremely high external LOC, you need to realize that you're ceding too much control to others or to fate. Practice stepping up and being less passive. Express your opinions more. Make an effort to take more control, no matter how small. Don't automatically give in and go along with what life hands you.

One more important point. Stepping up—being an active agent in your life—allows you to exert better control over what you feel. We've known about the connection between actions and emotions for over a hundred years. Still, most of us don't fully recognize the connection between our feelings (which are nearly impossible to control) and our actions (which are almost always in our conscious control). This is reflected in the wise words of William James, referred to as the father of American psychology:

Action seems to follow feeling, but really action and feeling go together; and by regulating the action, which is under the more direct control of the will, we can indirectly regulate the feeling, which is not.

Develop Your Own Personal Power Images

The image of yourself in your head has a very real impact. Engaging your imagination—using *power images*—is a mental action you can voluntarily take any time you want to enhance your self-efficacy.

The goal of this technique is to see yourself acting in a powerful way through an image that is personal to you. Next time you notice yourself daydreaming, you may discover that your mind has already invented an alternative reality—a positive, short movie-like clip—it's your creative imagination at work allowing you to escape boredom, frustration, or fear. Home in on this natural imaginative skill and bring it forth whenever you are feeling overwhelmed. In doing so, you can simulate successfully addressing a challenging situation by envisioning yourself acting to address it. This can improve your confidence and improve your performance when you must put your intentions into action. Often when people with agency look back on their early years, they report how important early power images were in preparing them to get to where they wanted to be. Power images are a tool allowing you to envision what a strong internal locus of control actually looks like when applied in your situation.

One study nicely illustrates the point. It asked a group of healthy, nondepressed women to close their eyes and focus on either sad or happy events from their real lives. The researchers observed distinct measurable changes in their brains on a PET scan. The lesson here is that you may be depressed (which is one of the lowest states of agency you can be in) not because your brain is wired that way but because you may be holding on to negative images, thoughts, and memories. Those ideas will send the brain moving down self-defeating paths, generating helplessness and hopelessness. Using power images can help to reverse this.

Uncover Your Primary Beliefs

We often ask our clients to do a short exercise in which they move to a quiet place where they can reflect without interruption. They think about how the world works and their place in it, and they write down whatever comes to mind. Here are some examples of the kinds of responses we typically get:

It's impossible to keep up . . .
It's a dog-eat-dog world we live in . . .
In this world, good things come to those who wait . . .
Things always work out the way they're meant to . . .
Politicians are all liars and schemers . . .
It is always best not to rely on others too much . . .

Now, write a few of your thoughts and beliefs down and say them out loud, and compare them in tone to those above. Note the degree to which none of these statements is provably right or wrong—that's what makes them beliefs; they are subjective statements. Further, note how strongly worded or rigid they are, using words like *always, all,* and *best,* which implies that they are somehow immutable laws of science rather than beliefs.

We suggest that they (and you) take a different approach to thinking about the world, one that allows a bit more flexibility and precision. Instead of "It's a dog-eat-dog world we live in," how about "There are supportive, warmhearted people as well as coldhearted, selfish people in the world." The key is to allow for more variation and less rigidity. This usually reflects reality more accurately.

Sometimes we are forced to update our beliefs after facing serious life events that might have been avoided. Our beliefs, left unchecked, can railroad us unintentionally onto harmful paths.

Brad started a drapery business with his wife, Pamela, in southwest Florida in the early 2000s, during an economy that was booming. They worked hard and took advantage of opportunities that came their way and were initially quite successful. The power of their success was infectious. Brad and Pamela bought a second property, then a third. They expanded their business and started dabbling in the stock market. "We started to feel that we were special, uniquely talented at what we did, and that we deserved all our success and that it would go on forever, but, looking back, everyone was doing great in those times," Brad told us.

Their belief about success wasn't based on a fanciful childhood fairy tale, although it did come to have the sound of wishful, almost magical thinking. It was fueled in part by the positive psychology movement that became popularized in the 1990s and was widely marketed in highly misleading, unscientific ways. Books, videos, and inspirational and motivational speakers flooded the market with promises of fast happiness and easy success. *If you want it, it will come. Believe in yourself and you will become rich and live the life of your dreams. The secret is just to think positively!* As the saying goes, a rising tide lifts all boats, and while the tide was in, all went swimmingly.

But boats also eventually sink when the tide goes out. When the Great Recession of 2008 hit, Brad and Pamela had to face their beliefs about success and adjust to the realities of a radically different, unforgiving economy. "We lost everything," Brad said. "It wasn't that we were especially talented or gifted at making money. We got caught up in the times. Had we seen things more realistically, we could have saved, not overinvested, and prepared for the eventual downturn."

Brad and Pamela weren't alone. Millions of people suffered foreclosures on their homes, lost their savings, and had to start over in the Great Recession. The depth of the downturn was exacerbated, if not caused, by greed and willful ignorance at the highest levels of business and government, including predatory lending practices and insufficient consumer protections, and yet, the signs of the excesses were there for anyone to see. Economic cycles are a well-known economic reality, but our beliefs can be blinding. They recruit our emotions and sometimes can function as a narcotic, offering us a false sense of euphoria. Again, beliefs must be examined and squared against what's actually occurring. Stay open to learning. Strive to be a perceptive person. Listen to a range of news sources. Don't surround yourself only with information sources or other people that confirm all your beliefs, because it leaves you vulnerable.

Back to your list of beliefs. What does your list of beliefs say about your worldview? Can you figure out where your beliefs originated? Your parents? Your upbringing or town or community? The times in which you grew up? A particularly formative experience? Many typically come from people who made a strong impression on you at a younger age.

Use Your Agency: Scrutinize your ideas and beliefs. Expose them to the logic of others. Check your facts and pay attention to the reputation and accuracy of the sources you consult. It forms the basis for all good decision-making.

Recognize that it's impossible for your beliefs to apply all the time and to every situation. Recognize their limitations and how, at times, they can be flat-out wrong. Try to widen or stretch your beliefs. By that, we mean make them more flexible and able to accommodate a wider range of real situations.

This isn't easy. Most difficult to challenge are *core beliefs*. These are basic beliefs about the world, about others, and about oneself, that are usually formed in childhood. They are constantly influencing us—shaping us—and they can be highly resistant to change. Again, we tend to adopt most of our beliefs uncritically, even automatically; it's as if they come in through the back door in the dead of night while we are sound asleep! Scribing them onto paper or even stating them out loud so you can hear how extreme and potentially distorted they are is a great first step toward consciously managing them.

Beliefs Aren't Values

There is a distinction between your beliefs and your values. Values are things we hold to be universal and unchanging as they apply very widely. They can often be found in familiar sayings and proverbs: Do unto others as you would have them do unto you. Honesty is the best policy. Winners never cheat, and cheaters never win. Values are useful guideposts for us to hold on to in terms of what is right, good, and what matters most. They inform our thinking, decisions, and our actions.

Beliefs, however, are often more specific—*Chevrolets are the best automobiles*—and reflect information we have or what we are aware of at a given time. They are much more similar to opinions but are often treated as unchanging values. When beliefs are held as firmly as values, it can make us highly emotional and play to our tribal tendencies. *Democrats/Republicans are anti-American. People in religion X are all terrorists.* There are many ways to understand political viewpoints, for example, and to appreciate and respect other religions.

Guard Against Magical Thinking

As we touched on earlier, inspirational stories by confident, successful people telling us it's possible to be anything we want, have anything we want—*Believe it and it will happen*—sometimes do us a disservice. Everyone enjoys feeling inspired by others, and we all seek out people and stories to motivate us—this book has its fair share of motivational anecdotes—but if you really want to build agency and make gains in your life, it won't happen through mindlessly embracing positive thinking and affirmations alone. Inspiration is only a starting point, a way to motivate yourself into action and change—you must figure out a path to action that works for you. From developing a career, to deciding whom to marry, to planning for retirement, you have to put in the time and energy to think carefully through the details and about what will realistically be required.

And to some degree, this warning applies to our faith as well. There are wonderful, deeply meaningful spiritual benefits that faith offers us.

There are health benefits to religious practices, as Vanderbilt University researchers recently reported. They found that regular attendance at worship services reduced stress and likely helped middle-aged men and women live longer, according to their study published in 2017. Even the most faithful and spiritual among us, however, understand that we must strive to be autonomous and self-reliant when it makes sense to do so. *God helps those who help themselves.* It's a reminder that we have within us the power to initiate, to think for ourselves, to tap into our potential and make positive life changes.

Managing Emotions and Beliefs When a Clinical Condition Is Involved

"I get lost in the abyss of my mind," Alan told us. "It's like being one of the prisoners in Plato's cave, chained to rocks."

Alan is an engaging young man in his mid-twenties with a wide, inviting smile. You'd never know that beneath his jovial façade he's obsessively focusing on details that aren't important. It's dominating his life at times. He was diagnosed with obsessive-compulsive disorder (OCD) and has been treated with medications and therapy on and off since age twelve. The OCD comes and goes, peaking when he's stressed.

Speaking with Alan was a great opportunity to test one of our strategies that we call *taking the big-picture view.*

Taking a step back and looking at the big picture was impossible for Alan when his OCD was flaring up. When anxiety occurs, your brain goes on high alert, even though there's rarely anything to be fearful about. Haven't you experienced this when you worry? You start focusing on small things, details. That's because small things might matter when you are in real danger. While your mind is hunting for potential threats, it fails to see the larger landscape that would calm you, prove that you are fine, in fact. Let's show you how this works by walking you through the technique we used with Alan, a fun, imagination-based technique that you can use anytime you feel anxiety rising and find yourself focusing on meaningless details.

First, we asked Alan what he meant when he said he was like a prisoner in Plato's cave. "My eyes are looking inward," he explained. "Like there's a cave wall, right? And my worries are the shadows reflected up on it. I know my thoughts mean nothing—but I can't stop focusing on them. I can't turn around and look out of the cave and see what is real. It drives me crazy." Alan also described his mind as, at times, like having CNN running over and over in his thoughts. It's like breaking news blaring at him every waking moment, but the news flashes are all highly unlikely things that could go wrong in his life. "It's so annoying," he said, shaking his head.

Alan is a highly visual person as evidenced by his descriptions of what he's seeing in his head. We decided to take advantage of that strength. If you're also a very visual person, consider guided-imagery techniques to substitute obsessive worries with pleasing and positive scenes under your control. Our coaching of Alan went something like what you see in the box that follows.

The Powerful Technique of Guided Imagery

Guided imagery is a tool that opens up possibilities and promotes agency (it's related to power images). It's all done in your head with your eyes closed, and you are typically guided by a script. It is commonly used in sports psychology to enhance athletic performance. It is often used to help people relax their bodies, reduce their anxiety, and achieve a grounded mental state. In its more complex application, people can be trained to envision different scenes where they are encountering a challenge or significant fear and watching themselves successfully moving toward better outcomes.

To understand its power, consider this simple guided-imagery exercise we used with Alan, who struggles with obsessive thoughts and worries that are getting in his way. It was an exercise to teach him how to shift perspective away from what was bothering him.

Start off with getting to a quiet place, sit or recline, and, if possible, record these words so that you can listen with your eyes closed:

See yourself lying in a field, and your head is turned toward the grass—you're staring at a bee moving around a flower. It's close to you. You're looking right at the stinger. You feel fear, right? Who wouldn't? Now, pick up your head. See yourself getting to your knees. Stay looking at that bee, but the stinger starts to become blurred, fades away. Now another step back, then another. The bee and that flower blend into a patch of colorful flowers. You keep walking backward—like a camera moving back—until the field resembles a Monet painting with blurred pleasant yellows dabbled with violet, red, and orange, and soon you see hills and a clear blue sky in the distance. Imagine the pleasant scent of those wildflowers. Imagine feeling a cool, gentle breeze on your skin. That bee and that stinger are still in that field, but you know they can't hurt you. They don't register anymore. It's only one of many tiny details that don't matter in the big picture.

With practice, use that series of images to prove to your mind that you can mentally step back from any unwanted thought or belief anytime you want.

Use Imagination Like a Time Machine

Your imagination can help you visualize yourself a day, a week, six weeks, six months, a year into the future. This is valuable as a tool because the magnitude of today's circumstances diminish when we project ourselves forward in time. Circumstances often don't feel as stressful when we consider them down the road.

Take this a step further to enhance your agency. Visualize yourself in a situation requiring high-performance. Envision your potential struggles and obstacles, but always end up with a great outcome. Try on a few power images for size just to see what your mind invents. Be playful with the exercise. Always see yourself succeeding.

In time, you'll be more comfortable with the possibility of making changes and taking on something new. First time up on a surfboard?

Teaching your son or daughter to dive? Nailing an interview or landing an account or winning over a new client? Envision the challenge before trying the real thing. See yourself sticking to it, and make sure your image includes seeing yourself relaxed and proudly smiling.

The Power of Psychotherapy

Psychotherapy can be an excellent way to enhance your skill at managing emotions and beliefs as you work at expanding your personal agency. There are many different forms of therapy. Two approaches will be discussed here—cognitive behavioral therapy (CBT) and psychodynamic psychotherapy. Both have strong theoretical underpinnings, have well-researched outcome studies, and have been around for decades. In some ways, they are opposite approaches but are complementary as well.

CBT, first introduced in the 1960s, was pioneered by the psychiatrist Dr. Aaron T. Beck at the University of Pennsylvania. CBT is usually brief; it's about managing symptoms, getting to goals through controlling how you behave, changing the environment around you, and digging deep to change negative thought patterns. Many of our principles overlap with this approach, but you'd be missing great opportunities to build agency if you thought CBT was the only valid approach.

Psychodynamic forms of therapy tend to be more open-ended, more exploratory, and seek to find deeper meaning in your life from delving into your memories, your history, all your life experiences that may have meaning. This allows you to construct an overall narrative of your life that can be uniquely valuable.

If you're feeling stuck in a difficult place and considering psychotherapy, it's good not to wait. This is especially true if you are experiencing symptoms of anxiety or depression, having trouble sleeping, relying heavily on drugs or alcohol to cope, or having anger outbursts, eating issues, or any number of problems that feel beyond your ability to control and are interfering with living your life as you want. We recommend you check with friends, family, or a trusted medical provider for a referral. You can then meet with a few therapists to see who you feel most comfortable with, of course selecting practitioners first for their qualifications and experience. You should feel connected and heard and want to return. Usually one or two meetings is enough to know if this is the right person for you, but don't rush to judgment either. Engage with them and be open. Ask them about themselves, their work experience, and what they think would be the best way to proceed after you've discussed your challenges.

Psychotherapy: The Underutilized Tool

Most people who could benefit from psychotherapy don't go. Reasons include accessibility to practitioners, insurance hurdles, costs in time and money, and the perceived stigma of seeking help for emotional problems.

The "worried well," as we like to call them, are people like our clients who are generally high-achieving, high-functioning, and living full, busy lives. Many do not need therapy in a formal, clinical sense, but they do benefit greatly from seeing a trained mental health professional from time to time—a mind coach of sorts—to help them manage their emotions and beliefs. When clinically indicated, we recommend longer-term psychotherapies, and in more severe situations, a medication consult in addition.

Maintaining balanced emotions and realistic beliefs is key to a productive life no matter who you are. It was psychoanalysis founder Sigmund Freud who noted that people depend on the capacity to work and the capacity to love (writing, in *Civilization and Its Discontents*, that "the communal life of human beings had, therefore, a two-fold foundation: the compulsion to work, which was created by external necessity, and the power of love"). If you're not adequately managing your emotions and beliefs, your capacities for both work and love will be compromised.

Mindfulness is another huge go-to approach with tremendous therapeutic benefits that we recommend. This includes the Buddhist practice of slowing things down and centering yourself through

(continued)

meditation. Again, it is also critical to focus on your body's needs. Nutrition, sleep, rest, respecting your body (as discussed in chapter 3), and engaging in regular healthy movement and outdoor activity will balance your neurochemistry and help you to manage your emotions.

Whether you enter into therapy or not, we recommend that you use any and all strategies to maintain healthy control over the feelings and thoughts in your mind. This, along with a body in a state of healthy physical balance, helps build your capacity for reasonable, intentional, planful thinking. A mind in balance is primed for extended thought, allowing you to analyze, use logic, and apply critical thinking to arrive at a good understanding of any issue—using your acquired insight to generate options, which you can then act on with full agency.

And it could lengthen your life. You've likely heard of the positive psychology movement and its many benefits. A study published 2016 in *The Journals of Gerontology* by researchers at Yale School of Public Health found that positive self-perceptions of getting older among people fifty years and up was related to living longer. The positive beliefs seemed to be a factor in helping lower stress-related inflammation. Why this happens isn't fully understood, and it likely isn't as simple as inserting a positive thought here and there into one's day. That may not be enough. Rather, it's more about maintaining a balanced, realistic view of everything, making sure that what is good in your life isn't being forgotten or eclipsed by distorted thinking and patterns of negative feelings.

Different Brains Respond in Different Ways to Similar Stimuli

People are working with different neurosystems, different hormone levels, different energy levels, and different life and cultural experiences that shape their feelings and thinking patterns. We each have different capabilities for dealing with strong emotions, and those capabilities may be stronger or weaker on any given day depending on how much sleep we've gotten, what kind of diet we've been eating, how many responsibilities and worries we're carrying. We point all this out to highlight the fact that you shouldn't make too much of any one feeling, thought, or belief, nor should you judge others as wrong because they respond differently to something or hold a different opinion.

Assessments such as the Strong Interest Inventory, 16pf (16 personality factors), Enneagram, and DISC Assessment (Decisiveness, Interactiveness, Stability, Cautiousness), just to name a few, are often used in organizational settings to facilitate personal discovery and self-awareness. No two people taking these type assessments are likely to come out exactly the same. This highlights the fact that we are all quite unique. Be open to this and keep learning about yourself; keep developing greater self-awareness.

Remember: You Are Not Your Beliefs and Emotions

Novelist and essayist Joan Didion wrote, "We tell ourselves stories in order to live." We all maintain a story line of our lives in order to comprehend and manage the world we live in. Beliefs, like emotions, are best when not fixed, but rather when they are allowed to evolve. The problem comes when we hold on to them as if they are synonymous with our identities—*I am my beliefs.*

Again, high-agency people use their beliefs as temporary guides to help them navigate as they gain experience and new learning. They distinguish their beliefs from the core principles and values they hold. They allow their beliefs to evolve as they learn. They are comfortable with ambiguity. They stay open to questioning their beliefs on a regular basis, understanding that both beliefs and emotions are cognitions separate from who they really are deep inside. This process allows them to keep their core values intact while they integrate real-life experiences and update what they know, becoming more perceptive and nuanced decisionmakers. All of this allows them to face new situations squarely through being more aware of their assumptions.

In many respects, this is the most challenging of the seven principles we detail in this book, but it's also the most rewarding for the clarity it will give you. As you become more skillful with the principle, you'll see the path ahead of you clearly and better know the direction in which you need to go.

YOUR AGENCY TOOL KIT

BE CLEAR: Distinguish between your values (universal) and beliefs (flexible in response to real evidence).

MONITOR EMOTIONS: Identify your feelings, recognize their value, and express them at the right time, in the right situation, and with the right level of intensity.

THEN, LET THEM GO: Don't fixate on your emotions: Talk them out, focus on your breath, meditate, and use other mind-body techniques to let them go.

PUT NAMES TO THEM: Name your strong emotions, worries, and negative beliefs to make them easier to manage.

EXPAND YOUR EMOTIONAL VOCABULARY: Work at more precisely defining your feelings and putting words to them.

PULL BACK: Practice pulling back your lens to shift your view to the broader landscape—it will protect you from getting caught up in minutiae.

CHANNEL ADRENALINE: Channel the adrenaline that fuels negative reactions by using power images, healthy movement, and other mind-body techniques.

TAKE CONTROL: Fight misperceptions that you aren't an active agent making your life happen—instead, for each situation, know how much control actually resides within you.

KNOW YOUR SINKHOLES: Be alert to patterns of thinking, feeling, and behaving that cause you to get stuck in "old, familiar places" pulling you down, sinking your confidence and resilience.

QUESTION ASSUMPTIONS: Challenge the assumptions you operate with—young people are apathetic . . . expensive wine always tastes better—it sets the stage for effective critical thinking and opens you up to trying new things.

USE YOUR INNER WISDOM

THE PRINCIPLE
Check Your Intuition

Intuition is an invaluable source of information to guide you, and when used wisely, it enhances creativity and the quality of your decision-making.

Intuition presents something of a paradox when it comes to agency. On the one hand, we've encouraged you to more actively pause, reflect, and think critically. On the other hand, we're asking you to rely on feelings that come to you immediately *before* you do any of these things.

Let's begin by saying that intuition probably isn't enough when it comes to certain kinds of important decisions. When possible, you want to check it against available evidence. For example, the guy who's selling you the car may intuitively strike you as an honest person (this is intuitive because you don't know anything about him), but you still want to look under the hood and check the tires.

How does intuition interact with agency? We can look to the phrase *trust your gut* for guidance. Allowing your intuition to guide you is another way of *trusting yourself,* or trusting your own judgment, which is based on an unconscious process that brings together whatever prior knowledge you have about the situation. In the case of the car salesperson, it might be based on the way he talked or expressed a willingness to let you more thoroughly check the car. You may not be aware that these things are coming into play, but they are important, *particularly* when something about a situation feels off or even dangerous.

We can think of intuition as an inner knowledge, comprised of a million data points that our brains have observed over the course of our lives. And when we use it, we express confidence in ourselves. That confidence is a big part of agency.

Consider Stanislav Petrov, described by the BBC as "the man who may have saved the world" by averting nuclear war. Petrov was a member of the Soviet Air Defence Forces in 1983, when alarms flashed indicating that several American missiles were inbound. In such instances, Petrov was supposed to alert his superiors so that they could quickly launch Soviet missiles the other way. His control panel informed him that the reliability of the alert was at the highest level. And yet he waited, even as the computer informed him of more missiles and eventually a strike.

It takes only about thirty minutes for an intercontinental ballistic missile to hit its target from halfway around the world. And yet Petrov waited. Why? "I had a funny feeling in my gut. I didn't want to make a mistake. I made a decision, and that was it." His gut told him something wasn't right. He placed a call to the duty officer in the Soviet army's headquarters and reported a system malfunction. If he had been incorrect, devastating nuclear explosions on Russian soil would have started within minutes.

Petrov credited his decision to both his training and his intuition. He didn't arrive at his judgment that it was a false alarm based on his hopes, his beliefs, or his feelings. Instead, he drew synergistically upon all his *ways of knowing,* using his intuition and skills combined with the limited data available at the time and all that he had learned as a human being in his forty-four years. Through use of his imagination and empathy, both of which are connected to intuition, he was able to fully imagine how the entire situation would unfold. Augmenting his intuition with logic led him to make the assumption that a nuclear first strike by the United States would not likely begin with just four or five missiles. He had been taught that a first strike by the United States would be massive and definitive, but that was not what appeared to be happening on his screens. "When people start a war, they don't start it with only five missiles," he told *The Post*. Of course, this was merely an assumption, and he could have been wrong, but he did rely on data and experience as well in making his decision.

The agency principle *Check Your Intuition* has a double meaning. It involves both the ability to *check in* and access your intuition as well as the ability to *keep it in check*, meaning to use it wisely as opposed to wildly.

When Intuition Kicks In— It's More Than Just a Hunch

Intuition is unconscious and automatic. It often happens as our brains take in subliminal flashes of information and nonverbal communications such as other people's tone of voice and body language.

David Myers put it this way in *Psychology Today*: "Cognitive science is revealing a fascinating unconscious mind that Freud never told us about: Thinking occurs not onstage but offstage, out of sight. Studies of automatic processing, subliminal priming, implicit memory, heuristics, right-brain processing, instant emotions, nonverbal communication and creativity unveil our intuitive capacities. Thinking, memory and attitude operate on two levels: the conscious/deliberate and the unconscious/automatic. 'Dual processing,' researchers call it. We know more than we know we know."

Defining and Locating Your Intuition

According to the *Oxford English Dictionary*, intuition is "the ability to understand something immediately, without the need for conscious reasoning." Swiss psychiatrist Carl Jung defined intuition similarly as "perception via the unconscious."

Because it is unconscious does not mean intuition is a passive process. Rather, intuition *makes rapid, beneath-the-surface mental connections.* Intuition is when your mind weaves perceptions together from the millions of stored bits of your memories and experiences. It is capable of creating a new, holistic understanding of a situation, almost always well before you arrive at a decision through conscious, logical thought.

Researchers are learning more about how intuition works. Intuition turns out to be an ancient evolutionary human ability, linked to a brain process called the *adaptive unconscious.* The cognitive psychologist Timothy Wilson was among the earliest to name this part of the mind: the unconscious, quick, automatic thinking that—with some practice and greater awareness—can be tapped for its valuable, efficient guidance. The concept of the adaptive unconscious was popularized in journalist Malcolm Gladwell's bestselling 2005 book *Blink,* whose evocative subtitle is *The Power of Thinking Without Thinking.* Psychologist Daniel Kahneman describes intuition as being fast, associative, and automatic ("System 1") thinking, contrasted with slow, analytical, and more bound by rules thinking ("System 2"). Intuition exerts a powerful influence, and when developed as a skill, it strengthens our ability to assess situations and make good decisions.

The Brain's Role in Intuition: A Different Part of the Brain Takes Over

If you've ever wondered how experts do complex mental tasks intuitively (and effortlessly), a study in 2012 in *The Journal of Neuroscience* offers a good introduction.

Anyone who has ever sat in a classroom knows that learning takes a lot of mental energy. It takes intentional focus and diligence. It involves a part of the brain we are hearing a lot about these days—the frontal cortex. The activities of the frontal cortex relate to Kahneman's slow, deliberate System 2 thinking.

But while a novice at any task or skill is consciously and laboriously

(continued)

working their frontal cortex, people with expertise at that same skill may be relying on less conscious, more intuitive areas of their brain—located in an altogether different region.

Here's what the study was about: Test subjects spent fifteen weeks learning and playing a Japanese board game called *mini-shogi*— which, in its full form, is a lot like chess, though considered more difficult. All subjects started out as novices. Researchers recorded neural scans as the mini-shogi players figured out their moves. The scans showed that with practice, the players got more skillful *and* relied less on conscious processes, using an area of the brain called the *caudate nucleus* rather than the cortex areas that we typically use for conscious and deliberate learning.

The main lesson is this: If you invest time learning something difficult, like a foreign language, a musical instrument, or complex dance steps, you will discover that there's a moment—a tipping point—where what was once hard and awkward suddenly becomes easier, more natural, and lots more fun. In time, with practice and rehearsal, intuitive thinking starts to take over and assist with many complex skills.

Another lesson from this is not to give up when a task you're learning is difficult. Keep practicing. Draw, paint, dance, write, ski, swim, cook, take up new activities you've always wanted to learn. Stick with it, as it is likely to become ever more rewarding as you gain experience!

Self-Awareness Sets the Stage for Effective Intuitive Thinking

We've already discussed the importance of understanding how your emotions and beliefs can guide or misguide you. We pointed out that adrenaline can produce irrational emotional reactions and that fixed, inaccurate beliefs can mislead you. It turns out both these things can also undermine your powers of intuition. If you are all over the place in terms of your emotions, you will likely not be effective at tuning in to your intuitive thoughts. Similarly, if you are an opinionated, defensive person who holds strong beliefs on all topics, you are likely to miss the subtle signals coming from the intuitive areas of your brain.

Given that none of us is perfect, how on earth do you start using something as elusive as intuition to gain agency?

Again, and somewhat paradoxically, it comes down to the *stop/reflect* part of the equation: *Do less and more intuition will come*. Intuition often kicks in when you quiet down your brain and take in the data around you at a given time and allow your brain some time to process it. First order of business is to learn to slow things down—to calm yourself. Without this first step, you will struggle to locate and use your intuition.

Check Your Intuition works in concert with *Manage Your Emotions and Beliefs*. As you develop greater agency, you will pick up a better sense of how these two principles work together and how they set you up for effective decision-making by preparing and priming you for the principle *Deliberate, Then Act*.

The Difference Between Intuition and Emotion

Intuition and emotion are close cousins, difficult to pull apart, but distinctly different. What makes it tricky to differentiate them is that they both often show up and speak to you through your body. They are both automatic. Additionally, they rely on each other and inform each other, and they are both sources of information that do not come through the reasoning centers of your brain. While it can be very difficult to tell the difference at times, with experience, it gets easier.

Most people describe emotions as being louder and more insistent, while intuitions can be quieter, subtler. Emotions typically come about as a direct response to something that has just happened, whereas intuition can surface when you are in a resting state with less external stimulation. However, intuitive perceptions do sometimes pop up in response to a specific stimulus. With an emotion, it is often easier to know what produced it. *She said I was acting selfishly, and it infuriated me.* An emotion typically shows up, you feel it, and it recedes, generally disappearing in fairly short order unless you purposely hold on to it. With intuition, by contrast, it often is more difficult to trace or articulate one exact source. *I am pretty sure that guy is trying to swindle me, but I can't exactly explain why.* A common experience that is related to intuition is déjà vu, often described as something you sense as familiar but just can't quite put your finger on why or how you know it.

Another subtle difference between emotion and intuition is that people often describe feeling them in different parts of their bodies. Some describe feeling intuition in the stomach or the lower part of the heart, perhaps why intuition is commonly referred to as a *gut feeling*. In contrast, emotions are often experienced higher in the body, in the upper chest area and into the throat and face. Feeling choked up by sadness or flushed with embarrassment would be common examples.

Intuitions are understood to tap into the reservoir of all our past experiences and to present an unconsciously derived synthesis of them. As such, they are an extremely valuable source of information. This is why it is useful to invest the energy to learn more about how to more fully access and develop this capability.

The Three Primary Types of Intuition

Intuition is a human ability that anyone can learn to access. It takes different forms, including these three primary types: *visceral (or ordinary) intuition, strategic intuition,* and *expert intuition.* Once you understand how these work, you can start to use them better to produce positive results in your life. Keep in mind, not everyone is highly intuitive by nature. For some, it will take practice.

INTUITION 1 OF 3:
Ordinary Intuition

This type of intuition is commonly referred to as *visceral* or as *a gut feeling* and is most useful in circumstances where there are complex social demands and few clues to navigate them.

For instance, so much of what people communicate to us isn't through words but rather through their body posture: how they sit and stand, the placement of their hands, whether their arms and legs are crossed. People's facial expressions also offer vital signals that can be intuitively registered if you develop the sensitivity to monitor them.

Own Your Agency: If you find yourself feeling anxiety or heart palpitations in the presence of someone, your intuition is picking up on signals that this is someone you can't trust. Pay attention, especially if you're typically comfortable around new people.

To use this form of intuition, start by learning to read the more obvious intuitive signals. Frequently referred to as a *sixth sense*, like a bodily hunch, this type of intuition typically registers physically. Your body, along with your brain, will signal you to make a decision and follow a course of action—you just need to pay attention and be willing to interpret this signal. Your heart may beat faster and your palms moisten, signifying anxiety. Some people report coolness in their hands or feet when they are about to make a *poor* decision. If this occurs immediately before a test or an important meeting, then it is likely just a passing feeling and situationally appropriate. But if it happens unexpectedly, with no apparent prompt, it likely is your intuition attempting to guide you.

Getting more in touch with these natural body changes is an important part of what intuition is all about. To do so, it is important to keep calm, get to quiet spaces, and set time aside to check in with and interpret your intuitive signals. Do this by focusing on your body—specifically, your heart rate and breathing. Are they elevated, even though you haven't been exercising? Muscles sometimes tighten as well during an intuitive moment, typically around the neck, shoulders, and forehead. Because these are common sensations, people are apt to write them off as everyday stress and miss the signal. "Butterflies" in your stomach are another common signal people report. You may experience goose bumps, and the hair will literally rise on your skin. What's happening on the inside? Your mind has picked up on something and has calculated that it calls for the release of some adrenaline to alert you. You may be under threat, or you may simply be having a strong emotional reaction, like hearing a patriotic song or recalling a fond memory of an old lost friend. Your brain will need to interpret which of these is the case.

Reflecting on your intuition can enable you to comprehend situations more deeply than rational thinking alone allows. *Why do I feel so positive when in the presence of a particular person? Why the strong pull to get closer? Is it because the person has many similar qualities to an important mentor who helped and influenced me in so many important ways?*

Listening to your intuition can also help you keep your stronger emotions and impulses in check—warning you of the potential danger in impulsively following a strong feeling. Intuition, in this case, acts to stop you from being misled and going down a wrong path. This occurs when your feelings about something and your intuitive body signals are not in alignment but rather are in conflict. For example, you might feel very excited and ready to buy a gorgeous sports car, but an inner nervousness makes you question the car's high cost and practicality. Or perhaps you feel gung ho about following others and jumping from an unfamiliar high-diving spot, but at the same time, you also hesitate as you notice your sweaty palms. In both cases, a part of you is intuitively responding—and if you allow it to consciously register—it forces you to pause and reflect further. You may still buy the new car or jump off the cliff, but after having given the decision more measured consideration.

Liz, a woman in her late thirties, actively practices this type of intuitive skill in her work at a highly successful insurance company. As a manager, she told us she pays close attention to how her body is responding during important meetings. Is she comfortable or uncomfortable? Tense or relaxed? Do the words people use match what her body is experiencing deep down? Everyone is nice and cooperative on the outside, she told us. Her coworkers are all polite. But as an African American in a company where there are few people of color, she's come across coworkers who at times have been passive-aggressive and indirectly antagonistic toward her ideas. She uses this intuitive information to address these issues openly and resolve them in a constructive way.

These assessments help Liz navigate social situations more accurately outside the office as well. For instance, sometimes she senses she's getting a negative body reaction, noticing her neck and shoulders tensing up, when she is out on a date. "I trust what my body is telling me," she said. "It's been a good way to figure out if I'm sitting across from someone I can potentially build a relationship with." Many have told Liz that she's a good judge of character and that she is able to read people quickly. To the extent this is true, Liz attributes it to working at effectively using intuitive thinking in her interactions with others.

Philosopher Eugene Gendlin conducted many years of research starting in the 1950s that showed that people's ability to achieve positive change in their lives depended on their innate ability to access a nonverbal, "felt sense" of their issues and life problems. He developed a six-step approach to help people learn to practice this on their own. He called his technique *Focusing,* and it is presented in his book of the same title. If you look online you will find many great resources that can guide you using the focusing approach. Gendlin believed people, through practice, could become skillful at both interpreting and using their felt sense, which is closely akin to intuition, as a way of knowing how to go about improving their lives. We cover this here as a way to connect better to your body knowledge to help develop your visceral intuition.

Gendlin suggests practicing this on your own with your eyes closed or with a partner with whom you can verbalize your process of defining your felt sense. You can practice the focusing techniques at any time and anywhere; it doesn't necessarily need to be in a highly controlled or formal environment.

Start by clearing a space through relaxing. Turn inward and ask yourself, *How am I? What is between me and feeling fine?* Let your "body" help you find the answer by tuning in to how your body is feeling. Create a simple list of what emerges. Then pick one problem to focus on from your list. What registers in the center of your body when you sense the whole of that problem? What's the felt sense (or bodily sense) that emerges? Try to get a handle on it—that is, identify one word, phrase, or image that comes out of this felt sense. What "quality" word best describes this felt sense? Some examples of quality words or phrases: heavy, jumpy, tightness in chest, stuck, stirred up. Next, try going back and forth between the word or phrase you have chosen and your original felt sense. Do they match well, or does it need adjustment? When you get a perfect match, just let yourself feel that for a minute or two. Next, ask yourself, *What is it about this problem that makes me so_____? What is the worst thing about this feeling? What is so bad about it? What should happen to address it?* And finally, welcome what shows up. Receive it, as Gendlin says. Be glad it spoke. Now that you have identified it and know where it is, you can come back to it later. Protect it from the critical voices that may try to interrupt.

INTUITION 2 OF 3:

Strategic Intuition

If ordinary intuition typically involves a reactive bodily sensation, then strategic intuition—our second type—shows up in your mind as a thought or solution. Popularized by business professor William Duggan of Columbia University, strategic intuition is particularly useful for big decisions, such as changing jobs, choosing a school, moving, or deciding to get married. People with higher levels tend to employ it at key moments of their lives. After giving serious thought to a problem, they'll step aside and let their unconscious start to do the deeper work. They occupy their minds with other things, and later in time, this form of intuition often arrives to guide them. This type of intuition arrives in its own time and cannot be forced to follow a specific time frame, but it can be encouraged.

Most of us have had an experience involving strategic intuition. They typically arrive as well-formed ideas in a flash. An insight presents itself after we've stopped worrying about it or have gotten busy focusing on something else. You can help prompt strategic intuition to happen through intentionally setting a problem you are worried about aside, often referred to as *incubation*. Go for a long walk, take a swim, drive, or bike ride, immerse yourself in cooking, shoot some hoops, flip through catalogs or read an article you've been meaning to get to, or chat with a friend to clear your head. Many people tell us they make it a practice to sleep on all their big decisions. Often when they aren't necessarily expecting it, a strategic insight appears to put them on a better course.

INTUITION 3 OF 3:

Expert Intuition

Expert intuition often involves highly trained individuals or teams operating at peak efficiency during especially stressful times. One memorable example of this came in the case of a plane making an emergency landing on the Hudson River back in 2009.

Captain Chesley Sullenberger described to ABC News the almost telepathic level of communication that went on between himself and his copilot as they were figuring out what to do to save the plane: "Jeff Skiles and I had to work almost intuitively in a very close-knit fashion without having a chance to verbalize every decision, every part of the situation. . . . By observing each other's actions and hearing our transmissions and our words to others, we were able to quickly be on the same page, know what had needed to be done, and begin to do it."

For true expert-level performance, particularly under pressure, years of experience can facilitate intuition by freeing the brain's attention and resources so it can be more reflexive in sizing up situations instantly, without being slowed down by step-by-step decision-making. Had panic spread in the U.S. Airways cockpit, all the experience in the world wouldn't have mattered. As with the other types of intuition, you need to get yourself to a place of relative inner calm to access it. Again, anxiety is an antagonist to accessing your intuition. Expert intuition, as with the other two forms, allows you to access your deep reserves of knowledge at important times and is a crucial lever that facilitates personal agency.

Intuition Often Intervenes in Times of Extreme Danger

Intuition can keep you from making a bad decision. It can also save your life.

We recently met a woman named Rena Finder, a concentration camp survivor, who literally saved her own life and that of her mother by following her intuition.

"I was ten when Germany invaded Poland on September 1, 1939, and went from being a little girl from a nice, middle-class family to being an enemy of the state, a nonhuman, an *Untermenschen*," she said with a slight Polish accent.

Relying on her intuitive wits, Rena found the wherewithal to survive many harrowing, near-unthinkable events. At pivotal moments, she was forced to make decisions that would have been impossibly difficult for someone of any age—consequential decisions amid narrowing options and a frightening, ambiguous future. "My mother asked me to go and speak with the office accountant to get us and my cousin on the list to work in Oskar Schindler's factory. We had the sense this would be a safer place to be."

When Rena showed up in Schindler's accountant's office alone (keep in mind she was a ten-year-old girl), she knew intuitively that she would have one, and only one, chance to appeal to this man. She entered his office, and as she sat down across from him, she recalled, she felt a strong sense that if she asked for three people to be put onto the list, the man would likely deny them all. "It was asking for too much. And then all would be lost," Rena added. She paused and then continued with great sadness in her voice. "At the final moment, I asked only for my mother and myself. He agreed."

Rena decided to come forward publicly to tell her life story late in life in response to a book by an historian who wrote that the holocaust never happened. Addressing school students and other groups, in her quiet, non-dramatic way, Rena emphasizes her primary point, "I was a witness to these events. And now in hearing my story, you too are a witness."

Anthony's Notes from the Office:
Listening to Intuitive Messages

Ignoring intuition can result in poor-quality decision-making—a fact that Rosa, a single mother of three, began to realize by the time of her second divorce.

After a life of struggle with a series of abusive and alcoholic partners, Rosa started paying more attention to what she describes as "that funny, strange feeling that comes up inside." So when her youngest son was among a handful of students being offered expensive gifts by his karate instructor, she registered her discomfort and insisted on returning the gifts.

Many of the other mothers were thrilled by the instructor's apparent generosity and accepted the man's explanation that their sons were being rewarded for their exceptional abilities. Being of modest income, these special favors were hard to refuse.

A few years later, Rosa read in the paper that the instructor had been accused of molesting some of his students. She was especially glad that she'd listened to her inner voice and backed off his overtures—and that she had taught her son to do the same.

Learning from Our Intuitive Connections with Animals

Dog lovers will tell you that their dogs are highly attuned to people's emotional states, and research is providing evidence that this may in fact have scientific merit. Many dogs know when you're upset and when you need comfort, and they respond to cues that you are worried or angry. A 2014 study in the journal *Behavioural Processes* reported that dogs show responses to hearing a baby cry that are similar to humans', such as alertness and elevations in salivary cortisol.

Dogs are a powerful agent in helping veterans cope with chronic, severe PTSD symptoms following tours of duty in Iraq and Afghanistan. As reported in *The New York Times* in 2012, service dogs are being used to reduce PTSD symptoms when typical medications and standard therapies aren't effective. One service dog, Devin, helps by guiding her owner through crowds, blocking people who come too close, sensing nervousness and placing a paw on her owner's lap, and licking her owner's face to wake her when she's having nightmares. Being in the presence of a dog lowers anxiety for many people. For example, dogs are frequently used in assisted-living facilities to visit the elderly, as they have a very calming effect.

Dogs, and horses as well, can be used to help us attend better to our intuitive gifts, as we will soon see. These animals are attuned to every nonverbal gesture—even the smallest movements matter. Animals use their sensory intuition in a highly functional way—to either get food or to prevent themselves from becoming food. Humans also pay extremely close attention to nonverbal gestures in social situations as well, for a larger variety of reasons. As you have likely read or heard, a large percentage of the communication occurring between people is actually nonverbal—conservative estimates are about 55 percent, and many are higher.

Debates continue as to the degree to which animals have intuitive skills as well as empathy and even problem-solving skills, but scientific research seems to be narrowing the divide. New frontiers are opening up in how animals and humans can work together—communicating through gestures and sounds rather than through spoken language—to learn and heal from the connection.

We witnessed such communication when we visited Jane Karol, a world-class equestrian expert. Along with her doctorate in clinical psychology, Jane melds her equestrian expertise into her practice of psychotherapy. At her barn in Concord, Massachusetts, she offers a unique form of therapy to children and young adults. Much of it is anchored to using and developing intuitive skills. With a horse as her co-therapist, she helps people who are anxious, timid, and at times struggling to find their own place in the world. She closely observes her clients' gestures toward the horses as a way to understand how they also relate to their fellow humans.

Studies indicate that horses respond to our gestures and our emotions. They read our posture and respond differently when we're snarling or angry (causing an increase in their heart rate) versus when we're smiling and appear happy, according to researchers from England, published by the Royal Society in 2016. Horses also respond to where we place our shoulders. If we are facing them head-on, it is experienced as more aggressive and pushes them away. Placing our shoulders slightly away from them invites them to come to us. Humans react similarly. If we open up space with our shoulders, and let our arms relax by our sides, people are more open to us. If we square off and cross our arms in front of us, other people sense aggression and will likely move away from us.

"Working with these extraordinary animals is an entirely intuitive process," Jane told us. Despite their tremendous physical power, horses are animals of prey, attuned to everything in their proximity and to their herd, and they register the tiniest of signals that danger may be nearby. "Communicating with horses, one needs to develop strong intuitive skills—there's no other way to interact cooperatively with them," Jane added. "You have to project physical confidence, be deliberate in your every movement and facial expression, and not be unpredictable or highly emotional, because these animals are reading you always."

Jane observes how the client relates to the horse as a source of therapeutic information. Paying close attention to how the client relates to her as well, she uses both sources of information to instruct her clients on how to see themselves more accurately. *See how the horse responded to you when you moved in that particular way?* This process helps her clients learn to trust themselves and their emotions, develop their own intuitive capacity, be more aware of their body language, and project confidence, all while riding and interacting with these tremendously powerful creatures. By learning more about how they relate nonverbally to the horses, the client learns how to better relate with the people in their lives, increasing their level of personal agency.

An Example from Jane's Case File

One of Jane's patients was a teenager with oppositional defiant disorder, meaning she was unable to realize the link between her obstreperous behavior and the aggression and anger she prompted in other people. One day, she moved her arms aggressively at the therapy horse and moved her whole body quickly (usually she was very good with the horses). The therapy horse, who is usually very calm, spooked dramatically and backed away from her. Jane explained what she did next. "In this moment, I could show her, in a way that she couldn't question, that her gestures, body position, tone of voice signaled aggression to the horse. The horse was not lying and did not have an ulterior motive. She couldn't argue with it. In that moment, her body lost the tension she was holding, she looked at the ground, and for the first time in her life (probably), she understood that her body position, gesture, and tone of voice caused fear and negative reactions in others—that she had to take responsibility for a part of her relational struggles. The horse's intuitive, instinctual response allowed her that gift of understanding."

Via this therapy learning occurs in two ways: You learn about yourself through the intuitive responses of the horse, and you learn to trust your own intuition in the building of your relationship to the horse. Jane notes, "You can't act impulsively around a horse. You imagine your way into what the horse is feeling, keeping your body calm, and using your body to develop trust with the horse given what you imagine the horse is experiencing."

Her years of working with and relating to horses, Jane says, have helped her personally to connect more empathically with other people. She listens respectfully to people she might disagree with, and, as we observed, her body language and tone of voice are open and inviting. By paying close attention to her own inner thoughts and impressions, she finds she can read the needs of her family, friends, as well as the people she counsels in her practice. "We are animals—animals teach us what we have forgotten within ourselves."

Initial Steps to Becoming a Better Intuitive Thinker

There are different ways to develop your capacity for intuitive thinking. Here are four time-tested methods:

- **Quieting your mind and focusing.** Gendlin's focusing techniques, which we noted earlier, are a terrific place to start. Also, previous agency principles can be helpful allies: *Control Stimuli* and *Associate Selectively*.

- **Shifting set.** Changing what your mind is currently focused on can help you keep from feeling bogged down. The easiest way to shift set is to get up and change your location or some of your typical routines. The previous agency principle *Move* is instrumental here. This works as a neurological jump start, waking up the brain and priming it for intuitive, reflective thought. Engaging in calming, simple, repetitive activities also helps. Many people have told us they have intuitive moments while on a leisurely drive, sitting in a soaking tub, showering, knitting, or cooking. One researcher told us she often walked to make copies, and while staring at the machine turning out page after page, she'd get interesting new ideas about a problem she was working on. Give your imagination space to roam. The ability to imagine primes the intuition pump. Einstein first had to imagine travel at the speed of light before he could come up with the theory of relativity.

- **Developing greater awareness of how you are thinking and feeling in the moment—otherwise known as** *mindfulness.* While you can't turn intuition on and off like a switch, techniques such as guided imagery, meditation, yoga, and tai chi can help you tune in to what is going on beneath the surface of your awareness.

- **Listening to your body.** You've likely experienced goose bumps or the hair rising on the back of your neck. These are clear and very dramatic intuitive body signals coming from your brain when it has made some important connection and is alerting you that something's potentially amiss.

Check in with Your Intuition— But Also Keep It in Check

Using your intuition as we are describing it here is an *active* process— you are actively monitoring, thinking about, and interpreting your intuitive thoughts. Feelings are a bit more of a reactive process; they occur all the time in response to some direct stimulus, and they come and go much like you breathe, in and out. Most simply stated, making the best use of your intuitive thoughts involves actively applying some rational thinking to your intuitions (recall Petrov, the Russian soldier from the beginning of this chapter).

If you choose to do something that is driven by strong sentiments alone, and you attribute the outcome (good or bad) to following your intuition, you may be fooling yourself. In this case, you were instead likely acting impulsively, not through the appropriate use of your intuition. With the exception of sudden visceral warnings (like goose bumps raising up on your skin) or when a strong feeling suddenly emerges while facing a potentially dangerous situation, intuition should be slowed down, monitored, and incorporated into a calm process of reflection. It's not doing something on a whim, or when your head isn't clear or you're filled with a rush of emotion. That's when you really need to keep intuition, and any strong emotions, in check.

Errors in Perception During High-Intensity Situations

Police officers often rely on their "inner expert" in highly charged emotional situations, such as the stop and search of a vehicle, when the ability to rapidly intuit and assess what is occurring could become a matter of life and death. Cops often call this intuition their *sixth sense,* and understanding what influences it and how to read it is now formally taught in police academies. Law enforcement professionals have told us that this sixth sense becomes a tool as important as their badges, handcuffs, or weapons. Training police officers in the use of this intuitive skill—getting them thinking about it and understanding it well before they put it to use on the streets—hopefully reduces the chance that an officer will rely on impulse alone at a critical moment.

But when strong emotions, such as fear or anger, enter into the mix, clearheaded thinking can easily get hijacked. Perceptions get distorted. Intuition is corrupted. Innocent people can be harmed, or worse.

Affective realism is worth visiting here to better understand what can go wrong in these high-intensity situations. At every moment, your brain is imposing its beliefs (and emotions) on what you think you are seeing, hearing, smelling, and touching, because it is trying to predict what comes next. As your brain attempts to make sense of the world around you, there is a strong tendency for it to shape every input to fit into what it already thinks it knows and what it expects is going on based on your emotions and beliefs.

It is important to be aware of this and aware of your limitations, particularly during charged moments; an important strategy is to take a second or two to slow things down. Take a breath. Step away from the action. Check in with others. If you are a police officer, seek backup. Get more information when possible. Remain open to the possibility that some of what you are seeing may not be being accurately perceived.

Here's a situation many people will recognize: getting an uneasy feeling when you're boarding a plane and the weather is bad. Tom flies thousands of miles per year for business, and when there's a thunderstorm or snowstorm, and he's feeling tired or stressed, and he doesn't want to make the trip, he can find himself wondering, for a moment, *Is this going to be the one in a million? Will this be the flight that gets in trouble?* We are back to the classic issue of trying to differentiate between a quick emotion, *I am feeling afraid,* and an intuition, *I'm having a very bad feeling that something is seriously wrong with this flight.*

But Tom is self-aware enough to know that when he is feeling tired or stressed, his perceptions can be unduly influenced by his emotional state. He also has some knowledge of flight safety practices because he is friends with a pilot. So when bad weather puts him on edge, he looks around himself for reasonable clues to keep his perceptions in check. Typically, when he does this, he sees calm flight attendants going about their preflight business and nothing out of the ordinary. While observing this and listening to the engines start up, and engaging rational thought as to how safe air travel actually is, he can tell himself that *the uneasy feeling he was experiencing is likely a passing emotion, not a reliable intuition,* and he can then let that uneasy feeling go.

> **Own Your Agency:** Fatigue and stress can make your intuition go off-kilter. Adjust accordingly.

Keeping your intuition in check also means giving the process enough time, letting your brain gather the data points it needs to intuit best. Not doing this can result in missed opportunities that you kick yourself for later. Julia is in her forties and successful in the field of biosciences, but in retrospect, she wishes she'd taken a different path in terms of her education. When she was eighteen and considering which college to attend, she visited the University of Chicago campus. She went in February, when the snow was high and a deep freeze had set in. To top it off, it was exam week, and a bitter north wind was whipping through campus. "Everyone looked exhausted and washed out," she remembers. "Touring the campus confirmed what I had expected—that it was a pressure cooker environment and no fun. I didn't stay there long and made up my mind immediately based on the first impressions I got, kind of on the spot, actually."

Julia didn't question her preconceived beliefs. She had been told by a high school friend that the school was too academic and that she would be unhappy there. She chose a different school for college, but as fate would have it, she went to the University of Chicago later for graduate school—and she loved it. "I wished I had gone as an undergrad," she says now. "Back when I toured the campus, I formed an impression that said that this would be a miserable place for me. If I had stopped and reflected more on the fact that it was frigid weather and exam week, I would have understood that I was being peremptory in my assessment—not making an adjustment for the particulars of the situation."

"Swiping Left" Is Based on Biases, Not Intuition

You may have just swiped away the love of your life.

On dating apps such as Tinder, two-dimensional, static head-shots of future partners about the size of a quarter don't really capture much. Sifting through people's profiles like a deck of cards is efficient, can be fun, can be discouraging, and yes, sometimes works out great—but know that you're working off your biases more than anything else in evaluating the qualities of a real flesh-and-blood, three-dimensional human being. Looking for a bright shiny object through a two-dimensional forum involves no intuition, as we define it.

When we meet people in real time, real space, and have multiple opportunities to meet and interact under low-stress circumstances, real bonds can begin to build.

So keep in mind, before you click or don't click, swipe left or swipe right, that you need to always be aware of your strong belief systems and biases that are in place long before you open the app. Be aware that you're working off first impressions that are limited and don't include access to the ineffable qualities that bring people together and keep them together. The result of this is that you likely will throw some great people to the curb.

"Rational Intuition" Is the Goal

The New York Times noted in its 2011 review of Daniel Kahneman's book *Thinking, Fast and Slow*: "Human irrationality is Kahneman's great theme." Kahneman and Amos Tversky, his longtime collaborator, pioneered research into many of the baseless decisions and unconscious errors we make when we *think* we are acting logically. For instance, their experiments defined the *anchoring effect*, which demonstrates that the way people answer questions can be misleadingly anchored by information they have just received, even if it has no relevance at all. In one test, subjects were shown a wheel of fortune that secretly only stopped on the numbers ten and sixty-five. After seeing the wheel turn and stop, the subjects were asked an unrelated question: "What is your best guess of the percentage of African nations in the United Nations?" People who had just seen the number ten guessed, on average, 25 percent. People who had just seen the number sixty-five guessed, on average, 45 percent. Their research illustrated the unreliability of most people's first "intuitive" responses to problem solving. What this points to is that when seeking to solve problems, especially more complex ones that require logical thought to arrive at a judgment, your first intuitive reaction should be monitored by your more methodical, controlled thinking skills. The less experience you have with complex problems, the less you should rely on intuition.

Turning to corporate actors, *Harvard Business Review,* in a 2003 article by Eric Bonabeau, an expert in artificial intelligences, goes as far as to warn business leaders, "Don't Trust Your Gut." A later article in the same journal, by Andrew McAfee, an MIT scientist, urges leaders toward "Less Intuition, More Evidence." Clearly, organizations need to be careful that they are collecting the right data and then drawing upon that data alongside human experience when making important decisions. What is this skepticism regarding intuition about? Another finding from Kahneman's research was that the slower, controlled, more analytical thinking takes more energy than the faster, more automatic intuitive-type thinking. If given a choice, most people simply prefer not to have to think that hard, which, in the case of decisions requiring logical thought, often leads to poorer-quality decision-making.

It is important to reiterate a crucial point here: Intuition is extremely valuable, but you need to be aware of its limitations. Best-case scenario: It is possible for your intuitive thoughts to be powerful and accurate contributors to your overall judgment. With practice, intuition can be called upon to assist in all decision-making, but it should rarely be used in isolation without some degree of monitoring by your slower, more analytical faculties. You always need to be in charge—the ultimate boss of all your cognition. As Kahneman notes, sometimes our preference for using our first intuitive idea to help us accurately solve a problem comes up empty—in which case we must switch to slower and more deliberate thinking. Again, you can allow your intuition to guide you, but you must realize that you are the chief quality control manager in your life and as such must effectively monitor the quality of your decision-making. In practice, many of the problems we face require us to employ both our intuitive as well as our analytical faculties to solve. We will be doing a deep dive on this in our next chapter, "Reflect, Decide, Act with Agency."

Having said all this, here is the paradox: When engaging in more creative endeavors like drawing or painting, or kinesthetic activities like skiing or tennis, the goal is to build your skill level to a place where you are almost purely using your intuitive faculty. Otherwise, your performance can be inhibited by being too analytical and self-conscious, often described as "getting stuck in your head." So while we've advised you to keep your intuition in check in most circumstances, there are times when you can let it run free. Related to this is something researchers call *flow*. Flow is experienced as deep, enjoyable states of consciousness when you are engrossed in an activity. It can be learned and further developed.

On the dance floor, behind a canvas, shooting hoops, and while imagining the possibilities of a better life, and yes, even tackling problems that require a fresh perspective and an innovative approach to solve— these are the types of moments and pursuits where fuller access to your intuition is most helpful. Let go of your observing eye. Censor your inner critic, push aside worries, and you may be surprised—and likely invigorated by—what flows early and more naturally to the surface.

When it comes to drawing, nothing is better than the first sketch.

—Pablo Picasso, in *Conversations with Picasso*

YOUR AGENCY TOOL KIT

ESTABLISH A SERENE MIND: Employ the agency principle *Control Stimuli* (see chapter 1, "A Clear Head") to quiet your mind and facilitate higher-quality intuitive thinking.

SHIFT SET: Get up and physically change your location or your typical routines frequently.

USE MINDFULNESS TECHNIQUES: These include meditation, which relaxes the mind and keeps you more present in the moment.

REMIND YOURSELF THAT AN INTUITION IS A HYPOTHESIS: As with any hypothesis, it should be confirmed through assessing its accuracy and reliability. Does it fit with other data?

APPLY ANALYTICAL REASONING: Generally, you are better off pairing intuitive thoughts with your logical reasoning to ensure your judgment is valid and applies to the situation at hand.

POSITION YOURSELF AS A LEARNER: Gather more information to confirm or reject your intuition.

MOVE: Throughout each day, walk or engage in any pleasant, repetitive physical movement to calm the mind and engage deeper intuitive thinking.

SLEEP ON BIG DECISIONS: Rest improves decision-making accuracy by allowing your strategic intuition time to work.

BE CREATIVE: Use your intuition to drive creativity, and allow your creativity to fuel your intuition!

REFLECT, DECIDE, ACT WITH AGENCY

THE PRINCIPLE
Deliberate, Then Act

Using a defined deliberation process allows you to make effective decisions, act with confidence to overcome obstacles, and open up new paths and opportunities.

The Final Agency Principle

We all like to think that we are effective captains of our own ships—capable of making decisions to steer ourselves through any condition to reach our desired destination. But here is some bad news: All of us engage in thinking habits that do not serve us well in terms of making decisions that keep us on the best course headings. We are far less rational and effective as decision-makers than we would like to admit, or even know, and most of us unwittingly fall into many of the same thinking traps over and over again. Simply put, our thinking is unreliable. The good news is that we can improve the reliability of our thinking with many of the principles and practices outlined in the book.

This final agency principle, *Deliberate, Then Act*, guides you on how to assess your current situation, generate and weigh your options in a contemplative, rational way before you make important decisions, and take clear, decisive action when required. Some decisions result in a minor course correction, while at other times you must make a more substantial decision that sends you in a totally new direction. Proper deliberation before taking action on matters large or small will help you avoid experiencing the regret many feel after acting on impulse.

All the other agency principles you have learned about thus far come to bear on your ability to make good decisions for yourself. Effective decision-making is so essential and foundational to the expression of human agency because we are, in many ways, the sum total of all the decisions we make during our lives.

In the course of our interviews, we uncovered valuable ways that expert decision-makers make decisions. Interestingly, we discovered areas of overlap common to effective decision-making. Read on and you will become familiar with some of the thinking skills and techniques that judges, physicians, police detectives, and business executives use in the course of their work. You will learn to refine your thinking skills and adopt a decision-making process to make important life decisions, much like these experts, to more effectively pursue your desired course.

The Battle Against Unreliable Thinking

For a moment, imagine yourself wearing a black robe and presiding over a courtroom as a sitting judge.

Your first case involves a woman in her midthirties who is in front of your bench for a bail hearing on first-degree murder charges. She's been indicted by a grand jury in Massachusetts for the murder of the father of her friend. The man had been stabbed to death while sleeping in his bed. There was a lot of evidence pointing to the woman, yet the case had gone cold for several years with no arrest. Police reopened the case after learning that this woman had issued a threat to her ex-husband: "I will kill you just like I killed that guy in Massachusetts."

Your task is to decide whether you will grant or deny this woman bail. Keep in mind that it is rare for someone accused of first-degree murder to receive bail. What do you think? Bail or no bail? And if you grant bail, will you make it high, like $1 million? Before you read any further, say aloud what your gut decision is.

If you are like most people, you are likely to automatically lean toward denying her bail or setting bail at an astronomical amount. Reading the basic details of the crime evokes emotion. Recall from previous chapters how System 1 thinking (fast, impressionistic, intuitive) operates and how it often quickly steps in when your emotions are stimulated. Thus far, System 1 is most likely the primary driver for your thinking about this case.

Now stop for a moment and ask yourself these questions:

- Can you describe the specific rationale or mental steps you used to arrive at your decision? Were you aware of any particular underlying beliefs that led you in the direction of making your decision?

- Are you in a positive mood at the moment—seeing people positively? Your frame of mind matters. What feelings emerged as you read the basic outline of the case? Did what happened to the victim shift your thinking toward being more negative?

- And lastly, do you believe in this: *It is better that ten guilty persons escape than one innocent suffer.* The English scholar William Blackstone wrote this in the late eighteenth century, and his writings have been highly influential in the development of U.S. law.

Now let's look a bit more deeply into the case. Below are a few more facts for you to reflect on before deciding the fate of this woman.

- The murder happened fourteen years earlier, and during most of the intervening years, the police were not actively pursuing the case.

- There were several other people also present in the house at the time of the murder. All evidence against the woman is circumstantial.

- The comment "just like I killed that guy in Massachusetts" was reported by a friend of the woman's ex-husband and is considered hearsay under the law.

• This woman was nineteen years old at the time of the crime, thirty-three years old at the time of her arrest, and she had no criminal record. She was living openly in Florida under her real name. Statistically, because she has a young child in her care, she is not a high flight risk.

Do these additional details change your thinking about whether to deny or issue bail in this case? Or not at all? In either case, your thinking likely has slowed down, shifting from System 1 into System 2 thinking (methodical, logical, and analytical). You may be reconsidering your initial judgment. There obviously is a lot at stake. Your decision could potentially take away an innocent person's freedom and consequently result in a minor child being taken from her mother's care.

For retired superior court judge Beth Butler, this case is one she is able to clearly call to mind years later. A perceptive, energetic woman with a warm smile, she met with us in a conference room at an old New England town library near her home.

"My ninety-four-year-old aunt often uses the word *discernment*," Butler said. "That's how I prefer to think of it. Judges and juries have to be discerning when assessing the credibility of witnesses and when weighing various evidence. You might have a hundred witnesses who were at the scene of a crime saying X but only one witness saying Y. And yet, that one witness may be the most credible."

Judges work to ensure that the trial process doesn't overload their minds or those of the jurors. They decide up front what evidence gets through the gate and what does not. They do this with a clear, transparent process that follows the rule of law. Up front, the legal process filters information to keep out that which is extraneous—and hence to also *keep in* the facts and evidence that are most relevant. This helps ensure that the deliberation process can be most effective and that our highly emotional, biased, and often irrational brains can arrive at a just decision.

Use Your Agency: Too much information can derail your thinking and confuse matters. Don't give everything you hear, see, or read

equal weight. Weigh credible sources more heavily. Pare information down to the facts most relevant to the decision you are considering. Filter out less relevant information up front to help yourself
focus.

"The safest thing to do in that case of the woman charged with
murder," Butler recalled, "was to set an incredibly high bail or deny it
altogether. There is considerable precedent for that—in fact, it is custom-
ary practice. That decision would have presented a low risk of public
criticism, and it would have eliminated the risk of her fleeing, but at the
same time, it would have had the highest chance of violating the rights
of a potentially innocent person." Interestingly, Judge Butler was at this
time in her career presiding over one of the most historic courtrooms in
the United States. It was in this same courtroom in 1921 that Nicola
Sacco and Bartolomeo Vanzetti, two first-generation Italian Americans, were sentenced to their deaths in the electric chair in a world-
famous trial for a crime they did not commit.

Butler had a process for helping her make her decision. First, she gave
herself time to decide. Important decisions need time and resources. She
considered what decisions had come before in this situation—legally,
these are called *precedents*. Good prior decisions can help guide future
decisions, although she knew she should decide this case on its own
merits. She talked with other judges. "I asked them what they thought
and what they would do," she said. "Consultation is so important. We
can learn from one another how best to decide."

After much deliberation, Judge Butler decided to set a low bail amount
for the accused woman. It wasn't an easy decision, bucking the strong
anti-crime public sentiments of the day. She told us that in recent memory she couldn't recall a time where this had happened in a first-degree
murder case.

In the subsequent legal proceeding where all evidence was weighed
and the credibility of the indictment against the accused woman was
openly evaluated, the woman was formally acquitted of all charges. She
returned to living her life in Florida and raising her child. Judge Butler

reported that the state prosecutor's demeanor post-trial indicated to her that he did not believe that an injustice had been served in the case.

The trial outcome is not the sole reason one could say that setting an affordable pretrial bail was the right decision. Judge Butler's difficult choice was made by scrupulously following the framework of the law as well as by using her own logical thinking process. She ensured that her emotions did not dominate. She did not allow a herd mentality to unduly influence her thinking process.

Put another way, Judge Butler's process is a good model because she slowed down and allowed herself to engage in more deliberative System 2 thinking, staying away from a snap judgment.

Your own process for deliberation should be as thoughtful, and you can keep it as simple as possible. You can start by asking yourself, *What am I seeing here? Do I need more time?* Or even asking just two words: *What's happening?*

What We Are Up Against

The other six principles in this book all feed into *Deliberate, Then Act.* As we've laid out in earlier chapters, we live during a time of increasing complexity and uncertainty. For most of us, the environments we inhabit are not conducive to good decision-making. Much too often, our brains are overstimulated by an excess of information and from the rapid rate of change and dislocation that we observe around us. Living in such an environment is mentally and emotionally taxing—and it increases anxiety. This stress and heightened emotion reduces the amount of personal energy available to reflect and deliberate in a methodical way on the more important decisions we must make. The result is that suboptimal or poor decisions are made with greater frequency.

Decision fatigue has become a growing problem. There are more choices confronting us every day that require us to navigate complex decision mazes. Health insurance plans, for example, typically are presented in detailed spreadsheets with a mind-numbing array of variables to consider. Just giving thought to it can be an exhausting undertaking. Multiply that many times over for the number of decisions we make each day, many with similar sets of complex options. When our energy is depleted, the quality of our decisions plummets.

The fact that life requires us to deliberate, decide, and make frequent choices means that developing an effective personal decision-making process has become critically important. The more grounded we are in terms of accurately perceiving what's happening around us and the more self-aware and less rushed we are, the better our overall judgment and decisions are likely to be.

One final point on what we are up against: A proliferation of powerful media platforms producing a cacophony of different voices in the virtual public square exist today, all vying for your attention and seeking to influence you. Fraud abounds. Gullibility has become an issue of such concern that it is being studied and debated by many experts. What is real and true cannot be assumed to be widely known and commonly understood. In this context, it has become necessary to define that most fundamental building block of effective thinking: facts. Facts are the bedrock of logical, intelligent thought and decision-making. Facts are verifiable. They are not someone's wishful interpretation of events. Facts enable us to use our minds to separate reality from fantasy, and we must make an effort to determine them if we are to exercise agency through making good decisions in our lives.

Thinking About Thinking

Judge Butler gave us insight into the way a judge weighs a complex decision. We can also learn from expert medical practitioners, who frequently make life-or-death decisions for the people in front of them.

As chief of experimental medicine at Beth Israel Deaconess Medical Center in Boston and Recanati chair of medicine at Harvard Medical School, Dr. Jerome Groopman is highly regarded both for his clinical prowess and for his outstanding writing about the practice of medicine. We caught up with him at his office a few blocks from historic Fenway Park. He recalled it was about ten or twelve years back when he undertook a deep dive into studying the decision-making practices of his physician colleagues.

It came about after he had been conducting medical rounds with interns, residents, and medical students. Something unexpected— "disturbing," as he put it—had occurred to him. Why weren't his students, this next generation of physicians, challenging each other, listening more carefully to patients, thinking openly, and reflecting more deeply about medical diagnosis and treatment? As an instructor, was he failing his trainees in some way? Was rigid reliance on evidence-based medicine and algorithmic decision trees constraining his students' thinking to the point it would prevent them from growing into discerning physicians, capable of thinking outside the box? That moment put him on a mission to find out more. He started turning to his colleagues in different areas of medicine and asking them, *How do you think?*

Surprisingly, Groopman told us, "Not one doctor to whom we posed that question had a clue as to how to answer. There was no *metacognition*." Metacognition is the mental task of stepping outside oneself and literally thinking about one's own thinking. "There was little self-awareness of the process of how they made their decisions, no triggers to warn them when they were moving into cognitive pitfalls, no stop-gaps or breaks to question their own process of making a diagnosis," he said. "These are highly trained physicians, and even they were just as susceptible to the evolutionary shortcuts we all take."

Metacognition Can Help Keep Unreliable Thinking in Check

Bias in decision-making and lack of awareness of how one thinks may help explain why medical diagnoses can be wrong and result in life-or-death consequences. For example, in a 2015 study of 286 patients seeking a second opinion from the Mayo Clinic, over 20 percent of initial diagnoses that had been previously assigned by the patients' primary care physicians were wrong. Medicine is part art and part science and is very complex and always evolving, so 100 percent accuracy in diagnosing may be impossible to achieve across all patients or all problems, but one has to wonder how many errors in medical decision-making can be avoided by teaching physicians to be more self-aware of their thinking processes and to follow simple rules in terms of how they think.

Groopman's wife, Dr. Pamela Hartzband, is also a medical doctor (she's an attending physician in the Division of Endocrinology at the Beth Israel Deaconess Medical Center), and she came up with a way to push back against automatic decision-making. "Pam developed a simple procedure when she was an intern in medical school many years back," Groopman says. "To her, it was like a game she played to stay sharp. She asked herself, *What if that other doctor who made the diagnosis is wrong? What else could it possibly be?* She made a concerted effort to always question before accepting an answer." Hartzband and Groopman collaborated on the book *Your Medical Mind: How to Decide What Is Right for You* (New York: Penguin, 2011), which emphasizes how partnering with other trusted, thoughtful, open-minded thinkers improves the decision-making process. They have introduced courses at Harvard Medical School to teach medical school students and practicing physicians about thinking rules that foster cognitive self-awareness, recognize bias, and increase the accuracy of making diagnoses.

Their approach to bringing awareness to decision-making is applicable outside of the medical field. A car mechanic should consider multiple causes of why an engine isn't running as it should. A contractor should ask what might be happening before replacing warped floorboards. A teacher ought to recommend testing if a student is falling behind in his or her reading level to help ascertain why. An unhappy worker should consider what's underlying her decision if she's thinking of quitting on an impulse.

People with agency often report using this feat of mind to better understand themselves and their thinking style more objectively, even if they didn't know the technical name *metacognition*.

Reflect back on a conversation you had earlier today and try to analyze it objectively. *How did I sound? Was I being defensive or aggressive when I was talking with my coworkers?* Metacognition will help you keep better track of—and help reduce—errors in your thinking and help you be more emotionally balanced and stable. Sometimes we call it *insight*, and it builds agency by giving you a more accurate read on how you think and feel. It keeps tabs on how others are likely perceiving you as well. When you metacognate, you are like your own consultant or trainer, giving helpful feedback to better yourself.

Metacognition steers you onto more realistic, thoughtful paths—facilitating critical thinking and putting you more in control. If you observe an emotion or thought that isn't helpful, flag it and alter it. If you observe yourself to be rushing to judgment, slow your thinking process down. Keep a critical eye on the quality of your thinking. People with greater agency monitor themselves more frequently to help them not veer off into irrational thinking.

To practice metacognition and think about one's own thinking, here are some takeaways from our conversation with Groopman:

- **Don't get seduced by shortcuts, and don't favor efficiency over accuracy.** Know when you're placing too much confidence in attractive charts, graphics, preset protocols, and computer algorithms. Are you accepting without questioning someone else's "frame" of the problem? Are you relying on others to do your deciding for you by accepting their conclusion too readily?

- **Name your mental steps. How did you arrive at your decision?** If you can't name your steps that led to a decision, be suspicious of that decision.

- **Always question your decisions and question how you make them.** Ask yourself, *Did I miss something? What if I've been making my decisions based on an erroneous starting point or piece of bad information? Are there other ways to approach making this decision? Am I questioning deeply enough?*

- **Recognize and remember your mistakes and your misjudgments.** Incorporate these memories into your current thinking to improve decision-making.

- **Stay open and self-aware.** Be open to learning from everyone. Be an active listener. Try to value many opinions. Also ask yourself,

*What's my thinking style, my personality? What are my biases? Do I
not ask questions because I want to be seen as competent? How might
my personality and ways of thinking influence how I make assessments
and reach conclusions?*

From our interviews with experienced decision-makers, all emphasized the importance of *not rushing*. Taking your time—even when others
or circumstances are rushing you—is essential to making accurate decisions. Consider the story below of another physician wrestling with this
issue within the context of a hectic emergency room.

Making Accurate Decisions
When Things Are Moving Fast

Thinking under extreme time pressure is not optimal, but it is inevitable that we will find ourselves in this situation at times. As Groopman
suggested, it is always best not to rush and get seduced by mental shortcuts. Use *all* the time available to you in making a decision. That means
slowing things down when possible. It means not allowing the external
setting to dictate the terms of your thinking. Speed typically decreases
accuracy—there is a direct relationship there.

Peter Shearer, M.D., is the associate director of the Mount Sinai Hospital Emergency Department in New York City. Athletic, with intelligent brown eyes and a compassionate demeanor, Shearer was surprisingly
relaxed as he discussed a typical hectic day in the Mount Sinai ER. Over
any given two-hour period, ER physicians like Shearer treat as many as
sixteen patients and are interrupted as many as forty times. Shearer's
decision-making needs to happen in a focused, organized manner and
at a rapid, intense pace, and it needs to be highly accurate. In his work,
knowing when to settle on a firm diagnosis versus deferring to gather
more information versus knowing when to take immediate and direct
action has life-and-death consequences. Knowing when to pause and reflect more deeply to ensure adequate deliberation has occurred can also
make all the difference for him and the patients he is treating.

Recently, a twenty-three-year-old student came to the Mount Sinai

ER asking for postexposure meds to prevent HIV and other STDs. She explained to Shearer that she'd had sex with a guy she'd met the night before and, upon waking, discovered drug paraphernalia lying around in his apartment. She was worried about HIV and hepatitis. She explained that she'd been out drinking the night before. The alcohol had clouded her judgment.

"While she was telling her story," Shearer explained, "something was telling me that things weren't quite adding up." The trainee who'd first taken her story missed it. Shearer reflected on an important intuitive moment. "There I was talking to her about something painful, embarrassing, and scary for her—in this crowded, noisy place, hoping to have a more private conversation and wanting to get more information from her. She relayed the same story to me again, but something inside kept telling me to ask her, 'Any chance you were coerced into sex?' Once I posed the question, everything changed. It was like a floodgate opened. She confided in me that she'd been date-raped. He was a friend of a friend. He'd been drinking heavily, too, and she couldn't get him to stop.

"Sometimes," Shearer said, "your intuition tells you to ask the more awkward question that most people don't want to ask. Even doctors feel awkward about asking certain questions and prying, but what I've learned is that the patient is often waiting for you to ask. Glad I picked up on that and did ask. For every one we catch, there are probably ten we miss."

Shearer was able to get this young, traumatized woman psychological counseling in addition to appropriate medical care, which helped set her on a better course than if he had simply treated her with postexposure medications. During his assessment, he was able to control external stimuli and not allow the hectic emergency room environment to force him to rush. This allowed him to pay greater attention to his expert intuition that told him something was amiss. He then applied his slower, more logical, deliberative thinking to the situation.

The Problem Is: We Prefer to Think Fast

We're all fast thinkers. We prefer to take mental shortcuts. We like to reach conclusions quickly but are often sloppy in our thinking habits. By contrast, slow thinking is simply harder to do. It requires more effort, and it's tiring. To give something deep thought—as when we learn something brand new or confront a puzzling, complex situation—takes more focus, concentration, and literal physiological energy, considering the fact that our brains eat up 20 percent of our bodies' energy. When Dr. Shearer hit the Pause button in the ER, took a moment to reflect on what he'd just heard from his twenty-three-year-old patient, and gave it his full attention, he lowered his risk of making an error, and he got it right. It was a conscious decision on his part to devote more energy to considering the patient he was treating. Devoting more of his brainpower to the task was the harder road to take, but it yielded a far better outcome for his patient.

As we've noted earlier, in 1974, Israeli psychologists Tversky and Kahneman published groundbreaking work on the ways that people make errors in judgment and decision-making. Despite possessing the talent to think logically, human beings often rely on mental short-cuts, or, as Kahneman refers to them, *rules of thumb*. While this greatly simplifies and dramatically speeds up the process of making thousands of judgments a day, it often comes with a significant amount of error.

Kahneman and Tversky describe the source of these errors in thinking, which take on predictable patterns, as *cognitive biases*. When you add time pressure and overstimulation into the mix, you can begin to imagine how often thinking errors occur for most of us.

The fact that these errors tend to be systematic is good news for achieving greater personal agency. If we are aware of our most common biases, we can work to keep our errors in thinking to a minimum, at least on the most important things. There's a glossary of biases on page 289. These are the biases we most often come across in our work, and they are worth having a look at to see which of them you might inadvertently be using. For example, when things work out well, do you catch yourself taking a little more credit than you might actually deserve? Likewise, when things don't go well, do you sometimes push the blame onto others for things that perhaps they don't have much control over? If so, don't be hard on yourself, but own up! These are just two of the many human biases that influence our thinking. Knowing where you are biased allows you to bring it to the surface to ensure that it doesn't lead you astray.

Deliberation Is an Active Process

Deliberation is an active process that requires energy. It can be learned and practiced. The overall goal of effective deliberation is for you to make appropriate and judicious use of both System 1 and System 2 thinking. In order to do this, you need to learn to use them together in a self-aware manner. The vast majority of the time, you are using System 1 ("fast") thinking because your brain has evolved to most readily perform this function. Your environment requires you to use mental shortcuts to think fluidly in your day-to-day life where you must make decisions frequently. Otherwise, you'd be thinking intensely about every detail or every single decision, and not much would get done. And yet, you can't and wouldn't be well served by living your life making only quick, intuitive decisions. There are clearly times when it is best to shift into intentional, slower thinking—thinking more analytically and methodically to arrive at a better decision. The key is knowing when it's worth the additional effort that this requires and learning how to do it effectively.

Ideally, you should call up System 2 thinking when you need to make bigger decisions and when the stakes are high. System 2 thinking also helps you sort out and make sense of the massive amount of information hitting you each day. Generally, System 2 thinking requires you to seek out accurate information to make an informed choice.

Review this checklist of questions. These are typical of the questions we ask our clients to get them thinking more about (and improving upon) their critical-thinking skills.

- How good are you at engaging in slow, deliberate thinking?
- Do you believe you have the capacity to think critically?
- Do you use a particular method?
- Do you take the time to pin down the most relevant facts?
- Is this something you do consciously for the bigger decisions?

Or

- Do you generally rush to a decision because it's quicker and easier and you just want to get it off your plate?
- Do you find yourself often getting distracted by the next thing demanding your attention?
- Do you tend to put off decision-making for as long as possible?

Be fair to yourself. If a highly educated expert like Dr. Shearer worries about making errors in his judgment, where in your life might you be making serious errors because you don't slow down your thinking or don't question how you think?

Again, in our experience, most people have not developed a reliable system to follow to keep their decision-making under their control. Few people try to step outside themselves to regularly observe how they employ their thinking skills. Surprisingly, many people don't even seek out the best information up front before making important decisions. In short, most people have serious gaps in their ability to think critically. We continue to be surprised how many people we work with find themselves rushing to judgment and looking back with regret.

Critical Thinking: Another Means to Keep Unreliable Thinking in Check

One concept has come up again and again throughout this book—critical thinking.

The potential to think critically resides in us all. While some may be better at it than others, anyone can learn to improve. Critical thinking is most important in situations where we have strong emotions about a topic and perhaps are getting our knowledge through taking mental shortcuts (politics, for instance). The most fundamental principle of critical thinking is to question things for ourselves and to be aware of the assumptions we are making. The goal here is not to question absolutely every last thing but to be a prudent person who is aware of the limitations of one's knowledge.

To engage critical thinking, your emotions and beliefs need to be held in check. This means that you need to start by suspending your fast, emotionally driven, and automatic thinking. In its place, engage slow, logical, and intentional thinking. The easiest way to do this is to get yourself somewhere quiet, uncluttered, and private, and tell yourself you're going there with a singular mission. You are going to spend time engaged in deep, reflective, logical thinking where you will question assertions, claims, and assumptions for their veracity and figure out a path forward. Below is a simple process that will help you to activate and engage your critical-thinking skills.

Critical Thinking in Everyday Life

There are many articles, books, courses, and adult education classes on how to develop critical thinking skills. Consider any or all of these resources and start simple. The points we describe below are inspired by the work of two experts, Linda Elder and Richard Paul, and are based on their article "Becoming a Critic of Your Thinking" from the Foundation for Critical Thinking.

Start by clarifying your thinking. Watch out for "vague, fuzzy, formless, blurred thinking," as Elder and Paul say. This is the type of thinking you're likely to have when rushing, distracted, and fatigued. One example is when you rely on overgeneralizations, such as *All banks are exactly the same, doesn't matter which you choose*. Resist thinking superficially. Challenge yourself to go deeper. Verify if your thinking is clear by running it by others and asking them if it sounds reasonable.

Also keep from straying off topic, and avoid making unjustified leaps in thinking. In other words, *stick to the point*. Don't meander. Stay focused and relevant to the main issue you are trying to critically think about.

Become a more adept questioner as well, and don't accept what others tell you unexamined. As Elder and Paul say, *question questions*. Ask yourself, *Have I asked the right questions, the best questions . . . enough questions?* Welcome questions (and feedback) from others, but be discerning and stick only to the questions or feedback of others pertinent to the topic and that really help to move you toward better thinking.

And last, try to be reasonable. This is easier said than done. First, acknowledge your fallibility. Realize you don't have all the answers. Don't be closed-minded. Be aware of your beliefs and biases. Elder and Paul note that the hallmark of a good critical thinker is the willingness to change one's mind upon hearing more reasonable explanations or solutions. An earlier-discussed agency principle, *Manage Your Emotions and Beliefs,* will also help you monitor and control strong feelings and beliefs that can derail your critical thinking.

Think Like a Detective

Superintendent Colm Lydon has a position with an enormous set of responsibilities. He's the chief of the Bureau of Intelligence and Analysis for the Boston Police Department, kind of the head of homeland security for the city. Critical thinking is second nature to him—something he engages in every day and all day. There is not much he has not seen, having served as a police officer for more than thirty years: terror attacks, homicides, gang violence, organized crime.

"Every single police officer is essentially a problem solver," Lydon told us. "Detectives are specifically trained to solve complex, ambiguous problems where there's little to guide them and when getting to resolution takes focus, time, persistence, and lots of patience."

The detective's process is similar to the judge's and to the mindful physician's, too. Here is a list of the key things Lydon focuses on: Use all the time you have at your disposal when making a decision. Hypothesize from initial evidence by envisioning all the ways something could have happened. Don't prematurely close off possibilities. Work toward planning several steps ahead in your thinking. Be open to new learning from others, and use good communication skills to draw people out. Be organized and aware of your mental steps as you study a situation. Have a curiosity and a drive to uncover and pursue the meaning behind the facts. Adhere to a code of values. Face problems directly, and prepare to take action. Put a process in place to learn from your mistakes. Persevere.

Like Judge Butler, detectives rely on a framework to guide them. They use scientific procedures to gather and maintain evidence, and they must be aware of and adhere to the rules of law. They are always thinking ahead in terms of putting their evidence together to make a case for the legal system and a possible trial.

Scan, Analyze, Respond, and Assess— A Reliable Model Used by Police Officers

One thinking framework in wide use by police officers, cited by Lydon, goes by the acronym SARA (Scan, Analyze, Respond, and Assess). Published in 1987 by William Spelman and John Heck, its tenets fit nicely into the principle of *Deliberate, Then Act*, and they can be applied to anyone working to solve a personal problem, particularly when feeling stuck. The model helps to keep your thinking organized as you reason through a complex issue. As you read through the four steps of the framework, test them out by applying them to a problem you are currently struggling with.

Start with *scanning*. Put attention to what you may be ignoring. Identify patterns and recurring issues. Be a tough-minded and astute observer. Identify relevant facts. Acknowledge openly and put a name to the problem. If you are dealing with a multipronged problem, prioritize the biggest issues. Once you have identified the problem, your second step is to start a non-emotional *analysis*. Put together the data points you have and start to identify potential causes and define the scope of the problem. *The problem I have in my marriage is possibly because _____. Work is a struggle because _____.* In your attempt at analysis, hypothesize what could be the root cause. Third, based on your analysis, brainstorm options and *respond* by identifying possible plans of action to achieve your desired outcome. *If X happens, I'll do Y . . . If Y happens, I'll do Z.* Run your plan by trusted others for feedback. Once you feel ready to move forward, go ahead and implement it. Finally, ask yourself, *How successful were the actions that I took? What resulted from it?* This is the *assessment* step. *Do I need to change my strategy or my plan? What should I modify to achieve a better outcome next time?* And most importantly, *What should I do from here?*

Take the story of our friend Carla. She'd been married for just ten months when her husband, Clay, accepted a job in a rural town hundreds of miles away. He then moved to the town, telling her he was going to scout out the area and find a place for them to live. Shortly after Clay got settled, he became increasingly evasive. He texted that he was busy with his new job and couldn't commit to when he could come back to see her or when he'd have a place for them to live. Then he went completely silent. Clay had family in the area, so Carla checked in with them, but they, too, were evasive.

Below, we apply the SARA model to the details of Carla's real-life situation. Again, this model can be helpful when attempting to assess and use logical reasoning to figure out an ambiguous, emotionally charged problem where you have little information to go on.

SCAN

Carla started by connecting the distancing behavior she was experiencing to some of Clay's earlier behavior. She recalled in their courtship how he'd often needed "space." She recalled that he'd only had one previous short-term relationship, and he never spoke much about the other woman. She pieced together relevant facts. One fact that stuck with her was when Clay first proposed moving, he had passed up many other positions that were geographically closer. She read through his text messages and listened to his voice mails, sifting them for potential meaning.

ANALYZE

Carla started to reflect on possible causes of what was happening. She considered that perhaps Clay had another life. Maybe he was having an affair? She also wondered if she had done something offensive inadvertently that had damaged their relationship. She compared various hypotheses to see what fit better with the facts and made more sense.

RESPOND

Carla sought guidance from close friends, who urged her to meet with a counselor for emotional support and to help her sort out what was happening. Meeting with the counselor helped her to think more clearly about options. Carla took certain actions. She reached out to Clay with carefully worded texts to document their correspondence. She started with positive and neutral texts, hoping to get a response. *Miss you. Just wondering how you are. How is the new job? Hope your family is okay.*

ASSESS

Clay finally responded and agreed to talk. He acknowledged he was having cold feet about being married and was feeling ambivalent about the move as well. Carla felt he sounded defeated. Having this new information allowed Carla to begin to assess the situation more accurately and consider her next steps. Carla decided to continue engaging with Clay before making any final decisions.

Using a model like this would make Carla less likely to make a rash, impulsive decision, such as taking preemptive legal action. While that's still an option, it's only one of several possible paths for her to take. Complex issues like these can take considerable time to figure out. It can be helpful to have a model that gives you a road map with steps to gain more information before taking decisive action. This is one reason why the SARA model has endured as a reliable method for police officers to use when facing complex problems.

Analyze Your Current Situation as Part of Effective Deliberation

A real estate investor and businessman named Tim told us that he was aware of the role that emotions and bias play in his thinking. "The capacity for *situation analysis* makes all the difference," he said when assessing the potential upside of a business opportunity. This helped him stay grounded and limit his losses in the real estate boom and subsequent 2008 economic crisis. "Sure," he added, "while there's a certain seduction to sizing something up fast and uncritically, because it gives you a green light to forge ahead quickly, it doesn't typically work out so well in business." Here, Tim preferred to use his critical-thinking faculties combined with a healthy amount of metacognition. He frequently questioned his own thinking. *What am I missing in my thinking about certain properties? What if I'm wrong?*

In this way, Tim exemplifies the agency principle of *Deliberate, Then Act*. While not an economist or even someone with an advanced business degree, over time through self-study and experience, he developed valuable expertise in the real estate business. Critical thinking and metacognition carried over to a solid awareness of himself and the social world. He was observant and thoughtful to the point of often being trenchant in his perceptions of larger trends, and he used his observations to inform his business decisions. He frequently pulled himself back from following the crowd. He described having made many mistakes over the years, but he consistently made an effort to learn from all these mistakes. While he appeared to move into action quickly, he attempted to do so thoughtfully rather than impulsively.

Develop Your Own Personal Framework

Tim, like the others whose stories we've shared in this chapter, operates with a framework that guides his decision-making. That's another thing these expert decision-makers share in common. Tim's framework ensures that certain conditions are true before he moves forward on a business idea. Are you a frequent viewer of the popular TV show *Shark Tank*? If so, what frameworks could you infer the investors use to guide their decision making? Masterful decision-makers, such as physicians, judges, and detectives, operate with the frameworks that their professional disciplines provide. But there are subtler frameworks in operation behind the scenes as well that function as critical infrastructure in decision-making.

A framework is many possible things. In general terms, it is something that helps you to organize your thinking, decision-making, and actions. It provides a structure that establishes boundaries to help you to see, appreciate, and focus more on what is inside the frame. In business, a framework can be as simple as a marketing strategy, a quarterly goal, a policy, or a process. It can also be more complex, like an overarching foundational premise, or a set of values and ethical guidelines, or an overall culture. In most practical terms, it's a lens to help you see more clearly to assess, plan, and take action in any area.

Paul's Notes from the Field: Continuous Learning as a Framework for Business Success

I caught up with two friends recently while on a consulting assignment in Virginia. John Luke, Jr., former CEO of MWV Corporation, is currently chairman of the board of WestRock Corporation and a member of several other corporate boards. Linda Schreiner, a business strategy expert, and now senior vice president of strategy at Markel Corporation, was chief human resources officer and a member of John's senior leadership team at MWV for many years. Along with a team of other talented executives, they built a strong organization culture around the framework of *continuous learning*.

John operates with the premise that senior-level executives don't need to have all the answers, "because it is impossible to know everything. Instead you must focus on partnering with others from whom you can learn—and from whom you can get help in making the kind of decisions you need to make." John referenced the *Harvard Business Review* article "In Praise of the Incomplete Leader" as providing an instructive framework for business leaders to meet the demands they face. Linda concurred on the relevance and applicabilty of this framework and added, "I've always seen my role as focused on bringing new learning into organizations to help other leaders to be more effective. For me this is a strategic imperative."

While Linda's expertise in business strategy informs all her thinking, her primary framework for much of her career has revolved around the work of organizational theorist Peter Senge of the MIT Sloan School, who wrote *The Fifth Discipline* in 1990 (and who co-authored the article referenced above). Building a "learning organization" culture to support the business strategy has been her passion in each of the organizations where she has been a leader. "In business, as in life, you must define the current reality and your desired outcomes and then deal with it. There is a need for a framework—even though there may be times when you need to adjust, or even throw out your framework, if it is getting in the way of the kind of inquiry you need to undertake." Senge, who is an engineer by training, has practiced meditation for thirty years. His model emphasizes the vital importance of active inquiry and deep reflection to effect transformational change in organizations.

Linda and John, through their leadership, augmented the learning organization framework with a focus on collaboration company wide to promote a learning-focused culture. They supported this culture with a core set of values and a strong business strategy that laid the groundwork for the type of tough-minded inquiry necessary to success. It allowed them to create an organization of strong decision-makers at all levels of the company focused on sustainable growth and profitability. With this they were able to shepherd the company through many business challenges and changes including complex mergers and significant acquisitions. All the while, their framework and collaborative approach helped them to create a successful business that was a rewarding and growth-inducing place for people to work.

The Role of Emotion in Decision-Making

Decisions are more prone to error when your emotions are running high. Emotions like anger, happiness, and fear speeds up your thinking. Elevated emotions make your brain think it needs to give you an answer *now*! Faster thinking pushes you to decide and take action prematurely, sidelining slower, deliberative thinking.

When you're upset, agitated, giddy, head over heels in love, or scared, know that you will tend to think more shallowly.

Psychologist Jennifer Lerner, cofounder of the Harvard University Decision Science Laboratory, describes two different types of emotions we should be on the lookout for when making important decisions: integral emotions and incidental emotions.

Integral emotions are relevant emotions. They arise from the decision at hand and should be considered and integrated into your decision-making process. For example, you may have positive associations to a neighborhood you grew up in as you return and give thought to potentially moving back there. Or perhaps you're deciding between two job offers at different companies. One job is with a company whose culture you immediately related to and felt comfortable in while the other left you cold. Those feelings should be factored in and integral to your decision. It is reasonable that they be factored in. Just don't let integral emotions completely drive the decision-making process.

Incidental emotions, on the other hand, aren't relevant to the decision you are making. They can be feelings carried over from something that simply happened to you earlier in your day. For example, if you are tense, suspicious, or irritated because you just spent forty minutes stuffed in a crowded, noisy subway car that broke down during your commute to work, it might not be the best time to interview prospective candidates for a key position at your start-up company. And yet, quite often people carry negative, unrelated emotions from one space into another and then attempt to make important decisions, unaware that incidental emotions are at play in the background.

There is not an exemption for positive feelings. Maybe you are in a happy-go-lucky, carefree mood. Maybe you're feeling excited after chatting with an attractive person on that same crowded train. It's put a spring in your step and left you in a highly optimistic state. That's terrific, but unless you are self-aware, your positive incidental emotions might bias you when it's time to make a judgment on the quality of a new candidate you're interviewing a few hours later. In short, incidental emotions—positive or negative—can make you think less incisively.

When Emotions Cloud Decision-Making

Hakim is an extroverted and highly reliable "black car" livery driver. He works for himself and has a large, stable group of satisfied clients. An eager learner, he enjoys engaging with his customers and always has an anecdote or two to relate. He shared this story on a recent trip to the airport.

Several years ago, shortly after he immigrated to the United States from Algeria, Hakim was having a conversation with his friend Omar, who worked with him in the same business. Omar had been in the United States for fifteen years and had methodically built up a business around his ownership of three taxi medallions. Owning a taxi medallion has long been a means of establishing wealth, and Omar felt proud of his accomplishment and secure financially knowing that each taxi medallion he owned was worth close to a million dollars.

"Are you aware of this whole Uber thing that is happening?" Hakim asked his friend. "You may want to think about if it is wise to continue holding on to all your medallions."

"Well, Hakim," his friend replied with skepticism and irritation, "I've lived here much longer than you, and medallions have been around for a long, long time. My uncle came here fifty years ago and is a wealthy man because of them. I know I'm safe holding on to them." Omar had his facts straight in terms of the points he made; medallions had certainly increased in value over the years in Boston. But was Omar correct that he was safe by being conservative, taking a wait-and-see approach? Why was he so angry at Hakim for raising the issue?

"A couple of years passed," Hakim continued, "and the value of Omar's medallions sank like a stone just like I warned him they might. He went bankrupt and lost his business, his home, too, and had so much stress that he had a stroke. It's a very sad situation. He just wasn't able to hear what I was trying to tell him—he couldn't see what was happening around all of us."

After all was said and done, Hakim and Omar had a conversation two years later about what had happened. Omar offered a regretful explanation, admitting that he had held an unshakable belief

(continued)

that taxi medallions were a stable store of wealth. His uncle had convinced him of this, and he trusted his uncle with his life. When Hakim called this into question, Omar had reacted with fear and anger. The whole idea had made him so intensely anxious that he angrily suspected Hakim might have had an ulterior motive, perhaps to buy them from him cheaply. Omar's fear, he told his friend, had been paralyzing. Not knowing what to do, the compromise position he reached within himself was deciding that simply waiting it out would be the safest thing. A massive shift in the taxi business had simply never occurred before, and therefore, he wanted to believe it was highly unlikely.

Omar had made a mistake that many of us frequently make—we believe we know more than we actually do and can fail to imagine what could possibly transpire. This, combined with his misdirected anger at Hakim, prevented him from taking in new learning and applying it to his situation.

Social Media and Decision-Making

To expand on earlier themes, living amid change and uncertainty encourages people to seek validation from others. More and more, this is being undertaken online through social media, often unwittingly. While online engagement might seem helpful, it often leaves people simply following like-minded individuals as opposed to truly opening themselves to new learning.

To the extent you compare yourself to others, and everyone does, beware of your need to be validated and how the opinions and feedback of others can influence your judgment and decision-making. In an age of overwhelm, people unconsciously seek more and more validation. They're feeling worried, off base, insecure—and the natural human tendency to want to check in with others is high. Social media becomes an easy go-to for this, but this approach comes with serious downsides. People snipe, are sarcastic, don't think through their feedback or the posts they send out quickly, or, even more frequently, inflate themselves (which makes the rest of us feel less than adequate). We're not suggesting you need to entirely unplug from social media, but we are recommending that you turn to people you trust when you are looking for support, in real time and in real ways (such as with more phone contacts and face-to-face meetings).

Impediments to Taking Decisive Action

Arriving at a good decision is the prerequisite to taking positive, productive action. Obsession, perfectionism, impulsivity, and procrastination—these are some of the most common and at times debilitating impediments to taking decisive action. At one time or another most of us have experienced these hindrances to our ability to exercise agency. Some of us experience one or more of these on a recurring basis. The underlying sources or pathways to "the big four" impediments are various and they do matter. This is where emotional awareness enters in. Your ability to reflect on and understand the source can allow you to identify and let go of it and move forward. For example, sometimes procrastination is caused by hypersensitivity to how you believe you are perceived or will be received by others. *She has written me off and no longer wants to hear from me.* This may be an erroneous perception that, through reflective scrutiny, can be rejected, allowing you to move into action. Simply stated, greater emotional granularity can often help you to reduce the grip these have on you.

For example, people who experience recurring obsession and perfectionism may be frequently anxious and worried. These people, in our experience, have a brain style that focuses on details and tends to think too far forward, worrying about future negative possibilities. Some people have so much fear of making the wrong decision that they obsess and overthink things to the point that they freeze, unable to pull the trigger on any action, even after they've effectively deliberated. Others focus on reaching perfection at all cost and their unrealistic expectations keep them stalled out in the deliberation phase. These are but a few examples of the underlying reasons why people get stuck.

Use Your Agency: If you tend toward being perfectionistic, beware of getting too caught up in slow, deliberative thinking. The goal is not to analyze absolutely everything to achieve perfection, as this can stymie important action you need to take. It will also use up considerable time and biological energy.

On the other end of the spectrum, impulsive people tend to be totally in the moment and do not engage in enough planning for the future. They often rush into action prematurely, have low risk aversion, and are impulsive—not fully thinking through the consequences of their actions. For example, people diagnosed with ADHD have a neurological style that can interfere with step-wise, slow decision-making, especially when they are frustrated by sitting for long periods or stuck indoors behind desks and screens or attending long meetings. People with this brain style seek out and require higher stimulation to keep their brains fully engaged. That's why, in our experience, we find them to be best at fluid, creative thinking rather than slow methodical thinking (they often prefer it!), although there are exceptions.

Procrastinators tend to avoid taking action until the last minute. Instead of rushing, they postpone engaging in the slower thinking that effective deliberation demands, especially if the task isn't interesting or of immediate appeal to them. Sometimes procrastination also happens because people are too distracted or busy, or unmotivated or depressed, or just plain exhausted. In short, there are many reasons behind why people procrastinate.

Minimizing the Impact of the Four Impediments

Where are you in this? Is there something that gets in the way of you taking positive decisive action? No matter what trips you up, here are key points of which to remind yourself:

- Life isn't about making the best decisions perfectly every time. It's recognizing that as you make each decision, new doors open up, and this is a good thing.

- There's a strong human bias against closing down options. We stay stuck in indecision because we fear losing something by closing doors. *Should I move or stay where I am? Should I seek a new job?* We often fixate on what we might lose rather than imagining ourselves in a new place with new possibilities after having made a choice. But the research is clear that when we are willing to be decisive and close down some options we end up in a better place, more satisfied with our decisions and more optimistic.
- The goal of good decision-making is not to completely avoid risk. In many cases, the goal is to understand and embrace *good risk*. Taking calculated risks won't guarantee each and every outcome that you desire, but it increases the chances, and the rewards are reaped over the long term, not necessarily the short term.

One of the most basic distinctions that you can make regarding the four impediments is to determine if, on balance, you tend to rush into action or if you avoid it. If you tend to rush, be aware that actions taken too quickly aren't likely to be effective, and you are all the more likely to act with impulse when you are angry, according to Jennifer Lerner, whom we mentioned earlier. The reason is that anger makes us perceive less risk and therefore we end up taking greater risk. Our thinking speeds up, and we have a false sense of control.

In short, don't make big decisions when you are angry or upset. Sleep on it, as the old saying goes.

Making Decisions When Angry and Frustrated

Kayla is a forty-two-year-old senior manager for an upscale restaurant group in New Mexico. She works hard and takes pride in having helped the company prosper, but she often catches herself stuck in work mode. Things move fast in the competitive restaurant world. She is valued for her ability to think on her feet and reach decisions quickly.

(continued)

Kayla was recently having her phone repaired, and her fifth-grade son tagged along. He was admiring the new phones on display. He started begging and lobbying really hard—*guilting her* was the term she used—to buy him his first mobile phone. That was an opportune moment to put on the brakes and engage System 2 thinking. Leave the store. Get calm. Get more information. Ask around. *What's a good age for a child to get a mobile device? What problems could arise? Should I draw up a behavior contract for my son to follow to ensure more appropriate use before purchasing the phone? Maybe he should spend some of his own chore money to buy it?*

Instead, her son's high emotions in the store stimulated her own emotions. She became frustrated, a bit angry. The salesman drove up her emotions further when he told her about time-limited offers and better data plans. She felt like she needed to act. All these emotions were incidental, not integral, to any decision she should be making about buying her son a phone. Before she knew it, her son was walking out with her to the parking lot carrying his new phone in a shiny store bag, and Kayla was already feeling she probably had made a mistake.

Procrastination is one of the most common impediments to taking action. We come across this continually in our work and sometimes in our own personal lives. Books abound to help with this: to help us get more motivated, to get into shape, to meet goals, to get organized. What is less commonly recognized is that the root of procrastination can be anxiety. In the age of overwhelm, we shouldn't be surprised that millions of people are shutting down, freezing up, avoiding, putting off, and becoming ever more unable to stay focused long enough to get themselves into productive action.

When anxiety is at the root of procrastination, consider a review of the first three behavioral principles to manage anxiety and high stress that may be stopping you from getting things done. Start by opening space in your mind to think more clearly and calmly (*Control Stimuli*). Secondly, secure social support and encouragement of others to support you in getting motivated (*Associate Selectively*), and thirdly, use movement (*Move*) to get energized and decrease feelings of helplessness. Now, take some action. Any action, no matter how small. If you're still stuck, break down your action into even smaller steps; for example, don't try to clean the whole house—clean one room, or clean one area of the room, like a desk or closet. Reward yourself for completing the smaller steps and then move on to the next.

Effective Deliberation and Action: A Six-Step Model

Here we are, nearly at the end of this book, and all roads have led to this simple but powerful thought: Effective deliberation is crucial when trying to do anything of importance. While many people with agency do not necessarily think of themselves as following a prescribed deliberation process, many of them are surprised to realize that they actually do in practice.

We have put together a model that incorporates a series of steps drawn from best practices to help you with your decision-making.

The capacity to see beyond your present circumstances—to see what "could be"—is central to agency. No matter where you are in life, no matter what you are dealing with, you can develop this ability. It is a critically important starting point when seeking to accomplish anything of significance.

Pulling from the ways that physicians, judges, and police officers think (and make decisions), coupled with the implications of Kahneman's *fast-versus-slow* dual-thinking framework, we have defined a six-step model to help you think in a more organized and deliberative manner:

1. **Set the stage.** Put yourself into a frame of mind and an environment conducive to reflection and exploration. Try to set enough time aside so you are not rushed. Take your emotional temperature, and try to get yourself into a relaxed, calm state.

2. **Focus, define, and deploy.** *Focus* on the issue at hand to adequately *define* and frame it. *Deploy* critical thinking to test out your assumptions. To do so, make sure that you:

- Clarify your primary objective and what is at stake.
- Ask open-ended questions (of yourself and others) to ensure you are giving adequate thought to framing the issue in the best possible way.
- Find the opportunity often embedded within the problem.
- Gather pertinent facts.
- Perform a bias check. (See the glossary of biases on page 289.)

3. Generate options. Allow conflicting ideas to surface. Put them all on the table. *Position Yourself as a Learner* by seeking counsel from others with related experience. Don't rush to judgment by narrowing the scope of your inquiry too soon. Check in with trusted others along the way for feedback on your thinking process.

4. Manage emotions. Ensure that strong emotions are not driving your thinking process. Be aware of both *integral* and *incidental* emotions (see page 269) that may be at work behind the scenes influencing your decision-making. Resist engaging in binary (either-or) thinking.

5. Draft a plan. Write out your thoughts. Read them out loud. Putting your thoughts and decisions into words (handwriting is most powerful) and hearing these words spoken aloud helps engage critical thinking. Your plan should simplify your options and incorporate the most important facts. You should be able to envision yourself successfully implementing it. Once completed, put your plan aside and focus elsewhere for a while. When you return to your plan, does it feel spot-on or does it need further development? If it does, don't be discouraged. Work through the changes and be glad that you didn't act prematurely.

6. Take action. When your plan feels solid, move into execution mode. You don't have to be 100 percent certain. In ambiguous situations or when information is less than perfect, higher-agency people typically follow an 80/20-type rule: They act when they have about 80 percent of the relevant information or when they feel 80 percent ready or justified to take action. Plan to make midcourse corrections as needed.

It's nearly impossible to be 100 percent correct or to perfectly anticipate all outcomes. Think through possible midcourse corrections during the deliberation phase, which bolsters your confidence to move forward. Once you are in the action stage, reassess as you go, making changes as necessary.

Effective decision-makers don't see the world as a binary place in which a right decision versus wrong decision will always be clear at the outset. They take action believing that there is most often a way to fix, salvage, change, and improve an outcome as they move forward.

Creating Lives on Their Own Terms: Two People/Two Paths

As a twenty-one-year-old single, unemployed mother, Kris found herself with only a few dollars in her pocket, resting alongside a rural road with her three-year-old son. Having set out on foot more than an hour earlier to buy breakfast at the nearest market, both she and her son were tired. He pointed to an orange tree across the road, loaded with ripe oranges glistening in the California sun. She told him it wouldn't be right to take the fruit—the oranges didn't belong to them. But he was hungry. She looked into his eyes and, in that moment, she says, a surge of something akin to knowingness passed through her. *We are going to be okay, he and I.* The torturing self-doubt about her capability to build a life where she could adequately care for him somehow lifted. A small kernel of a plan emerged. Kris gathered herself.

Kris picked the orange and decided at that moment that everything had to change. She went that day to a shopping mall, applied to every single store, got a job, and eventually made enough money to go back to the Midwest where she had family and could start taking classes and get a steady job.

Thirty years later, Kris is now director of process improvement for a global Fortune 200 manufacturing company. With no formal college degree, she has achieved Six Sigma Master Black Belt certification, the highest level of proficiency in the empirical, statistical quality management techniques of her field. With a rich and fulfilling personal, spiritual, and community life, Kris helps entire functions and departments within her company to intelligently work through challenges to realize their goals. And she volunteers her time and skill to help disadvantaged communities all over the world to become stronger, healthier places to live.

Kris encountered many tough trials along the way requiring her to take stock, cope with tough challenges, and make difficult decisions. From her father, a career military man, she learned discipline and order, as well as the importance of enjoying life along the way. From her mother, a remote, withholding person, she was called upon to dig deep to overcome emotional scars, gaining life-changing insight through therapy and spiritual practice. Experimenting with various paths, she developed a passion for figuring things out and for bringing order to disorder.

Pause to imagine the intelligence and perseverance it took for Kris, an African American woman on her own from an early age, to succeed both within corporate America and on her own terms in pursuing a role of great personal meaning for her. That's where her passion and agency took her.

In addition to agency, Kris demonstrates grit. According to author Angela Duckworth, an associate professor of psychology at the University of Pennsylvania and author of *Grit: The Power of Passion and Perseverance*, grit is "passion and perseverance." In her 2014 TED Talk, Duckworth said that grit is "having stamina . . . sticking with your future, day in, day out, not just for the week, not just for the month, but for years."

We have seen this resolute persistence in many people with high agency once they have decided on a well-considered, definitive goal and are ready to act.

Agency requires that they exercise good judgment by not calling upon this persistence in the wrong set of circumstances, to avoid getting stuck on paths not authentic to who they really are or who they want to become. Agency requires the patience, courage, and wherewithal to experiment and try out different identities. It also entails the capacity to know when to quit doing something and set new goals.

Mal had a different path to creating a life on his own terms. Unlike Kris, Mal was born with a script that his father had written about the way his son's life should unfold. He experienced a privileged post-war 1950s New England childhood where opportunity abounded. After attending Dartmouth College on a hockey scholarship and graduating with an MBA, he landed a prized job on Madison Avenue as an account manager for Young and Rubicam, a premier advertising agency. Think *Mad Men*, the popular TV series, and you get the picture. As a young man in 1960s Manhattan, Mal was living many people's concept of the ideal life. Great money, two-martini lunches, Broadway plays. But there happened to be a problem, he says: *I felt it wasn't my life.* Mal and his wife spent a week in 1968 at the Esalen Institute, a retreat center in Big Sur, California, taking part in a series of seminars as part of the human potential movement.

Within a year of his first trip to Esalen, Mal had taken a leave of absence from his job on Madison Avenue, never to return. Following a teaching position of many years at Esalen, he took himself to study at an Ashram in India, living for ten years in a rural town with cows moving around unpaved roads. "I saw people living on almost nothing and they were very much enjoying their lives," he recalled, a tone of surprise suffusing his voice these many years later. "It killed the American dream for me—the pursuit of material objects. I asked myself, what would I be missing?" He went against all the expectations of his father and the society around him. Many people simply didn't understand and reacted with anger, but Mal remained resolute. "I experienced an epiphany that I couldn't put into words. I found something I was looking for but hadn't even known I'd been looking. It was the truest part of myself, beyond what I might think, beyond concepts or beliefs I held."

As a teacher he has had a profound impact on the lives of many. Now living with his wife in the San Francisco Bay Area, he told us, "I have become the man I wanted to be. I gained more fulfillment, more self-respect, by the path I followed—even though it involved a great many difficult moments and may not have come for twenty years."

People with high agency like Kris and Mal step back, reflect, and think for themselves. They don't reflexively follow other people's expectations or the societal "script" laid out for them. They tap their intuition and trust themselves, and enlist their decision-making skills to move onto paths of their own choosing.

Personal success is not equivalent to high achievement. As *Grit* author Duckworth emphasizes, you must be passionate if you are going to stay focused and persist long enough to make something your own, whatever that may be. That's where agency comes into play. You need to locate what you are truly interested in pursuing in your life. It isn't following the herd or your family's expectations automatically. It requires equal parts reflection, learning, and experimentation to come to know your true passion. Rest assured, your intuition will let you know when you've found it, as it did for Kris and Mal.

Use Your Ability to *Deliberate, Then Act* to Create a Life on Your Own Terms

People with high levels of agency focus on determining both where they stand and what their options are. They possess confidence in their ability to make decisions and to act upon them. This capability is a key differentiator in terms of the ability to take one's life in the desired direction.

For this reason, the seventh principle is of critical importance in your journey to build greater agency and create the life you most want. The more you work on this last principle—and the more you can move fluidly among all seven principles highlighted in this book—the more nimble and effective you will become in your approach to decision-making, and the more natural and obvious will be your awareness of when you've arrived at the moment for action. In fact, you will be setting the agenda and becoming the leader to whom others look for guidance, and on your way to discovering and leveraging the agency within you.

YOUR AGENCY TOOL KIT

GET A PROCESS: Establish, and become skillful at using, a specific deliberation process to make effective decisions.

DIVIDE IT UP: Separate your deliberation process from taking action on important matters.

BE AWARE: Know the salient differences between objective facts and your emotions, beliefs, wishes, and desires. Know how the latter influence your decision-making.

FEED YOUR BRAIN: Eat, exercise, rest, and get adequate sleep to ward off mental depletion so that your mind is prepared to do the heavy work required to make decisions.

CREATE SPACE: Make room in your head for competing thoughts and feelings to help you generate more creative ideas and solutions.

LEARN FROM MISTAKES: Engage in after-action reviews to learn from your errors as well as your successes.

BE ON ALERT: Know when your emotional System 1 thinking is being stimulated or manipulated by an outside source.

ENGAGE METACOGNITION: Accurately assess the quality of your own thinking.

BE EMOTIONALLY AWARE: Guard against allowing your feelings to derail your thinking process and cause you to make poor decisions.

KNOW YOUR THINKING TRAPS: Be familiar with the more common thinking traps you fall into so that they don't impede a reliable and accurate deliberation process.

BE DECISIVE: Once you have thoughtfully deliberated, don't get stuck in indecision by engaging in endless what-ifs. Act before events unfold and act on you.

VERIFY: For big decisions, don't rely entirely on someone else's opinion (even if they are an expert) without verifying the facts and thinking it through for yourself.

CONCLUSION

We started this book by reminding you that for every action you take, *including reading this book*, you have a choice. The problem is that most of us are so overwhelmed half the time we have trouble giving ourselves the necessary space to make choices that are both consistent with our values and point us toward the life we want to lead.

It's our hope that the principles and practices outlined in this book will help you achieve two intertwined goals: 1) Develop the skill and confidence to make good decisions at important times in your work and personal life, and 2) Develop the perspective to identify what you need to change in order to live your life the way you want to live it.

With these goals in mind, here are some simple reminders to keep you on the path toward greater agency:

- Actively monitor the things to which you give your attention. The many moments we are distracted, or distract ourselves, add up to minutes, hours, and days of missed opportunities to experience something richer, more lasting, fulfilling, and life-changing.

- Seek the company of good people, those who both support your positive aspirations, and aren't afraid to challenge you when you need it. Minimize time spent with people who undermine you or are overly ingratiating.

- Take care of yourself by exercising, eating well, and developing good sleep habits. Each of these things is directly tied to your personal agency.

- Press yourself to be open to learning by asking questions, seeking out new perspectives, and surrounding yourself by people who are curious about and open to new things.

- Actively monitor your emotions and beliefs by developing the habit of reflecting on them. At moments when you find yourself seeking distractions, consider whether you're avoiding strong feelings or emotions. It's impossible to get the life you seek until you are really in touch with what you believe and feel about the things life has to offer.

- While it's important to be open to others, remember too that only you, through quiet personal reflection, can know what you want and what is best for you. Trust and follow your intuition, while of course remaining open to information that suggests another direction.

- Use reason and deliberation over passion when making important decisions while never losing sight of your passion. Locate and use it to determine and pursue your own path in life.

If there's one thing we learned in the course of researching and writing this book, it's that developing and maintaining agency requires a commitment to these practices. It's not the case that once you develop a healthy sense of agency you can stop giving thought to it and simply let yourself go. Many of the people described in this book—those who successfully developed greater agency—emphasize that it is an ongoing process that takes energy, practice, and patience. So that even in times when they feel exhausted or overwhelmed, they have learned to remind themselves that effort put toward agency-enhancing behavior now will always pay off in the long run.

The next time you sense something happening around you—or within you—that doesn't feel quite right, don't ignore it and reflexively press on. Exercise the discipline to stop. Pay attention to that signal. If the path you are on doesn't seem right, pause, reflect, and get off. Put yourself onto a better path. If that path isn't apparent, take the time to create and design one for yourself. Others may end up following your lead.

Finally, with greater agency, you will have greater influence over your life *and* greater impact on the lives of others. How you decide to use that power is a matter of deep importance to yourself, to those you love and care for, to those you work with, and to all the communities you touch. Be ethical. Be considerate. Be measured. While agency doesn't come with a built-in moral or ethical navigation system, the seven principles help you to stay grounded and steady, maintain open-mindedness, pursue continuous learning, and increase your self-understanding, self-control, and understanding of others. And, in practice, the seven principles also encourage you to push yourself each day to develop greater acceptance and empathy toward others and consider the longer-term consequences of your actions. In other words, to become a humanist.

Our hope and most fervent wish for you:

Use your power of agency to do some good in your life and in the world. The world needs you.

Define success on your own terms. Make creative choices. Live your values and your passion . . . Don't be afraid to go your own way.

Plant a tree. Help it grow. Maintain your connection to the earth.

Above all . . . Use your power of agency wisely to be the person you most want to be in the world. Enjoy your life.

METHODOLOGY

We conducted over a hundred in-depth structured interviews with people across the country. We identified interview subjects through professional and personal contacts, articles, and news stories. We made every effort to include a diverse group of men and women, of varying age, race, socio-economic status, vocation, sexual orientation, and geographic location. Our procedure was guided by the classic case study, qualitative approach. This is an intensive open-ended study of individuals in order to provide rich data, often used in the early stages of developing theories and new ideas in social science. The questions we used were standardized but designed to be open-ended and flexible. This encouraged interview subjects to speak freely and allow for deeper conversations to emerge.

Participants were told that we were interviewing a range of people to learn more about how people face challenges in their lives. Participants were informed their stories could be included in a book. They were told that the goal of these interviews was to record real-life examples about the behaviors and the ways of thinking that they used when coping with difficult situations to identify priniciples of agency in action.

Interviews were supplemented with archival information found in public records, books, journals, newspaper and magazine articles, and online sources such as recorded speaking events. Interviews were arranged in various locations: people's homes, their workplace, or a mutually convenient location, such as a public library. Some interviews were conducted via video conference or by telephone when face-to-face meetings weren't feasible. All interviews were conducted in one or two sessions and lasted between one and four hours in length.

Development of the Agency Practices Inventory

The development of the Agency Practices Inventory involved an adapted version of the survey design process recommended by Artino and colleagues (2014). This multi-step process began with a search of the research literature related to human agency and a series of interviews with a diverse sample. Candidate inventory items were developed based on a synthesis of the literature and interviews; we then conducted pilot testing of candidate items with a sample of 380 adults recruited from Amazon MTurk. In addition to completing candidate items, participants in this pilot study also completed measures of self-efficacy and hope, which we expected would correlate with agency, and a brief demographic questionnaire. Item range and variance, reliability, and convergent validity were evaluated using the pilot data. Based on this analysis, some candidate items were removed from the inventory, some were revised, and some new items were developed. The revised inventory was then piloted with a new sample of 327 adults from Amazon MTurk, and statistical analyses were again used to evaluate the psychometric properties of the inventory. The revised inventory demonstrated acceptable psychometric properties and, as expected, indicated that agency was positively correlated with both self-efficacy and hope.

GLOSSARY OF BIASES

Eight Thinking Traps to Guard Against

Researchers have identified many cognitive biases—so many, in fact, that they are too numerous to list here. The large number of biases discovered by researchers is evidence that we humans are prone to think in distorted ways and, for the most part, are oblivious to it. We refer to the more common ones we see in our work as *thinking traps*.

When you can, read through those eight biases and ask yourself if you can recall a time when you may have relied on these types of thinking shortcuts. Put a checkmark next to those that sound familiar. Underline key words or phrases that apply to you in the descriptions.

Being aware of these common thinking traps allows you to get them under control. Realize that you tend to rely more on these biases when you are more emotional, when in a rush, fatigued, or anytime you lower your mental guard and let your mind run on autopilot.

THE BIAS: Attribution Error

The Solution: Blame situations, not people.

When something goes wrong, we tend to blame the personalities and characters of others rather than taking the time to fully consider the situation. *Rene clipped the meeting short this morning. She's an impulsive, inconsiderate person.* Chances are Rene cut the meeting short because her schedule that day was overbooked. But what often come to mind first are *dispositional* explanations. Don't underestimate the power that situations have over everyone. Situational factors often drive people to act the way they do. Assign blame to people less, but at the very least consider the situation more fully before you judge.

THE BIAS: Confirmation Bias

The Solution: Stop justifying half-baked, uninformed beliefs.

There are many ways we arrive at false beliefs, but keeping them alive is often the role of the confirmation bias. It's cherry picking. We're continuously filtering for and focusing on incoming data points that confirm our current beliefs, attitudes, and opinions. Everyone does this, and it frequently gets in the way of effective decision-making. One way to know that you are engaging this bias way too much? You rarely struggle to form your opinions and to make decisions—everything seems to fit quite neatly into your worldview all the time to the extent that you don't need time to think or make decisions; you just stick to what you already know and reject what's new or different. We all like seeing the world as a stable and predictable place, but the problem is it isn't, and to learn and adapt, we have to think our way through challenges—this requires not reflexively confirming what we already know or what we prefer to believe.

THE BIAS: Anchoring Effect

The Solution: Beware how first inputs anchor your brain and hijack your thinking.

This bias, which has been studied extensively by researchers, in many ways can be considered the grandparent of all biases. How it works is that your mind becomes tethered to an arbitrary piece of information (often a number or a value) that has been presented to you. The *anchoring effect* operates to pull, tug, or nudge you in the direction of this arbitrary "anchor" that has entered (and stays stuck in) your mind as a reference point. Extensive research has shown that such an anchor will exert considerable influence over your decision-making even when it is completely arbitrary. The research also shows that the anchoring effect is hard to avoid, even by experts who are aware of it.

There are many different ways that anchoring operates in our lives.

Take, for example, those prices scribbled prominently on the windshields of used cars. You are anchored to that price, whether it is reasonable or sky high, the moment your eyes see it. Everything in the negotiation with the salesperson will be tethered to that. Chances are, if you start your negotiation from there, you will likely end up paying too much. Still not convinced you're affected by anchors? One of our favorite examples comes from the work of psychologist Dan Ariely, currently at Duke University. When he was a professor at MIT, he asked MBA students to write down the last two digits of their social security numbers. Afterward, he had them place bids on various luxury items, like Belgian chocolates, computer accessories, and bottles of wine. Business students with higher social security numbers bid significantly higher for these items.

The bottom line is that to address this bias, you must realize that bigger decisions deserve more research and analysis. Look for anchors when making large purchases, researching schools, or deciding on what doctor or medical practice will be caring for you. Sticker prices and advertising anchor us, setting an expectation of what something is worth. And be wary of those "Ten Best" or "Top" lists we commonly see. Those also use the anchoring effect to influence our choices.

THE BIAS: Self-Serving Bias

The Solution: Give credit where credit is actually due.

When things go well, whether we had a hand in it or not, we like to take credit. When things go badly, we tend to assign blame to others or outside factors beyond our control. *My teacher grades too hard . . . The finance and marketing teams dropped the ball . . . The playing court was slippery from last night's rain.* A little self-serving bias is not bad, as it keeps our self-image sturdy and our mood positive. Think of people who are the opposite and are overly self-critical. They may hesitate on making needed decisions and can act in self-defeating ways. The trick is to not let this bias take over and become your default way of explaining every-thing away. To do this, be less defensive. Take responsibility. Acknowl-edge your shortcomings. Lay claim only to what you had a real hand in creating or effecting. Try to be more truthful with yourself and with others, and always give credit where credit is due.

THE BIAS: Bandwagon Effect

The Solution: Follow the herd less.

This is related to groupthink and the impulse we experience to follow the herd, even if it goes against our own beliefs and our own values. Groups can exert a powerful effect. We're wired to align our thinking, emotions, and behaviors with groups of people. We've all experienced the strong pull of watching people dancing, laughing, applauding, or singing, and suddenly, we get the strong urge to join in. When activities or ideas are positive, it's a way to connect with others and bond over these social moments. The problem is deferring to groups to decide important things that we should decide for ourselves. Make sure you don't auto-matically follow the herd. Don't lose your independence. Keep your critical thinking always at the ready.

THE BIAS: Halo Effect

The Solution: Don't be shined on or misled.

Whether accurate or not, first impressions are powerful. What you see or hear first can influence everything else you think about a person thereaf-ter. Research has shown that physically attractive people, for example, are judged to be nicer, smarter, and more trustworthy, regardless of their true character or abilities. Wealth, athletic skills, and celebrity often lead to this same *halo effect*. The halo effect can happen when teachers decide what grades to give students. It happens in hiring and promotion deci-sions in work settings. Ask yourself this: Would you choose your sur-geon or trust a pilot because they are good looking or entertaining? People do. The halo effect, like all biases, is a common shortcut we take, but people with agency learn to rely less on their initial impressions. When the stakes are high, take your time and think critically to realistically assess what is both true and relevant about another person.

THE BIAS: Intergroup Bias
The Solution: Don't be tribal, unless purely for fun.
This is the classic *us versus them* way of thinking. Sometimes referred to as *tribalism,* it's related to groupthink and to the bandwagon effect discussed earlier. We often prefer (or reject) ways of thinking and behaving based on the groups we affiliate (or don't affiliate) with. Identifying with a group is often positive. It can offer us support and resources. It can also be relatively harmless, such as a friendly school rivalry. But beware that this bias can also lock us out of opportunities to expand, to learn, to enjoy new experiences, and to connect with people outside our normal social spheres. In its darkest form, intergroup bias is at the core of reinforcing stereotypes and fueling divisive, hostile attitudes toward "others." Like all biases, it is based on fast thinking, as it packages up the complexities in the world quickly and comes with massive distortions that can lead to negative outcomes. To guard against intergroup bias, expose yourself to new people and new places regularly. In short, anything that's a bit off the beaten path for you can accomplish this. Reach out to people you don't know, smile and nod at people next to you, and strike up a conversation—ask someone about the book on their lap or where they got their eyeglasses that you like, inching further out into the rich, interesting world outside yourself.

THE BIAS: Gambler's Fallacy
The Solution: Keep superstitious thinking in check . . .
Don't try to control what you can't.
We often see patterns in the things around us. That's because the human brain is designed to look for all possible associations, even ones that aren't there. Gamblers fall prey to this quite readily. A twenty-eight-year-old client of ours was regularly betting on sports, mostly with friends in office pools and weekend poker games, and it climbed to a fever pitch

during the World Series and March Madness. At one point, his gambling "hobby" got way too serious, and he owed thousands of dollars to a bookmaker. The main reason his gambling got out of control, he told us, was superstitious thinking. He saw a relationship between his actions and outcomes that were outside of his control, and he believed he could influence them. He linked his winning or losing to such things as the night of the week, the person who dealt the playing cards, or what his girlfriend said to him the morning of a playoff game. He saw his mind "slipping off the rails," as he put it, into these false patterns. Smartly, he had the awareness that he needed help. He was motivated to change and willing to do the hard work required. This included meetings at Gamblers Anonymous, coming clean to his girlfriend and parents, and corrective cognitive and behavioral strategies that he practiced daily. These strategies moved him from magical, emotional (System 1) thinking to more logical (System 2) thinking. This allowed him to get his life back on track.

BIBLIOGRAPHY

AAP News. "Children's Hospitals Admissions for Suicidal Thoughts, Actions Double During Past Decade." May 4, 2017. http://www.aappublications.org/news/2017/05/04/PASSuicide050417

Ahlskog Erik, J., Yonas E. Geda, Neill R. Graff-Radford and Ronald C. Petersen. "Physical Exercise as a Preventive or Disease-Modifying Treatment of Dementia and Brain Aging." *Mayo Clinic Proceedings* (2011): 86(9), 876–884. https://www.ncbi.nlm.nih.gov/pmc/articles/PMC3258000/

Albuquerque, Natalia, Kun Guo, Anna Wilkinson, Carine Savalli, Emma Otta and Daniel Mills. "Dogs Recognize Dog and Human Emotions." *Biology Letters*: January 13, 2016. Published 13 January 2016. DOI: 10.1098/rsbl.2015.0883 http://rsbl.royalsocietypublishing.org/content/12/1/20150883

Alfini, Alfonso J., Lauren R. Weiss, Brooks P. Leitner, Theresa J. Smith, James M. Hagberg and J. Carson Smith. "Hippocampal and Cerebral Blood Flow after Exercise Cessation in Master Athletes." *Frontiers in Aging Neuroscience* (2016): August 5, 2016. https://www.frontiersin.org/articles/10.3389/fnagi.2016.00184/full

American Academy of Ophthalmology. "Is Too Much Screen Time Harming Children's Vision? The American Academy of Ophthalmology Helps Parents Separate the Facts from Fiction." ScienceDaily. 2018. https://www.sciencedaily.com/releases/2018/08/180806162718.htm

American Psychological Association. "APA's Survey Finds Constantly Checking Electronic Devices Linked to Significant Stress for Most Americans." February 23, 2017. https://www.apa.org/news/press/releases/2017/02/checking-devices.aspx

American Psychological Association. "Data on Behavioral Health in the United States." 2018. https://www.apa.org/helpcenter/data-behavioral-health.aspx

Anderson, Simon P. and André De Palma. "Shouting to be Heard in Advertising." HAL Archives-Ouvertes.fr, 2012. https://pdfs.semanticscholar.org/5a51/d1316f856687661388787579df00f1e21a2a.pdf

Ariely, Dan. *Predictably Irrational.* New York: HarperCollins Publishers, 2008.

Artino, Anthony R., Jeffrey S. La Rochelle, Kent J. Dezee and Hunter Gehlbach. "Developing Questionnaires for Educational Research: AMEE Guide No. 87." Medical Teacher (2014): 36 (6), 463–474.

Balko, Radley. "Was the Police Response to the Boston Bombing Really Appropriate?" *The Washington Post* (Washington, DC). April 22, 2014. https://www.washingtonpost.com/news/the-watch/wp/2014/04/22/the-police-response-to-the-boston-marathon-bombing/?utm_term=.69285a75967b

Barnett, Tracie A., Aaron S. Kelly, Deborah Rohm Young, Cynthia K. Perry, Charlotte A. Pratt, Nicholas M. Edwards, Goutham Rao and Miriam B. Vos. "Sedentary Behaviors in Today's Youth: Approaches to the Prevention and Management of Childhood Obesity—A Scientific Statement from the American Heart Association." *Circulation* (2018):138, 142–159. https://www.ahajournals.org/doi/10.1161/CIR.0000000000000591

Barrett, Lisa Feldman. "Are You in Despair? That's Good." *New York Times* (New York, NY), June 3, 2016. https://www.nytimes.com/2016/06/05/opinion/sunday/are-you-in-despair-thats-good.html?_r=0

Barrett, Lisa Feldman. *How Emotions Are Made*. Boston: Houghton, Mifflin, Harcourt, 2017.

Barrett, Lisa Feldman and Jolie Wormwood. "When a Gun Is Not a Gun." *New York Times* (New York, NY), April 17, 2015. https://www.nytimes.com/2015/04/19/opinion/sunday/when-a-gun-is-not-a-gun.html

Bayda, Ezra. *Being Zen*. Boston: Shambhala Publications, Inc., 2002.

Bazelon, Emily. "How 'Bias' Went From a Psychological Observation to a Political Accusation." *New York Times Magazine* (New York, NY). October 18, 2016. https://www.nytimes.com/2016/10/23/magazine/how-bias-went-from-a-psychological-observation-to-a-political-accusation.html

Beck, Julie. "How to Get Better at Expressing Emotions." *The Atlantic*, November 18, 2015. https://www.theatlantic.com/health/archive/2015/11/how-to-get-better-at-expressing-emotions/416493/

Begley, Sharon. "Happiness Is Contagious?" *Newsweek*, December 12, 2008. https://www.newsweek.com/happiness-contagious-221368

Bekoff, Marc, and Jane Goodall. *The Emotional Lives of Animals: A Leading Scientist Explores Animal Joy, Sorrow, and Empathy—and Why They Matter*. Novato, CA: New World Library, 2008.

Ben-Ner, Avner, Darla J. Hamann, Gabriel Koepp, Chimnay U. Manohar and James Levine. "Treadmill Workstations: The Effects of Walking While Working on Physical Activity and Work Performance." *PLoS One* (2014): 9(2). https://www.ncbi.nlm.nih.gov/pmc/articles/PMC3930588/

Bennett, Jessica. "On Campus, Failure Is on the Syllabus." *New York Times* (New York, NY). June 24, 2017. https://www.nytimes.com/2017/06/24/fashion/fear-of-failure.html

Biglan, Anthony. *The Nurture Effect*. Oakland, CA: New Harbinger Publications Inc., 2015.

Bilton, Nick. "The American Diet: 34 Gigabytes a Day." *New York Times* (New York, NY), December 9, 2009. https://bits.blogs.nytimes.com/2009/12/09/the-american-diet-34-gigabytes-a-day/

Blackstone, William. "Blackstone's Commentaries on the Laws of England, Book the Fourth—Chapter the Twenty-Seventh: Of Trial, and Conviction." Yale Law School, The Avalon Project. http://avalon.law.yale.edu/18th_century/blackstone_bk4ch27.asp

Blatt, Sidney J. *Polarities of Experience*. Washington, D.C.: American Psychological Association, 2008.

Bohn, Roger E. and James E. Short. "How Much Information? 2009 Report on American Consumers Global Information." Industry Center University of California, San Diego, December, 2009. http://group47.com/HMI_2009_ConsumerReport_Dec9_2009.pdf

Bonabeau, Eric. "Don't Trust Your Gut." *Harvard Business Review*, May 2003. https:// hbr.org/2003/05/dont-trust-your-gut

"The Brain on Stress: How Behavior and the Social Environment 'Get Under the Skin.'" *Agency for Healthcare Research and Quality*, Rockville, MD. http://www.ahrq.gov /professionals/education/curriculum-tools/population-health/mcewen.html

Brookfield, Stephen D. *Developing Critical Thinkers: Challenging Adults to Explore Alternative Ways of Thinking and Acting.* San Francisco: Josey-Bass, 1987.

Brookfield, Stephen D. *Teaching for Critical Thinking.* San Francisco: John Wiley & Sons, Inc., 2012.

Brown, Peter C., Henry L. Roediger III, and Mark A. McDaniel. *Make It Stick: The Science of Successful Learning.* Cambridge, MA: Belknap Press, 2014.

Browne, M. Neil and Stuart M. Keeley. *Asking the Right Questions.* Englewood Cliffs, NJ: Prentice-Hall Publishers, 2003.

Bruce, Marino A., David Martins, Kenrik Duru, Bettina M. Beech, Mario Sims, Nina Harawa, Roberto Vargas, Dulcie Kermah, Susanne B. Nicholas, Arleen Brown et al. "Church Attendance, Allostatic Load and Mortality in Middle Aged Adults." *PLOS ONE* (2017): 12(5): e0177618. https://journals.plos.org/plosone /article?id=10.1371/journal.pone.0177618

Burnett, Bill, and Dave Evans. *Designing Your Life.* New York: Alfred A. Knopf, 2016.

Bybee, Kevin A. and Abhiram Prasad. "Stress-Related Cardiomyopathy Syndromes." *Circulation* (2008): 118, 397–409. https://www.ahajournals.org/doi/abs/10.1161 /circulationaha.106.677625

Byers, Dylan. "Facebook: Russian Ads Reached 10 Million People." *CNN*, October 3, 2017. https://money.cnn.com/2017/10/02/media/facebook-russian-ads-10-million /index.html

Cain, Susan. *Quiet.* New York: Crown Publishers, 2012.

Canadian Paediatric Society, Digital Health Task Force. "Screen Time and Young Children: Promoting Health and Development in a Digital World." January 2018. https://academic.oup.com/pch/article/23/1/83/4823532

Carola Salvi, Emanuela Bricolo, John Kounios, Edward Bowden and Mark Beeman. "Insight Solutions Are Correct More Often than Analytic Solutions." *Thinking & Reasoning* (2016): 22(4), 443–460. https://www.ncbi.nlm.nih.gov/pmc/articles/PMC5035115/

Center for Problem-Oriented Policing. The SARA Model. http://www.popcenter.org /about/?p=sara

Centers for Disease Control. "Prevalence and Most Common Causes of Disability Among Adults—United States, 2005." *MMWR Weekly* (2009): 58(16), 421–426. https://www.cdc.gov/mmwr/preview/mmwrhtml/mm5816a2.htm

Children's Hospital of Philadelphia. "Is Screen Time Making Our Kids Unhappy?" 2018. https://www.chop.edu/news/health-tip/screen-time-making-our-kids-un happy

Christakis, Nicholas A. and James H. Fowler. "The Spread of Obesity in a Large Social Network over 32 Years." *New England Journal of Medicine* (2007): 357, 370–379. https://www.ncbi.nlm.nih.gov/pubmed/17652652

Cisek, P., and J. Kalaska. "Neural Mechanisms for Interacting with a World Full of Action Choices." *Annual Review of Neuroscience.* (2010): 33, 269–298. http://www .cisek.org/pavel/Pubs/CisekKalaska2010.pdf

Clark, Andy. "Whatever Next? Predictive Brains, Situated Agents, and the Future of Cognitive Science." *Behavioral and Brain Sciences.* (2013): 36, 281–253. https://www.fil.ion.ucl.ac.uk/~karl/Whatever%20next.pdf

Cleveland Clinic. "Women & Cardiovascular Disease." 2018. https://my.clevelandclinic.org/health/diseases/17645-women—cardiovascular-disease

Cole, Diane. "The Joy of Learning to Play an Instrument Later in Life." *The Wall Street Journal* (New York, NY), April 23, 2017. https://www.wsj.com/articles/the-joy-of-learning-to-play-an-instrument-later-in-life-1492999441

"The Components of Multiple Intelligences." *MI Oasis.* http://multipleintelligencesoasis.org/about/the-components-of-mi/#box-6

Cosmides, Leda, and John Tooby. "Evolutionary Psychology and the Emotions." In *Handbook of Emotions,* 2nd Edition, edited by Michael Lewis and Jeanette M. Haviland-Jones. New York: Guilford Press, 2000.

Crum, Alia J., Peter Salovey, and Shawn Achor. "Rethinking Stress: The Role of Mindsets in Determining the Stress Response." *Journal of Personality and Social Psychology.* (2013): 104(4), 716–733. http://goodthinkinc.com/wp-content/uploads/CrumSaloveyAchor_RethinkingStress_JPSP2013.pdf

Csikszentmihalyi, Mihaly. *Flow.* New York: HarperPerennial Modern Classics, 1998.

Damasio, Antonio. *Descartes' Error: Emotion, Reason, and the Human Brain.* New York: Avon Books, 1994.

Dao, James. "Loyal Companion Helps a Veteran Regain Her Life After War Trauma." *New York Times* (New York, NY), April 28, 2012. https://www.nytimes.com/2012/04/29/us/loyal-companion-helps-a-veteran-with-post-traumatic-stress-disorder.html

Davis, Matthew A., Lewei A. Lin, Haiyin Liu and Brian D. Sites. "Prescription Opioid Use Among Adults with Mental Health Disorders in the United States." *Journal of the American Board of Family Medicine* (2017), 30(4), 407–417. http://www.jabfm.org/content/30/4/407.long

Dean, Joshua T. "Noise, Cognitive Function, and Worker Productivity." Department of Economics, MIT. November 11, 2017. https://economics.mit.edu/files/13747

Diaz, Keith M., Virginia J. Howard, Brent Hutto, Natalie Colabianchi, John E. Vena, Monika M. Safford, Steven N. Blair and Steven P. Hooker. "Patterns of Sedentary Behavior and Mortality in U.S. Middle-Aged and Older Adults: A National Cohort Study." *Annals of Internal Medicine* (2017): 167(7), 465–475. http://annals.org/aim/article-abstract/2653704/patterns-sedentary-behavior-mortality-u-s-middle-aged-older-adults

Dietz, Robert. "Single-Family Home Size Increases at the Start of 2018." *National Association of Home Builders.* May 21, 2018. http://eyeonhousing.org/2018/05/single-family-home-size-increases-at-the-start-of-2018/

Dreyfus, Hubert, and Sean Dorrance Kelly. *All Things Shining.* New York: Simon & Schuster, Inc., 2011.

Druskat, Vanessa Urch, Fabio Sala, and Gerald Mount, eds. *Linking Emotional Intelligence and Performance at Work.* New York: Routledge, 2013.

Duch, Helena, Elisa Fisher, Ipek Ensari, Marta Font, Alison Harrington, Caroline Taromino, Jonathan Yip and Carmen Rodriguez. "Association of Screen Time

Use and Language Development in Hispanic Toddlers: A Cross-Sectional and Longitudinal Study." *Clinical Pediatrics* (2013): 52(9), 857–65. https://www.ncbi.nlm.nih.gov/pubmed/23820003

Ducharme, Jamie. "A Lot of Americans Are More Anxious Than They Were Last Year, a New Poll Says." *Time*, May 8, 2018. http://time.com/5269371/americans-anxiety-poll/

Duckworth, Angela. *Grit*. New York: Simon and Schuster, Inc. 2016.

Duenwald, Mary. "Power of Positive Thinking Extends, It Seems, to Aging." *New York Times* (New York, NY), November 19, 2002. https://www.nytimes.com/2002/11/19/science/power-of-positive-thinking-extends-it-seems-to-aging.html

Duggan, William. *Strategic Intuition: The Creative Spark in Human Achievement*. New York: Columbia Business School Publishing, 2013.

Dunckley, Victoria L. "Gray Matters: Too Much Screen Time Damages the Brain." *Psychology Today*, February 27, 2014. https://www.psychologytoday.com/us/blog/mental-wealth/201402/gray-matters-too-much-screen-time-damages-the-brain

Dweck, Carol. *Mindset: The New Psychology of Success*. New York: Random House, 2006.

"Early Release of Selected Estimates Based on Data from the National Health Interview Survey, 2015." CDC. https://www.cdc.gov/nchs/nhis/releases/released201605.htm

Edelman, Gerald M. *The Remembered Present: A Biological Theory of Consciousness*. New York: Basic Books, 1990.

Elder, Linda and Richard Paul. "Becoming a Critic of Your Thinking." *The Foundation for Critical Thinking*. http://www.criticalthinking.org/pages/becoming-a-critic-of-your-thinking/478

Elder, Linda and Richard Paul. "Critical Thinking Development: A Stage Theory." *The Foundation for Critical Thinking*. http://www.criticalthinking.org/pages/critical-thinking-development-a-stage-theory/483

Elliott, Anthony. *Subject to Ourselves: Social Theory, Psychoanalysis, and Postmodernity*. Boulder, CO: Paradigm, 2004.

Engelmann, Jan B., C. Monica Capra, Charles Noussair and Gregory S. Berns. "Expert Financial Advice Neurobiologically 'Offloads' Financial Decision-Making under Risk." *PLOS ONE* (2009): 4(3): e4957. https://journals.plos.org/plosone/article?id=10.1371/journal.pone.0004957

English, Tammy and Laura L. Carstensen. "Selective Narrowing of Social Networks Across Adulthood Is Associated with Improved Emotional Experience in Daily Life." *International Journal of Behavioral Development* (2014): 38.2, 195–202.

Epstein, Mark. *Thoughts Without a Thinker*. New York: Basic Books, 1995.

Facione, Peter A. *Think Critically*. Englewood Cliffs, NJ: Pearson Education, 2011.

Facione, Peter A. and Noreen C. Facione. *Thinking and Reasoning in Human Decision Making*. Millbrae, CA: The California Academic Press, 2007.

"Facts and Statistics." *Anxiety and Depression Association of America*. https://adaa.org/about-adaa/press-room/facts-statistics#

Fadel, Charles, Maya Bialik, and Bernie Trilling. *Four-Dimensional Education*. Boston: The Center for Curriculum Redesign, 2015.

Feagin, Joe R., Anthony M. Orum, Gideon Sjoberg, eds. *A Case for the Case Study.* Chapel Hill, NC: University of North Carolina Press, 1991.

Fligstein, Neil, Orestes P. Hastings and Adam Goldstein. "Keeping Up with the Joneses: How Households Fared in the Era of High Income Inequality and the Housing Price Bubble, 1999–2007." *Socius* (2017): 3, 1–15. http://journals.sagepub.com/doi/pdf/10.1177/2378023117722330

Florida House Experience. "#bodypositive: A Look at Body Image & Social Media." 2018. https://fherehab.com/news/bodypositive/

Fonagy, Peter, Gyorgy Gergely, Elliot Jurist, and Mary Target. *Affect Regulation, Mentalization and the Development of Self.* New York: Other Press, 2005.

Ford, Brett Q., and Maya Tamir. "When Getting Angry Is Smart: Emotional Preferences and Emotional Intelligence." *Emotion.* (2012): 12(4), 685–689. https://www.researchgate.net/publication/221810160_When_Getting_Angry_Is_Smart_Emotional_Preferences_and_Emotional_Intelligence

Fowler, James H. and Christakis Nicholas. "A Dynamic Spread of Happiness in a Large Social Network: Longitudinal Analysis over 20 Years in the Framingham Heart Study." BMJ (2008): 337, a2338. https://www.bmj.com/content/337/bmj.a2338+

Fox, Andrew S., Regina C. Lapate, Alexander J. Shackman, and Richard J. Davidson eds. *The Nature of Emotion: Fundamental Questions.* New York: Oxford University Press, 2018.

Frie, Roger, ed. *Psychological Agency.* Cambridge: The MIT Press, 2008.

Gardner, Howard. *Harvard Graduate School of Education.* https://howardgardner.com

Garten, Ina. *The Barefoot Contessa.* https://barefootcontessa.com/about

Gendlin, Eugene T. *Focusing-Oriented Psychotherapy.* New York: The Guilford Press, 1996.

"Generation M2: Media in the Lives of 8- to 18-Year-Olds." *Kaiser Family Foundation Study,* January, 2010. https://kaiserfamilyfoundation.files.wordpress.com/2013/04/8010.pdf

Ghezeljeha, Tahereh Najafi, Maryam Nasari, Hamid Haghani and Habiballah Rezaei Loieh. "The Effect of Nature Sounds on Physiological Indicators Among Patients in the Cardiac Care Unit." *Complementary Therapies in Clinical Practice* (2017): 29, 147–152. https://www.researchgate.net/publication/319925833_The_effect_of_nature_sounds_on_physiological_indicators_among_patients_in_the_cardiac_care_unit

Goldstein, William M. and Robin M. Hogarth, eds. *Research on Judgement and Decision Making: Currents, Connections and Controversies.* Cambridge, UK: Cambridge University Press, 1997.

Goleman, Daniel. *Focus.* New York: HarperCollins Publishers, 2013.

Goleman, Daniel. *Working with Emotional Intelligence.* New York: Random House, 1998.

Gore, Al. "Al Gore Warns That Trump Is a 'Distraction' From The Issue Of Climate Change." Fresh Air: August 2, 2017; Philadelphia, PA: WHYY Radio. https://www.npr.org/programs/fresh-air/2017/08/02/541159469/fresh-air-for-august-2-2017

Grabar, Henry. "How Much Will the Boston Lockdown Cost?" *Citylab.* April 19, 2013. https://www.citylab.com/equity/2013/04/what-will-boston-lockdown-cost-city/5350/

Graber, Mark L. "The Incidence of Diagnostic Error in Medicine." *BMJ Quality & Safety* (2013): 22:ii21-ii27. https://qualitysafety.bmj.com/content/22/Suppl_2/ii21

Gregory N. Bratman, Gretchen C. Daily, Benjamin J. Levy and James J. Gross. "The Benefits of Nature Experience: Improved Affect and Cognition." *Landscape and Urban Planning* (2015): 138, 41–50. https://www.sciencedirect.com/science/article/pii/S0169204615000286

Groopman, Jerome. *How Doctors Think*. New York: Houghton Mifflin Company, 2007.

Groopman, Jerome. *The Measure of Our Days*. New York: Viking Penguin, 1997.

Groopman, Jerome and Pamela Hartzband. *Your Medical Mind*. New York: Penguin Books, 2012.

Gross, James J., and Lisa Feldman Barrett. "Emotion Generation and Emotion Regulation: One or Two Depends on Your Point of View." *Emotion Review*. (2011): 3(1), 8–16. https://www.ncbi.nlm.nih.gov/pmc/articles/PMC3072688/

Haase, Lori, April C. May, Maryam Falahpour, Sara Isakovic, Alan N. Simmons, Steven D. Hickman, Thomas T. Liu and Martin P. Paulus. "A Pilot Study Investigating Changes in Neural Processing after Mindfulness Training in Elite Athletes." *Frontiers in Behavioral Neuroscience* (2015): 9, 229. https://www.ncbi.nlm.nih.gov/pubmed/26379521

Hallowell, Edward M. and John J. Ratey. *Driven to Distraction*. New York: Random House, 2011.

Hamblin, James. "Exercise Is ADHD Medication." *The Atlantic*. September 29, 2014. https://www.theatlantic.com/health/archive/2014/09/exercise-seems-to-be-beneficial-to-children/380844/

Harris, Sam. *Waking Up*. New York: Simon & Schuster, 2014.

Hawkins, Jeff, and Sandra Blakeslee. *On Intelligence*. New York: St. Martin's Griffin, 2004.

Heath, Chip, and Dan Heath. *Decisive*. New York: Crown Business, 2013.

Heck, John E. and William Spelman. "Problem Solving." *Police Executive Research Forum* (1987). https://www.ncjrs.gov/pdffiles1/Digitization/111964NCJRS.pdf

Higgins, Tory E. "Making a Good Decision: Value from Fit." *American Psychologist* (2000): 55, 1217–1230. https://www.ncbi.nlm.nih.gov/pubmed/11280936

Higgs, Suzanne and Jason Thomas. "Social Influences on Eating." *Current Opinion in Behavioral Sciences* (2016): 9, 1–6. https://www.sciencedirect.com/science/article/pii/S235215461500131X

Hillman, Charles H., Matthew B. Pontifex, Darla M. Castelli, Naiman A. Khan, Lauren B. Raine, Mark R. Scudder, Eric S. Drollette, Robert D. Moore, Chien-Ting Wu and Keita Kamijo. "Effects of the FITKids Randomized Controlled Trial on Executive Control and Brain Function." *Pediatrics* (2014): September 2014. http://pediatrics.aappublications.org/content/early/2014/09/24/peds.2013-3219

Hintzen, Katy. "The Consequences of Children Spending Less Time Outdoors." Michigan State University Extension, July 2, 2015. http://www.canr.msu.edu/news/the_consequences_of_children_spending_less_time_outdoors

Hoang, Tina D., Jared Reis, Na Zhu, David R. Jacobs, Jr., Lenore J. Launer, Rachel A. Whitmer, Stephen Sidney and Kristine Yaffe. "Effect of Early Adult Patterns of Physical Activity and Television Viewing on Midlife Cognitive Function." *JAMA Psychiatry* (2016): 73(1), 73–79. https://www.ncbi.nlm.nih.gov/pubmed/26629780

Hofferth, Sandra L. "Changes in American Children's Time—1997 to 2003." *Electronic International Journal of Time Use Research* (2009): 6.1, 26–47.

Hofferth, Sandra L. and John F. Sandberg. "How American Children Spend Their Time." *Journal of Marriage and Family* (2001): 63, 295–308. https://pdfs.semanticscholar .org/85de/6403c2c2e8631e44d00db818109180d958df.pdf

Hohwy, Jakob. *The Predictive Mind.* Oxford: Oxford University Press, 2013.

Holland, Dorothy, William Lachicotte, Debra Skinner, and Carole Cain. *Identity and Agency in Cultural Worlds.* Cambridge: Harvard University Press, 1998.

Holman, E. Alison, Dana Rose Garfin and Roxane Cohen Silver. "Media's Role in Broadcasting Acute Stress Following the Boston Marathon Bombings." *Proceedings of the National Academy of Sciences* (2014): 111 (1) 93–98. http://www.pnas.org /content/111/1/93

Holt, Jim. "Two Brains Running." *New York Times* (New York, NY), November 25, 2011. https://www.nytimes.com/2011/11/27/books/review/thinking-fast-and-slow -by-daniel-kahneman-book-review.html

Huber, Brittany, Megan Yeates, Denny Meyer, Lorraine Fleckhammer, and Jordy Kaufman. "The Effects of Screen Media Content on Young Children's Executive Functioning." *Journal of Experimental Child Psychology* (June 2018): 170, 72–85. https://www.sciencedirect.com/science/article/pii/S002209651730646X ?via%3Dihub

Huitt, William. "Critical Thinking: An Overview." *Educational Psychology Interactive.* http://www.edpsycinteractive.org/topics/cognition/critthnk.html

Hygge, Staffan and Igor Knez. "Effects of Noise, Heat and Indoor Lighting on Cognitive Performance and Self-reported Affect." *Journal of Environmental Psychology* (2001): 21, 291–299. https://pdfs.semanticscholar.org/0416/23140ae6afb0e419ff9 e13a4003da56dcc0b.pdf

Immordino-Yang, Mary Helen, Joanna A. Christodoulou and Vanessa Singh. "Rest Is Not Idleness: Implications of the Brain's Default Mode for Human Development and Education." *Perspectives on Psychological Science* (2012): 7(4), 352–364. http:// journals.sagepub.com/doi/abs/10.1177/1745691612447308

The International Focusing Institute—Building on the Work of Eugene T. Gendlin. http://www.focusing.org/sixsteps.html

Jabr, Ferris. "Why Your Brain Needs More Downtime." *Scientific American*, October 15, 2003. https://www.scientificamerican.com/article/mental-downtime/

Janet K. Freburger, George M. Holmes, Robert P. Agans, Anne M. Jackman, Jane D. Darter, Andrea S. Wallace, Liana D. Castel, William D. Kalsbeek and Timothy S. Carey. "The Rising Prevalence of Chronic Low Back Pain." *Archives of Internal Medicine* (2009): 69(3), 251–258. https://www.ncbi.nlm.nih.gov/pmc/articles /PMC4339077/

Jones, Jeffrey M. and Zacc Ritter. "Americans See More News Bias; Most Can't Name Neutral Source." *Gallup.* January 17, 2018. https://news.gallup.com/poll/225755 /americans-news-bias-name-neutral-source.aspx

Joseph, Richard J., Miguel Alonso-Alonso, Dale S. Bond, Alvaro Pascual-Leone and George L. Blackburn. "The Neurocognitive Connection Between Physical Activity and Eating Behavior." *Obesity Reviews: An Official Journal of the International*

Association for the Study of Obesity (2011): 12(10), 800–812. https://www.ncbi.nlm
.nih.gov/pmc/articles/PMC3535467/

Jung, Carl G. *Psychological Types,* edited and translated by Gerhard Adler and R.F.C.
Hull. Princeton, NJ: Princeton University Press, 1976.

Juster, Thomas F., Hiromi Ono and Frank P. Stafford. "Changing Times of American
Youth: 1981–2003." Institute for Social Research University of Michigan, November 2004. http://ns.umich.edu/Releases/2004/Nov04/teen_time_report.pdf

Kagan, Jerome. *What Is Emotion? History, Measures, and Meanings.* New Haven, CT:
Yale University Press, 2007.

Kahneman, Daniel. "A Perspective on Judgment and Choice: Mapping Bounded Ra-
tionality." *American Psychologist* (2003): 58(9), 697–720. https://www.ncbi.nlm.nih
.gov/pubmed/14584987

Kahneman, Daniel. *Thinking, Fast and Slow.* New York: Farrar, Straus and Giroux,
2011.

Kegan, Robert. *In Over Our Heads.* Cambridge: Harvard University Press, 1993.

Kent, Robert G., Bert N. Uchino, Matthew R. Cribbet, Kimberly Bowen and Timothy W. Smith. "Social Relationships and Sleep Quality." *Annals of Behavioral Medicine* (2015): 49(6), 912–917. https://www.ncbi.nlm.nih.gov/pubmed/25976874

Kessler, Ronald C., Matthias Angermeyer, James C. Anthony, Ron de Graaf, Koen
Demyttenaere, Isabelle Gasquet, Giovanni de Girolamo, et al. "Lifetime prevalence and age-of-onset distributions of mental disorders in the World Health
Organization's World Mental Health Survey Initiative." *World Psychiatry* 6.3
(2007): 168–176. https://www.ncbi.nlm.nih.gov/pmc/articles/PMC2174588/

King, Patricia M. and Karen Strohm Kitchener. *Developing Reflective Judgment.* San
Francisco: Jossey-Bass Publishers, 1994.

Klepeis, Neil E., William C. Nelson, Wayne R. Ott, John P. Robinson, Andy M. Tsang,
Paul Switzer, Joseph V. Behar, Stephen C. Hern and William H. Engelmann. "The
National Human Activity Pattern Survey (NHAPS): A Resource for Assessing Ex-
posure to Environmental Pollutants." *Journal of Exposure Analysis and Environmental
Epidemiology* (2001): 11, 231–252. https://www.nature.com/articles/7500165

Koch, Christof. "Intuition May Reveal Where Expertise Resides in the Brain." *Scientific American*, May 1, 2015. https://www.scientificamerican.com/article/intuition
-may-reveal-where-expertise-resides-in-the-brain/

Koepp, Gabriel A., Graham Moore and James A. Levine. "An Under-the-Table Leg-
Movement Apparatus and Changes in Energy Expenditure." *Frontiers in Physiology* (2017): 8, 318. https://www.ncbi.nlm.nih.gov/pmc/articles/PMC5435803/#

Kramer, Adam D. I., Jamie E. Guillory and Jeffrey T. Hancock. "Emotional Contagion Through Social Networks." *Proceedings of the National Academy of Sciences*
(2014) 111, 8788–8790. http://www.pnas.org/content/111/24/8788

Kramer, Adam D. I., Jamie E. Guillory and Jeffrey T. Hancock. "Experimental Evidence of Massive-Scale Emotional Contagion Through Social Networks." *Proceedings of the National Academy of Sciences* (2014): 111 (24), 8788–8790. http://www
.pnas.org/content/111/24/8788.full

Kross, Ethan, Philippe Verduyn, Emre Demiralp, Jiyoung Park, David Seungjae
Lee, Natalie Lin, Holly Shablack, John Jonides and Oscar Ybarra. "Facebook

Use Predicts Declines in Subjective Well-Being in Young Adults." *PLOS ONE* (2013): 8(8): e69841. https://journals.plos.org/plosone/article?id=10.1371/journal .pone.0069841

Lefèvre, Marie, Marie-Christine Carlier, Patricia Champelovier, Jacques Lambert, Bernard Laumon, and Anne-Sophie Evrard. "Effects of Aircraft Noise Exposure on Saliva Cortisol Near Airports in France." *Occupational and Environmental Medicine,* August (2017): 74(8), 612–618. https://www.ncbi.nlm.nih.gov/pubmed /28442544

Lennon, Sharron J., Kim K. P. Johnson, and Jaeha Lee. "A Perfect Storm for Consumer Misbehavior: Shopping on Black Friday." *Clothing and Textiles Research Journal* (2011): 29, 119–134. http://journals.sagepub.com/doi/abs/10.1177/0887302X11401907

Lerner, Jennifer S. and Larissa Z. Tiedens. "Portrait of the Angry Decision Maker: How Appraisal Tendencies Shape Anger's Influence on Cognition." *Journal of Behavioral Decision Making* (2006): 19(2), 115–137. http://psycnet.apa.org/record /2006-05240-004

Lerner, Jennifer S., Ye Li, Piercarlo Valdesolo and Karim S. Kassam. "Emotion and Decision Making." *Annual Review of Psychology* (2015): 66, 799–823. https://www .annualreviews.org/doi/abs/10.1146/annurev-psych-010213-115043

Levitin, Daniel J. *The Organized Mind.* New York: Penguin Random House, LLC, 2014.

Levy, Becca R. and Avni Bavishi. "Survival Advantage Mechanism: Inflammation as a Mediator of Positive Self-Perceptions of Aging on Longevity." *The Journals of Gerontology: Series B* (2018): 73(3), 409–412. https://academic.oup.com/psychsocgerontology /article-abstract/73/3/409/2631978?redirectedFrom=fulltext

Levy, Becca, Martin Slade and Stanislav V. Kasl. "Longitudinal Benefit of Positive Self-Perceptions of Aging on Functional Health." *The Journals of Gerontology: Series B* (2002): 57, 409–417. https://www.researchgate.net/publication/11190453 _Longitudinal_Benefit_of_Positive_Self-Perceptions_of_Aging_on_Functional _Health

Li, Qing, Kanehisa Morimoto, Maiko Kobayashi, Hirofumi Inagaki, Masao Katsumata, Yukiyo Hirata, Kimiko Hirata, Hiroko Suzuki, Yingji Li, Yoko Wakayama, et al. "Visiting a Forest, but Not a City, Increases Human Natural Killer Activity and Expression of Anti-Cancer Proteins." *International Journal of Immunopathology and Pharmacology* (2008): January 1, 2008. https://www.ncbi.nlm.nih.gov /pubmed/18336737

Lin, Ling-Yi, Rong-Ju Cherng, Yung-Jung Chen, Yi-Jen Chen and Hei-Mei Yang. "Effects of Television Exposure on Developmental Skills Among Young Children." *Infant Behavior Development* (2015): 38, 20–26. https://www.ncbi.nlm.nih.gov /pubmed/25544743

Lipshaw, Jeffrey. *Beyond Legal Reasoning: A Critique of Pure Lawyering.* New York: Routledge, 2017.

Liu, Fengqin, Simone Sulpizio, Suchada Kornpetpanee and Remo Job. "It Takes Biking to Learn: Physical Activity Improves Learning a Second Language." *PLOS ONE* (2017): 12(5): e0177624. https://journals.plos.org/plosone/article?id=10.1371 /journal.pone.0177624#sec014

Macmurray, John. *The Self as Agent.* Amherst, NY: Prometheus Books, 1999.

Maier, Steven F. and Martin E. P. Seligman. "Learned Helplessness: Theory and Evidence." *Journal of Experimental Psychology: General* (1976): 105, 3–46. https://pdfs.semanticscholar.org/bd0b/38c23bb66a0762b0023b0306c86411f47edc.pdf

Makary, Martin A. and Michael Daniel. "Medical Error—The Third Leading Cause of Death in the US." *BMJ* (2016): 353 :i2139. https://www.bmj.com/content/353/bmj.i2139

Malt, Barbara, and Phillip Wolff. *Words and the Mind: How Words Capture Human Experience.* New York: Oxford University Press, 2010.

Manjoo, Farhad. "I Ignored Trump News for a Week. Here's What I Learned." *New York Times* (New York, NY), February 22, 2017. https://www.nytimes.com/2017/02/22/technology/trump-news-media-ignore.html

Martin, Jack, Jeff Sugarman, and Janice Thompson. *Psychology and the Question of Agency.* Albany, NY: State University of New York Press, 2003.

Maume, David J. "Social Ties and Adolescent Sleep Disruption." *Journal of Health and Social Behavior* (2013): 54, 498–515. https://www.ncbi.nlm.nih.gov/pubmed/24311758

Mayo Clinic. "Chronic Stress Puts Your Health at Risk." 2016. https://www.mayoclinic.org/healthy-lifestyle/stress-management/in-depth/stress/art-20046037

McAfee, Andrew. "The Future of Decision Making: Less Intuition, More Evidence." *Harvard Business Review,* January 7, 2010. https://hbr.org/2010/01/the-future-of-decision-making

McManus, Ali M., Philip N. Ainslie, Daniel J. Green, Ryan G. Simair, Kurt Smith and Nia Lewis. "Impact of Prolonged Sitting on Vascular Function in Young Girls." *Experimental Physiology* (2015): 100(11), 1379–87. https://www.ncbi.nlm.nih.gov/pubmed/26370881

"Median and Average Square Feet of Floor Area in New Single-Family Houses Completed by Location." https://www.census.gov/const/C25Ann/sftotalmedavgsqft.pdf

Merchant, Nilofer (2013). "Sitting Is the Smoking of Our Generation." *Harvard Business Review,* January, 14, 2013. https://hbr.org/2013/01/sitting-is-the-smoking-of-our-generation

Mercier, Hugo, and Dan Sperber. *The Enigma of Reason.* Cambridge: Harvard University Press, 2017.

Metz, Cade. "How Facebook's Ad System Works." *New York Times* (New York, NY). October 12, 2017. https://www.nytimes.com/2017/10/12/technology/how-facebook-ads-work.html

Modell, Arnold H. *Imagination and the Meaningful Brain.* Cambridge: The MIT Press, 2003.

Monroe, Rachel. "#Vanlife, the Bohemian Social-Media Movement." *The New Yorker,* April 24, 2017. https://www.newyorker.com/magazine/2017/04/24/vanlife-the-bohemian-social-media-movement

Morin, Amy. "3 Important Ways Your Childhood Shaped Who You Are." *Psychology Today,* September 4, 2017. https://www.psychologytoday.com/us/blog/what-mentally-strong-people-dont-do/201709/3-important-ways-your-childhood-shaped-who-you-are

Morishima, Takuma, Robert M. Restaino, Lauren K. Walsh, Jill A. Kanaley, Paul J. Fadel and Jaume Padilla. "Prolonged Sitting-Induced Leg Endothelial Dysfunction

Is Prevented by Fidgeting." *American Journal of Physiology-Heart and Circulatory Physiology* (2016): 311, No. 1. https://www.physiology.org/doi/abs/10.1152/ajpheart .00297.2016#

Mueller, Pam A. and Daniel M. Oppenheimer. "The Pen Is Mightier Than the Keyboard: Advantages of Longhand Over Laptop Note Taking." *Psychological Science* (2014): 25 (6), 1159–1168. http://journals.sagepub.com/toc/pssa/25/6

Myers, David G. "The Powers and Perils of Intuition." *Psychology Today,* November 1, 2002. https://www.psychologytoday.com/us/articles/200211/the-powers-and-perils -intuition

National Institute of Mental Health. "Transforming the Understanding and Treatment of Mental Illnesses." 2017. https://www.nimh.nih.gov/health/statistics/any -anxiety-disorder.shtml

The National Trust. "The Humble Stick Revealed as the Must-Have Toy for Summer." July 27, 2016. https://www.nationaltrust.org.uk/news/the-humble-stick-revealed -as-the-must-have-toy-for-summer

Ochsner, Kevin N., and James J. Gross. "The Cognitive Control of Emotion." *Trends in Cognitive Science.* (2005): 9(5), 242–249. https://www.sciencedirect.com/science /article/pii/S1364661305000902

Oppezzo, Marily and Daniel L. Schwartz. "Give Your Ideas Some Legs: The Positive Effect of Walking on Creative Thinking." *Journal of Experimental Psychology: Learning, Memory, and Cognition* (2014): 40(4), 1142–1152. http://psycnet.apa.org /record/2014-14435-001

O'Neil, Cathy. *Weapons of Math Destruction.* New York: Crown Publishing Group, 2016.

Park, Bum Jin, Yuko Tsunetsugu, Tamami Kasetani, Takahide Kagawa and Yoshifumi Miyazaki. "The Physiological Effects of Shinrin-Yoku (Taking in the Forest Atmosphere or Forest Bathing): Evidence from Field Experiments in 24 Forests Across Japan." *Environmental Health and Preventive Medicine* (2010): 15(1), 18–26. https://www.ncbi.nlm.nih.gov/pmc/articles/PMC2793346/

Parkinson, Carolyn, Adam M. Kleinbaum & Thalia Wheatley. "Similar Neural Responses Predict Friendship." *Nature Communications* (2018): 9, 332. https://www .nature.com/articles/s41467-017-02722-7

Paul Gauguin (1848–1903). *The Metropolitan Museum of Art.* https://www.metmuseum .org/toah/hd/gaug/hd_gaug.htm

Pinker, Steven. *How the Mind Works.* New York: Norton, 1997.

Plemmons, Gregory, Matthew Hall, Stephanie Doupnik, James Gay, Charlotte Brown, Whitney Browning, Robert Casey, et al. "Hospitalization for Suicide Ideation or Attempt: 2008–2015." *Pediatrics,* May, 2018. http://pediatrics.aappublications.org /content/early/2018/05/14/peds.2017-2426

Pozen, Robert C. *Extreme Productivity: Boost Your Results, Reduce Your Hours.* New York: HarperBusiness, 2012.

Primack, Brian A., Ariel Shensa, César G. Escobar-Viera, Erica L. Barrett, Jaime E. Sidani, Jason B.Colditz and Everette James. "Use of Multiple Social Media Platforms and Symptoms of Depression and Anxiety: A Nationally-Representative Study Among U.S. Young Adults." *Computers in Human Behavior* (2017): 69, 1–9. https://www.sciencedirect.com/science/article/pii/S0747563216307543

Raichlen, David A., Pradyumna K. Bharadwaj, Megan C. Fitzhugh, Kari A. Haws, Gabrielle-Ann Torr, Theodore P. Trouard and Gene E. Alexander. "Differences in Resting State Functional Connectivity Between Young Adult Endurance Athletes and Healthy Controls." *Frontiers of Human Neuroscience* (2016): November 29, 2016. https://www.frontiersin.org/articles/10.3389/fnhum.2016.00610 /full

Ratey, John, J. *Spark: The Revolutionary New Science of Exercise and the Brain.* New York: Little, Brown and Company, 2013.

Reetz, David R., Carolyn Bershad, Peter LeViness and Monica Whitlock. "The Association for University and College Counseling Center Directors Annual Survey." *The Association for University and College Counseling Center Directors* (2016): https://www.aucccd.org/assets/documents/aucccd%202016%20monograph%20 -%20public.pdf

Reynolds, Gretchen. "Get Up, Stand Up!" *New York Times* (New York, NY), September 13, 2017. https://www.nytimes.com/2017/09/13/well/move/get-up-stand-up .html

Reynolds, Gretchen. "Why Fidgeting Is Good Medicine." *New York Times* (New York, NY). Sept. 14, 2016. https://www.nytimes.com/2016/09/14/well/move/why-fid geting-is-good-medicine.html

Ritchie, Hannah and Max Roser. "Mental Health." OurWorldInData.org, April 2018. https://ourworldindata.org/mental-health

Robinson, Thomas N., Jorge A. Banda, Lauren Hale, Amy Shirong Lu, Frances Fleming-Milici, Sandra L. Calvert and Ellen Wartella. "Screen Media Exposure and Obesity in Children and Adolescents." *Pediatrics* (2017), 140, 2016–1758. https://www.ncbi.nlm.nih.gov/pmc/articles/PMC5769928/

Rook, Karen S., and Susan T. Charles. "Close Social Ties and Health in Later Life: Strengths and Vulnerabilities." *The American Psychologist* (2017): 72.6, 567–577. https://www.ncbi.nlm.nih.gov/pubmed/28880103

Russo, J. Edward, and Paul J. H. Schoemaker. *Winning Decisions.* New York: Doubleday, 2002.

Safina, Carl. *Beyond Words: What Animals Think and Feel.* New York: Macmillan, 2015.

Salganik, Matthew J., Peter Sheridan Dodds and Duncan J. Watts. "Experimental Study of Inequality and Unpredictability in an Artificial Cultural Market." *Science* (2006): 311, 854–856. http://science.sciencemag.org/content/311/5762/854

Sax, David. *The Revenge of Analog.* Perseus Books, LLC, 2016.

Schumann, Karina, Jamil Zaki and Carol S. Dweck. "Addressing the Empathy Deficit: Beliefs About the Malleability of Empathy Predict Effortful Responses When Empathy Is Challenging." *Journal of Personality and Social Psychology* (2014): 107(3), 475–493. http://ssnl.stanford.edu/sites/default/files/pdf/schumann2014_empathy Deficit.pdf?width=85%&height=85%&iframe=true

Schwartz, John. "Learning to Learn: You, Too, Can Rewire Your Brain." *New York Times* (New York, NY). August 4, 2017. https://www.nytimes.com/2017/08/04 /education/edlife/learning-how-to-learn-barbara-oakley.html

Scriven, Michael and Richard Paul. "Defining Critical Thinking: A Statement By Michael Scriven & Richard Paul for the National Council for Excellence in Critical

Thinking Instruction." https://www.crc.losrios.edu/files/cassl/DefiningCritical
Thinkingc2.pdf

Scutti, Susan. "'Alarming' Rise in Children Hospitalized with Suicidal Thoughts
or Actions." CNN, 2017. https://www.cnn.com/2017/05/05/health/children-teens
-suicide-study/index.html

Seligman, Martin E. P. *Learned Optimism: How to Change Your Mind and Your Life.*
New York: Alfred A. Knopf, 1991.

Seligman, M. E. P., and Maier, S. F. "Failure to Escape Traumatic Shock." *Journal of
Experimental Psychology* (1967): 74, 1–9. https://homepages.gac.edu/~jwotton2
/PSY225/seligman.pdf

Shane, Scott and Vindu Goel. "Fake Russian Facebook Accounts Bought $100,000 in
Political Ads." *New York Times* (New York, NY). September 6, 2017. https://www
.nytimes.com/2017/09/06/technology/facebook-russian-political-ads.html

Sherman, Lauren E., Ashley A. Payton, Leanna M. Hernandez, Patricia M. Greenfield
and Mirella Dapretto. "The Power of the Like in Adolescence: Effects of Peer Influence on Neural and Behavioral Responses to Social Media." *Psychological Science*
(2016): 27, 1027–1035. https://www.ncbi.nlm.nih.gov/pmc/articles/PMC5387999/

Silva, Clarissa. "Social Media's Impact on Self-Esteem." *Huffington Post.* February 22,
2017. https://www.huffingtonpost.com/entry/social-medias-impact-on-self-esteem
_us_58ade038e4b0d818c4f0a4e4

Simon, Jonathan. *Governing Through Fear: How the War on Crime Transformed American
Democracy and Created a Culture of Fear.* New York: Oxford University Press, 2007.

Slife, Brent D. "Free Will and Time: That 'Stuck' Feeling." *Journal of Theoretical and
Philosophical Psychology* (1994): 14, 1–12. http://psycnet.apa.org/record/1995-13451
-001

Smith, Alan L., Betsy Hoza, Kate Linnea, Julia D. McQuade, Meghan Tomb, Aaron J.
Vaughn, Erin K. Shoulberg, and Holly Hook. "Pilot Physical Activity Intervention
Reduces Severity of ADHD Symptoms in Young Children." *Journal of Attention
Disorders* (2011): 17, 70–82. http://journals.sagepub.com/doi/abs/10.1177/108705
4711417395?legid=spjad%3B17%2F1%2F70&patientinform-links=yes

Smith, Amy Victoria, Leanne Proops, Kate Grounds, Jennifer Wathan and Karen
McComb. "Functionally relevant responses to human facial expressions of emotion in the domestic horse (Equus caballus)." *Biology Letters* (2016): DOI: 10.1098/
rsbl.2015.0907 http://rsbl.royalsocietypublishing.org/content/12/2/20150907

Smith, Harrison. "Stanislav Petrov, Soviet officer credited with averting nuclear war,
dies at 77." *The Washington Post* (Washington, DC), September 18, 2017. https://
www.washingtonpost.com/local/obituaries/stanislav-petrov-soviet-officer
-credited-with-averting-nuclear-war-dies-at-77/2017/09/18/78c6b0e6-9c80-11e7
-9083-fbfddf6804c2_story.html?utm_term=.5f1b02411de7

Smoller, Jordan. *The Other Side of Normal.* New York: William Morrow, 2012.

Spreng, M. "Possible Health Effects of Noise Induced Cortisol Increase." *Noise Health*
(2000): 2(7), 59–64. https://www.ncbi.nlm.nih.gov/pubmed/12689472

Stein, Steven. *The EQ Leader.* Hoboken, NJ: John Wiley & Sons, Inc., 2017.

Sternberg, Robert J., Henry L. Roediger III, and Diane F. Halpern eds. *Critical Thinking in Psychology.* Cambridge, UK: Cambridge University Press, 2007.

Storrs, Carina. "Americans Are Fatter Than Ever, CDC Finds." CNN, May 25, 2016. https://www.cnn.com/2016/05/25/health/americans-health-obesity-diabetes /index.html

"Stress Effects on the Body." American Psychological Association. https://www.apa.org /helpcenter/stress-body.aspx

"Stress in America: Our Health at Risk." American Psychological Association, Washington D.C. https://www.apa.org/news/press/releases/stress/2011/final-2011.pdf

"Studies Show Normal Children Today Report More Anxiety than Child Psychiatric Patients in the 1950s." American Psychological Association, December 14, 2000. https://www.apa.org/news/press/releases/2000/12/anxiety.aspx

Swanson, Larry W. *Brain Architecture: Understanding the Basic Plan*. New York: Oxford University Press, 2012.

Taleb, Nassim Nicholas. *Hidden Asymmetries in Daily Life*. New York: Random House, 2018.

Tang, Yi-Yuan, Britta K. Holzel, and Michael I. Posner. "The Neuroscience of Mindfulness Meditation." *Nature Reviews Neuroscience*. (2015): 16(4), 213–225. https:// www.nature.com/articles/nrn3916

Tarnas, Richard. *The Passion of the Western Mind*. New York: Crown Publishers, Inc., 1991.

Tavris, Carol, and Elliot Aronson. *Mistakes Were Made (but not by me)*. Orlando, FL, Harcourt, Inc., 2007.

Taylor, Charles. *Sources of the Self*. Cambridge: Harvard University Press, 1989.

Teri, Linda, Rebecca G. Logsdon, and Susan M. McCurry. "Exercise Interventions for Dementia and Cognitive Impairment: The Seattle Protocols." *The Journal of Nutrition, Health & Aging* (2008): 12.6, 391–394. https://www.ncbi.nlm.nih.gov /pmc/articles/PMC2518041/

Thompson, Jeff. "Is Nonverbal Communication a Numbers Game?" *Psychology Today*, September 30, 2011. https://www.psychologytoday.com/us/blog/beyond-words /201109/is-nonverbal-communication-numbers-game

Tierney, John. "Do You Suffer from Decision Fatigue?" *New York Times Magazine*, August 17, 2011. https://www.nytimes.com/2011/08/21/magazine/do-you-suffer -from-decision-fatigue.html

Tomasello, Michael. *A Natural History of Human Thinking*. Cambridge: Harvard University Press, 2014.

Tomopoulos, Suzy, Benard P. Dreyer, Samantha Berkule, Arthur H. Fierman, Carolyn Brockmeyer, and Alan L. Mendelsohn. "Infant Media Exposure and Toddler Development." *Archives of Pediatric & Adolescent Medicine* (2010): 164 (12), 1105–1111. https://www.ncbi.nlm.nih.gov/pmc/articles/PMC3095486/

Torsheim, Torbjørn, Lilly Eriksson, Christina W. Schnohr, Fredrik Hansen, Thoroddur Bjarnason and Raili Välimaa. "Screen-based Activities and Physical Complaints Among Adolescents from the Nordic Countries." *BMC Public Health*, 2010. https:// bmcpublichealth.biomedcentral.com/articles/10.1186/1471-2458-10-324

Tversky, Amos and Daniel Kahneman. "The Framing of Decisions and the Psychology of Choice." *Science* (1981): 211, 453–458. https://faculty.washington.edu/jmiyamot /p466/pprs/tverskya%20framing%20of%20decisions%20&%20psych%20o%20 choice.pdf

Tversky, Amos and Daniel Kahneman. "Judgment Under Uncertainty: Heuristics and Biases." *Science* (1974): 185, (4157), 1124–1131. http://psiexp.ss.uci.edu/research/teaching/Tversky_Kahneman_1974.pdf

Twenge, Jean M. "The Age of Anxiety? Birth Cohort Change in Anxiety and Neuroticism, 1952–1993." *Journal of Personality and Social Psychology* (2000): 79, (6), 1007–1021. https://www.apa.org/pubs/journals/releases/psp7961007.pdf

Vanderbilt University Medical Center. "Study Finds Sharp Rise in Suicide Risk for Children." VUMC Reporter, 2018. http://news.vumc.org/2018/05/17/study-finds-sharp-rise-in-suicide-risk-for-children/

Walle, Eric A., Peter J. Reschke, and Jennifer M. Knothe. "Social Referencing: Defining and Delineating a Basic Process of Emotion." *Emotion Review* (2017): 9, 245–252. http://journals.sagepub.com/doi/abs/10.1177/1754073916669594?journalCode=emra

Wan, Xiaohong, Daisuke Takano, Takeshi Asamizuya, Chisato Suzuki, Kenichi Ueno, Kang Cheng, Takeshi Ito and Keiji Tanaka. "Developing Intuition: Neural Correlates of Cognitive-Skill Learning in Caudate Nucleus." *The Journal of Neuroscience* (2012): 32(48), 17492–17501. http://www.jneurosci.org/content/32/48/17492

Ward, Adrian F., Kristen Duke, Ayelet Gneezy and Maarten W. Bos. "Brain Drain: The Mere Presence of One's Own Smartphone Reduces Available Cognitive Capacity." *Journal of the Association for Consumer Research* (2017): 2:2, 140–154. https://www.journals.uchicago.edu/doi/abs/10.1086/691462

Ward, Brian W., Tainya C. Clarke, Colleen N. Nugent and Jeannine S. Schiller. "Early Release of Selected Estimates Based on Data from the 2015 National Health Interview Survey." National Center for Health Statistics. May 2016. https://www.cdc.gov/nchs/data/nhis/earlyrelease/earlyrelease201605.pdf

Webb, Christine E., Maya Rossignac-Milon and Troy E. Higgins. "Stepping Forward Together: Could Walking Facilitate Interpersonal Conflict Resolution?" *American Psychologist* (2017): 72(4), 374–385. http://psycnet.apa.org/record/2017-19038-005

Williams, Florence. "Take Two Hours of Pine Forest and Call Me in the Morning." *Outside Magazine*, November 28, 2012. https://www.outsideonline.com/1870381/take-two-hours-pine-forest-and-call-me-morning

Williams, R. N. "The Human Context of Agency." *American Psychologist* (1992): 47, 752–760. http://psycnet.apa.org/record/1992-34951-001

Wilson, Timothy D. "Self-Knowledge and the Adaptive Unconscious." *Neurosciences and the Human Person: New Perspectives on Human Activities Pontifical Academy of Sciences* (2013): Scripta Varia 121. http://www.pas.va/content/dam/accademia/pdf/sv121/sv121-wilson.pdf

Wilson, Timothy D. *Strangers to Ourselves: Discovering the Adaptive Unconscious.* Cambridge, MA: President and Fellows of Harvard College, 2002.

Wilson, Timothy D., David A. Reinhard, Erin C. Westgate, Daniel T. Gilbert, Nicole Ellerbeck, Cheryl Hahn, Casey L. Brown and Adi Shaked. "Just Think: The Challenges of the Disengaged Mind." *Science* (2018): 345(6192), 75–77. https://www.ncbi.nlm.nih.gov/pmc/articles/PMC4330241/

Winerman, Lea. "By the Numbers: Our Stressed-out Nation, Americans Are Worried About the Future of Their Country in These Tense Political Times, According to

APA's 2017 Stress in America Survey." *Monitor on Psychology* (2017): 48(11), 80. https://www.apa.org/monitor/2017/12/numbers.aspx

Wolpert, Stuart. "The Teenage Brain on Social Media: The Findings in a New UCLA Study Shed Light on the Influence of Peers and Much More." *UCLA Newsroom*, May 31, 2016. http://newsroom.ucla.edu/releases/the-teenage-brain-on-social-media

Woodbine, Onaje. *Black Gods of the Asphalt: Religion, Hip-Hop, and Street Basketball.* New York: Columbia University Press, 2016.

World Health Organization. "Depression and Other Common Mental Disorders: Global Health Estimates." 2017. http://apps.who.int/iris/bitstream/handle/10665/254610/WHO-MSD-MER-2017.2-eng.pdf

Yong, Min Hooi and Ted Ruffman. "Emotional Contagion: Dogs and Humans Show a Similar Physiological Response to Human Infant Crying." *Behavioural Processes* (2014): 108, 155–165. https://www.sciencedirect.com/science/article/pii/S0376635714002472?via%3Dihub

Zagorski, Nick. "Using Many Social Media Platforms Linked with Depression, Anxiety Risk." *Psychiatric News* (2017). https://psychnews.psychiatryonline.org/doi/full/10.1176/appi.pn.2017.1b16

Zenger, Jack and Joseph Folkman. "Getting 360 Degree Reviews Right." *Harvard Business Review*, September 7, 2012. https://hbr.org/2012/09/getting-360-degree-reviews-right

Zucker, Donna M. "How to Do Case Study Research." *Teaching Research Methods in the Social Sciences* (2009). https://scholarworks.umass.edu/cgi/viewcontent.cgi?article=1001&context=nursing_faculty_pubs

ACKNOWLEDGMENTS

This book represents years of work on a complex and far-reaching topic: human agency. The path to conceptualizing the book wasn't linear and required help from many talented people along the way. It was our long-held ambition to convey the ideas in the book to make the human journey a bit easier and clearer at this challenging juncture in human history. To the extent we succeeded it is largely due to the generous assistance of some smart, dedicated, and empathetic people who deserve our utmost gratitude.

First, our thanks go to the tireless and visionary Todd Schuster and the brilliant and creative Jane Von Mehren, our agents at Aevitas Creative Management. Without their sustained interest and support the project would never have gotten off the ground. They partnered with us in bringing shape to many nascent ideas, pivoting as necessary to rein the project in when it was veering off course. Both brought a sense of levity and order to a fundamentally messy and challenging endeavor. Their candid, constructive criticism was essential and they secured the best possible home for the project at St. Martin's Press.

Tim Bartlett, our editor, and the tremendously talented team at St Martin's Press, recognized the seeds of something uniquely powerful in the seven principles. Our first meeting with them was a high-energy exchange of ideas that made us feel an immediate bond. Tim encouraged us to pause and reconceptualize at a crucial point in the project, all the while lending his thoughtful expertise. He pushed us hard when it was needed, and it made the book immeasurably stronger. As we jumped through our hoops, Tim demonstrated great personal agency by remaining calm, measured, and ever supportive. Alice Pfeiffer was omnipresent, thankfully, to keep the wheels on the bus at every sharp turn. The entire St. Martin's team took us in and enthusiastically and competently guided the project along to what it is today. Laura Clark, Martin

Quinn, Gabi Gantz, Eric C. Meyer, among many other unsung heroes, all contributed to shape and bring the project into the world so that others might experience it.

Several other people who pitched in tirelessly and partnered with us early on deserve our sincere thanks. We dubbed this group *Team Agency* as they were instrumental in moving all aspects of the project forward. Our stellar writing consultant/coach Leslie Brokaw brought our ideas into literary shape, helping us to organize the vast amounts of material into a coherent whole. Rachel Oblath lent statistical expertise and research acumen as well as feedback on every chapter, Christopher Coutsoukis helped at every juncture (a man of endless talents), Marty Buss Smith added her marketing and social media guru status into the mix, and Mindy Crowley offered her expert psychological insights on key aspects of the book. Their assistance and advice continues to be necessary and deeply valued.

Samantha Marshall helped us to rework an early version of the proposal. Ellen Berlin and Nancy Lynch were always standing by to help us bring this book into the world at large. We'd also like to thank friends Michele Millon, April Prewitt, Ed Prewitt, Jennifer Ash, Lori Wiggins, Deborah Rosenbaum, Justin Blinder, Alexandra Dunk, Dobbie Newman, and Steve Graham for reading key portions of the manuscript and offering their input and expertise. John Butman deserves a special callout for helping to shape early concepts and plant early seeds that, with some nourishment, grew into this book.

Thanks also to the support and encouragement of Shauna Mullan Smith, Carl Cwiok, Katherine Stevens, Dr. Stephen Tang, Evan Lamont, Bill Munger, and Karen Rao, who lent their help and support along the way. And to those whose prior mentoring has had a deep and lasting influence: Peter Kassel and James P. McSherry.

We can't thank our clients enough. There are so many people we work with who trust us and have shared their stories while being patient and encouraging during the writing phase, in particular, Paul's corporate clients Linda Schreiner, Sue Davies, and Stephanie White. These are people who show us how agency works every day.

Many late dinners at our beloved Boston haunts fueled long discussions that were essential. Some of what you have read was scribbled on napkins and coasters under the flickering light of table candles. Thank you Niamh "Snowy" Quinn, Anne Marie McDonnel, Chee Lau, the crew at Pomodoro and The Abbey, and Kay Mills of Naples, Florida.

Finally we thank our many fellow psychologists who have advanced the field of study through their painstaking research, practice, and authorship. On the shoulders of giants we stand.

Our apologies if we inadvertently missed anyone among the many generous and caring people, the helpers, readers, thinkers, friends, and family, who never seemed to tire of our obsession to bring agency out of the obscurity of academia and make it accessible to those of us who need it most.

Writing the book was an enormous learning experience for us and we hope that our readers will discover the same.

INDEX